IN THE ZONE

*Notes on Wondering
Coast to Coast*

Blayney Colmore

To order additional copies of this book, contact:
Xlibris Corporation
1-888-795-4274
www.Xlibris.com
Orders@Xlibris.com

CONTENTS

I
Notes From Zones 4 & 10

II
Essay and Commentary

III
Poetry

IV
Fiction/Short Story

To Lacey who practiced and tried to teach me tough love
before it became a cliché.

"You had a church full of people eager to hear the Gospel and instead you told them that ridiculous story."

She was angry, her late husband had been a preacher and, from past encounters I knew it was about a lot more than my Easter sermon. The sermon had been redone at 4am Easter morning. I walked down to the church, as was my habit, an hour before services were to begin, and stopped in the 24 hour restaurant next door for a cup of tea. The waitress was distraught.

"That homeless guy who hangs out on your church porch came in here and stole my pocket book! I'm getting damn sick and tired of your bleeding heart causing problems for all the rest of us."

I expressed my embarrassed condolences, got my tea and walked next door to the church. As I entered the sanctuary I smelled smoke. The flower guild had decorated the church the night before and I was afraid some greens had caught fire. As I raced around the darkened church the smell got stronger but I couldn't find where it was coming from. Finally I walked up the chancel steps and saw smoke streaming through the lattice window behind the choir stalls.

I hit the crash bar on the door and rushed onto the porch, where the homeless man was passed out, a bonfire he had built to get warm roared beside him. The waitress' pocket book served as his pillow.

I tried without success to shake him awake. Finally, after pouring a pot of water from the kitchen onto the flames, thoroughly smoking up the church, I pulled the pocket book form beneath his head, went next door and returned it to the waitress.

Forty minutes later the other clergy arrived to prepare for the Great Vigil of Easter. The Vigil begins with the lighting of the Easter fire, but we were all reformed smokers, none of us had matches. A handful of parishioners had already gathered on the front porch for what the purists consider the central liturgical drama of the church year. But without matches we couldn't begin.

"Oh, yeah," I had a brainstorm, "I think I know where we can find a match." I ran through the church and up the chancel steps, out onto the side porch where the homeless man was still sleeping soundly. As he lay on his side I patted him down like a cop looking for weapons. He didn't stir. In his breast pocket the rattle of wooden matches. I reached into his pocket and took the match box. We rekindled the first fire of Easter.

Later, in the sermon, I talked about the search for something to ignite the first fire of Easter, the Light of Christ. Although I had polished an Easter sermon over the prior couple of weeks, as I described the morning's events, it became the sermon. The homeless man who had stolen the pocketbook unwittingly provided the Light of Christ. His story became the Easter story.

Three times more, at the 7:30, 9:00 and 11:30 services, I told the homeless man story. My carefully crafted manuscript became lining for the birdcage. And in the eyes of the woman who accosted me, I became what the lining in the birdcage is for.

Over the course of thirty years as a parish priest in the Episcopal Church two problems plagued me and plagued my parishioners. The first was that I liked to hang out more than I liked to run an organization. The second that I believed too much. creeds felt like a straightjacket.

Orthodoxy, the drive to precisely define religious truth, never attracted me. So when the combination of my mother's inheritance, and a retirement offer from the Church Pension Fund made it possible for me to survive without my pastor's salary, I decided to spare my parishioners and myself and try another idiom to explore what I have always imagined to be boundary-less reality.

This collection of short stories, reflections, essays, poems and screeds is that idiom. Much of it has been sent out through e-mail, Notes From Zone 10 (California) and Notes From Zone 4 (Vermont), the two disparate places between which we have divided the past five years. My wife Lacey, a gardener, suggested Zones 10 and 4, the horticultural zones of the two places. Lacey's work as an interior designer differs markedly between the two zones, and perhaps my writing does, too.

I had thought by this time I would be publishing the novel(s) I have been working on the past many years. One of them has reached the end but is not yet ready for prime time, two others are at various points.

I have been writing these shorter pieces to keep up my morale while I slog through the novel(s). With some encouragement from some of you, some urgency at my advancing age, coupled with my growing affection for the shorter pieces, I decided to go ahead and put them into print. The novel(s) may or may not follow.

Though they may follow no single theme, they may, like the drunk street person who unconsciously provided the Easter fire, uncover a sliver of light reality sometimes provides when we give up trying to capture life's meaning and succumb to despair.

Many pieces, you will recognize, were written in response to specific times and events. The terrorist attacks on September 11, 2001, which uncovered our vulnerability, nothing new, but now our illusions became a sham. Aging, which we are all doing, and I sometimes feel I my focus is locked onto, lurks unsubtly in just about every piece.

As I look back over the writing I am surprised at how often Viet Nam comes up. And Martin Luther King and John Kennedy's assassination. Politics, especially the dramas Bill Clinton provided for eight years, creeps in, too. All you would expect from someone who came of age in the notorious 1960s.

My third grade Sunday School teacher, Mrs. Williams, instead of scolding me when I drifted from the lessons she had prepared, discovered me dabbling in poetry one day and encouraged me to do more. Thanks to her I wrote poetry for a couple of years more, then abandoned it as frivolous, until four years ago when, frustrated in my novel writing, I let the pen go free one day. Though my classically trained friend, Louis, says my poems are the sad refuse of the damage done to poetry by Walt Whitman, it has become my favorite way to write. Without Mrs. Williams' support I likely would have been intimidated by the likes of Louis.

I would love to be your Mrs. Williams, encouraging you, when you find the old orthodoxies narrow and unconvincing, to wonder, not why you can't fit into the fast food explanations for things, but how much larger and more challenging the possibilities may be.

I was about two-thirds of the way through this book when our Norfolk Terrier died. In my years in the parish I buried hundreds of people, many about whom I cared deeply. But I rarely grieved them as I have that dog. I take that as a clue that there is more buried beneath the surface of my life, and maybe yours, than we have bargained for. If this writing succeeds it will give us courage to look there, trusting that whatever we uncover, because it is a piece of reality, must not, cannot be permanently driven into exile.

My quarrel with most writing of this sort is that rather than pressing deeper into the shadows it provides comfort too soon and explanations we neither asked for nor trust,. As I grow nearer my death, I find answers less compelling than the abyss.

I am perhaps most proud of my title as Writer In Residence at the Museum of Contemporary Art, San Diego, conferred on me four years ago by the Museum's fearless director, Hugh Davies. The Museum inspires me every day as I walk through its exhibits, always tweeking, challenging, refusing orthodoxy and willing to suffer the slings and arrows of conventional tastes on behalf of its mission to extend our boundaries.

The writing is of various sorts. The first section is made up of Zone Notes. I began sending these out in the winter of 1997, one of the bleakest periods of my life. The sense that they were reaching another human may have saved me from suicide during two weeks in January when Lacey was back working in California and I was holed up in our wrecked farmhouse in rural Vermont. The dog and the cat also deserve credit. Section two contains essays and commentary. The poetry in the third part is blank verse. Finally a small collection of short stories.

Lacey, my wife for more years than I expected anyone to be able to live with me, is my grounding to earth. She does not share my cosmic ambiguity, but she does, thank God, share my days on earth.

You will not find the holy grail here, but a fellow wonderer, seeking courage, and company.

I

Notes From Zones 4 & 10

These notes were sent out over a five year period, every couple of weeks as the spirit moved. They are collected here in no particular order and you should feel free to dip into them at random. I have searched for some organizing principle to figure out what themes may have been triggered by the different Ph in the soil of California and of Vermont, but I have found none.

I have dated them when I can find a date.

The Zone Notes began with about eight people who graciously agreed to be my trial group. Somehow the list grew like a snowball rolling downhill; last I counted it was nearing 400. My ISP cancelled my account one day accusing me of sending pornography. When I tried to explain, I think I made them even more suspicious.

I'd love to hear from you at *blayneyc@earthlink.net* and would be happy to put you on the list to receive these Notes, until the list gets too large for my laptop to manage, or my ISP kicks me off. There is no charge for the Zone Notes, just, I hope, the charge you get from reading them.

SHEMA
WHY GOD WON'T GO AWAY*

Notes From Zone 4

Justin, Martyr May 31, 2001

Perhaps you know about the
posterior superior parietal lobe, the
orientation adjustment area in your
brain,
a small spongy knob that alerts you to everything that
isn't you,
the way we mostly measure,
pretty much
everything. Helps you not to stumble.

Watch that step
kiss that frog
smell the flowers
the busy little knob shows up in a SPECT** image red hot
navigate the freeway
freeze your computer
measure news of a friend's death,
it's your gyroscope, filtering the brain's information,
suggesting strategy:
stand up, sit down, fight, fight, fight.
Helps you figure how to keep yourself
intact.

But meditate, sit silently, pray, do a ritual, and the SPECT image
    shows cool
green and blue,
the brain stops sending information about what's out
there, so the knob ceases its vigil.
But it's still at work, just not processing information
out there, but
in here
quietly, calmly.

Ask the subject, what's up?   "It's all
One."
The Orientation Adjustment Area, receiving no outside
    information,
unable to mark a border between self and outside world, says, "It's
    all
One."
Bingo.
See why God won't go away?
God's hot wired into the circuitry.

*Inspired by a new book, Why God Won't Go Away, by Andrew Newberg,
    M.D. Ballantine Books. 2001

**single photon emission computed tomography, a high-tech imaging tool that
    detects radioactive emissions.

CALIFORNIA APOCALYPSE

Notes From Zone 10

Feast of the Epiphany 2001

[Manifestation of the Christ to the Gentiles]

When we woke the other morning
I thought maybe we had slept through the
day
grainy refracted light suggested dusk not
dawn
or could this be the day appointed
apocalypse
now?

Not now, not right after Alan
Greenspan
had given us back our big
boom.

The day felt warm, welcoming, but the
sun
rose
orange, purple, brown
muted
Spielberg ominous
the ocean
cast in molten bronze, sea
lions

raising Cain as if the
leviathan
were upon them
people walking
on the beach
greeted
each other silently solemnly with a nod so as
not
to intrude on the liturgy
we acknowledged but
couldn't comprehend.

The dog's fur stood straight on her
back
and the cat set herself at the window as if the whole world was a
    bird
feeder
Ash began to fall and we turned on the
radio
to hear that a passing motorist 40 miles east had dropped
a cigarette
from the car window and several thousand acres in
east county
were on
fire.

Later that
day
NPR's Marketplace mentioned the utilities in
California
were out of cash, billions burned, broke, belly up
and their lenders on the slippery
slope
of non-
existence. Alan's alchemy quickly
collapsed.

California showing the
Way
the world winds
down
rolling dice
with kilowatts
blind man's bluff before the inexorable terms of parching
wind and brush
human hubris
hammering habitat where aeons of earthquake fire and water
have ordained
abstinence.

Did Dinosaurs discern the data denoting their
demise
perched on promontory
Lands End
speculating on their successor?
Do we?

That ghostly millennium morning I thought I saw the perfect
wave
curl and roll
catch the mysterious metallic gray heavens in its
break
pause at its peak promising perhaps
this California cresting
moment
was the
Big One.

CAPSTONE'S HONEY BEAR, ALYSSUM, IS DEAD

The Ides of December 2001

Capstone's Honey Bear, known to those who love her as Alyssum, is dead, a few months shy of her fourteenth birthday. A Norfolk Terrier of noble birth and elegant disposition, she died in our arms this morning at 9:15am. The past seven months she suffered from congestive heart failure slowing her from the friendly-to-all-but-rodents dog, first greeter of any who came to our door, to sedentary old lady even tolerating chipmunks on the bird feeder.

We first met her in Roseland, California at her breeder's, an original in Apple computer who had cashed out and turned his dreams of perfection to a line of Norfolks. He required that we fly up, spend a night and have dinner with him and his wife while they vetted us to see if we were fit companions for Alyssum. Lacey's protestations that her family had always raised this breed would not satisfy him; he insisted on his own inspection. She was three weeks old, twice the size of a baked potato, but her warm personality and terrier tenacity were unmistakable. She squirmed in Lacey's arms as Lacey cooed in her ear, "You're mine."

When Alyssum was ten weeks Lacey flew to Sacramento to pick her up. When she arrived home we opened her crate in the front hall and she catapulted herself out after the full grown Siamese who had come around to satisfy her curiosity. They finally called an uneasy truce that lasted until the cat's death in a coyote ambush two years later.

Though she was California born, Alyssum flourished in Vermont where stone walls, moles, voles, mice, snakes, chipmunks and badgers, aroused her instinct as consummate ratter. In the fall, when the nights grew cold and mice moved indoors, she took up relentless patrol of the house. The cat would tease and play with mice, but Alyssum dispatched them in a single disgusting gulp.

One sunny afternoon two falls ago, Lacey looked out our kitchen window and watched a cheeky bloated varmint waddling toward the vegetable garden for a brazen daylight raid. She opened the door and Alyssum tore after the animal which was nearly twice her size. Alyssum rolled the animal twice before it realized it outweighed her and counter attacked. Lacey separated them with her tennis racket while I cornered the dog and brought her inside.

Last summer Alyssum made her customary leap from floor to chair from which she kept watch over the back yard, and missed her jump, falling onto her back. She looked puzzled, shook herself, and made a second attempt, which was only barely successful. A few days later we heard a frightful thumping as if something was ricocheting off the walls in the front hall, and ran just in time to see Alyssum hit the bottom step after a free fall down the steep wood stairs.

The vet said her heart sounded like a broken washing machine. She never again attempted the jump to the chair. Nor did she take long walks with us. But her love of food and people were undiminished. Her hearing went, but if she could smell or see you when you came home she gave you a royal greeting. If you went to the next room to get your glasses, she would rise from her nap and follow you, always choosing to be with you. She was unfailingly good company.

Two weeks ago she began to refuse food, we knew we were near the end. The lab tests came back yesterday, showing her entire system was shut down and we decided we couldn't make her go on like this. Or was it that we couldn't go on like this? How awesome, unnerving it is to decide a living being you love will die. Lacey and I talk a lot as we age about how we hope we won't have to linger when we've had enough. But deciding when enough has been reached feels way weightier than talking about it.

This morning Alyssum could hardly lift her head. Before we took her to die, stalling I suppose, Lacey carried her out to see if she could pee. As Lacey was holding her up, Fin, the fox terrier Alyssum has always responded to with vigorous sexual enthusiasm, walked by with Ray, her Irish handler. Alyssum somehow sensing Fin, wagged her tail one last time. Ray removed his glasses and dabbed his eyes.

CARIBBEAN SHOOTOUT

April Fool 2000

So there's this third world, (stupid expression but there it is) choleric woman running the marina on the tiny western Caribbean cay, a decidedly first world motor sailor, a competent and confident first world Dutch mate, and a week's worth of trash in plastic bags, as volatile a mix as the fertilizer that blew up the Federal Building in Oklahoma City. The year before, the boat moored offshore and dinghied in to use the marina facilities because the shallow water could take her only at flood tide.

This time, as the first world Dutch mate, competent confident woman, drove the dinghy to the dock, with a guest who needed to make a phone call, an owner who craved land based exercise, and five plastic trash bags bulging like Santa's sack, she was met by a swarthy, gesticulating, shiny hair and mustached Latin man in khaki shirt and pants, motorcycle black boots, and highway patrol Polaroid sunglasses that reflected back to her the Dutch woman's own resolute image. No, he said sternly, shaking his head, you cannot dock here, private marina. I can come here, the Dutch woman insisted, I did it last year and I must let these people go ashore. No, he said, you must leave. Just get off the dinghy, the Dutch mate calmly instructed her passengers, I'll take care of this, and they did.

Here's what was new since last year, the marina manager, an excitable easily offended western Caribbean woman with tight boundaries who was the second and current wife of the Mayor, and who was now striding rapidly down the dock shouting and waving her arms, No, you can't come here, you are not using the marina, this is for the private use of our guests, leave now. The Dutch mate steered the dinghy 100 yards south to a barge, tied the dinghy to the barge and began unloading the bags to take to the dumpster into which she'd thrown trash last year. No, shouted the marina woman, you may not use our dumpster, the Dutch woman shrugged, put the bags back on the dinghy, padlocked the dinghy and walked off to find a taxi and go shop for the evening meal. To all appearances, provocative costly appearances, the Dutch first world competent confident mate was unmoved, untouched by the aggressive opposition of the excitable marina manager.

The dinghy passengers reassembled a few hours later at the barge where the Latin man with the mirror glasses and the excitable Caribbean marine manager woman waited. The barge, she shouted, also belongs to the marina and you must leave at once or I will call the police. Don't get so excited, the Dutch mate counseled, we're paying customers, we'll be in tomorrow at high tide to buy gas. No, the excitable Caribbean woman rebuked the Dutch mate, you are not parked here, you will not come here. Now starting to feel the pressure, the Dutch mate started the outboard. What about the trash, the recently land based exercised owner asked the Dutch mate, who said, just put it on the dock, a gesture akin to Kruschev pounding his shoe on the UN desk, no way, the trash returned to the first world motor sailor in the dinghy under the now seething supervision of the bloody but unbowed Dutch mate.

Day two, the captain ferried the owner and wife and four guests to the marina dock for sightseeing, the trash accompanies them, the Latin mirrored glasses man awaits, warning them not to dock, Just get off the boat and walk over to the taxi, instructs the captain, the Latin man entered into strenuous conversation with the taxi/guide instructing him not to bring them back here, ever. The first worlders had the strongest feeling that the marina manager lady lurked nearby.

As the taxi van was reentering the city after the day's sightseeing, the driver's cell phone rang, he answered and handed the phone to the owner who carried on a subdued conversation, then asked the driver, Do you know where the police station is, he did and they went where the Dutch competent confident mate was being held for trespassing. Checkmate. At the jail the owner met the Minister of Tourism who released the competent Dutch woman with apologies and advised the owner to find a different dock, he agreed, but not before they had to return to find the captain who was hovering offshore to pick them up, and when they entered the parking lot to tell him to meet them elsewhere, the excitable marina manager instructed the Latin mirrored glasses man to lock the gate so the owner, his wife, the four guests, the competent Dutch mate and the taxi/guide were now held hostage. The excitable marina manager called the police demanding to know why they had released the competent Dutch mate and insisting she would not open the gate until the police returned and rearrested her, a stalemate that was to drag on for the next three hours, while the taxi/guide tried futilely to persuade her to release them, the police were clearly giving them all ample time to sort it out themselves.

After two and a half hours one of the guests, an old labor negotiator, figured he could not make things worse, so, after phoning the American Embassy to let them know there was a, however benign, hostage situation in progress involving US citizens, approached the excitable marina manager who was seated on a wooden bench on one corner of the marina dock with her husband the Mayor who had arrived after being summoned by the marina manager on her cell phone. Excuse me, the labor negotiator guest said to the marina manager, may I speak with you a moment, You may, she granted, her husband the Mayor stared off in the opposite direction toward the horizon. I've just spoken with the police, the old labor negotiator lied, and they tell me you're waiting for us to pay what we owe before you will let us go, I've come to settle with you. Darling, the excitable marina manager replied, this is a matter of stealing, of someone using facilities that she hasn't paid for, refusing to pay and offending me, she is arrogant and I'm afraid it's not so simple as paying, this is stealing, thievery, and if I was to come onto your property in the US without permission I would be shot dead and no one would care because I had been wrong, you people must learn some day to bear the consequences of your actions, she has done wrong, a criminal act and I will hold up my head knowing I have done right, the old labor negotiator looked over to the husband/Mayor who continued to study the horizon.

I have not come to defend her actions, the old labor negotiator said, but to see if there's some way we might set this matter right before it becomes more than any of us wish, Darling, she said again and the old labor negotiator listened carefully to hear if this darling was an endearment or a warning, deciding it was the former, the excitable marina manager said, I sense you have a pure heart, you are a good man, the old labor negotiator quelled his Yankee instinct to demur at anyone attributing to him too much virtue, and I respect you, but this woman is evil and someone must make her pay for her disrespect. They were well into the third hour, and though dusk approached the sun was still hot and the first worlders had been on the road all day and were missing their afternoon tea, I know you know we're Americans, the old labor negotiator said gently, and if this goes on much longer I will have to let the embassy know, Do what you must, darling, she answered and the old labor negotiator, worried that he might have misread her, fell silent for several moments before saying, I only wish we might back up so you

could understand that we respect your right to control who uses
your marina and do not intend to challenge that right. Perhaps,
the marina manager said, there might be some . . . at which
point two police vans pulled up to the locked gate, seven
policemen, one police woman who was the ranking officer, a
bevy of automatic weapons, followed by a Tourism Ministry
officer on his bicycle, the critical mass now moved to the front of
the parking lot as the mustachioed Latin man unlocked the gate
admitting the considerable constabulary.

Where is the justice, the excitable marina manager demanded to
know from the police woman officer, I pay my taxes and you give
protection to this woman thief, where is the justice, What is it
you want, the police woman asked, her face without expression,
I want justice, the excitable marina manager shouted, How
much money do these people owe you for your services, the
stolid police woman wanted to know, At least $1300 dollars for
all the times they have come into my marina without
permission, was her excited answer, US dollars the police woman
asked, Look, the excitable marina manager said, that would be
blood money, it's not about money, it's about right and wrong, the
police woman was utterly still, silent, for several moments, So if I
tell them they're wrong and they're never to come back here, you'll
be satisfied, the police woman asked, and for the first time looked at
the husband/Mayor who, knowing he was in a minefield said, Ask
her, don't ask me, she's the one who's been offended, and she did
and somehow, in a moment too subtle and exotic for the first
worlders to discern what had happened, the crisis passed.

The eight first world motor sailors would regale each other for
the next two days with different versions of what had happened
and why, perhaps they would never know that they had played
parts prepared for them from before they were born, played
them as well as if they had been rehearsing their roles since their
parents' sex had created them, which they had.

CYBEREXTINCTION

Notes From Zone 4

Summer Solstice 2000

I'm making a couple of assumptions; that you're not a cyber junkie and that you don't read Wired magazine. So you may not have read or even heard about Bill Joy's article, "Why the Future Doesn't Need Us." I'm going to summarize, even perhaps caricature it in hopes of drawing you into conversation and, I hope, persuading you to read it (*www.wired.com/wired/archive/ 8.04*).

Joy is cofounder and chief scientist of Sun Microsystems, one of the most influential figures in computing. He was a pioneer of the Internet, godfather of Unix and architect of the software systems Java and Jini.

Joy believes we're right on the cusp of creating an artificial intelligence of such complexity that it will have an independent existence, that it will be able to reproduce itself. He envisions the day, not far off, when the 'nervous system' of this entity will be so much more efficient and speedy than ours that we will become its slave. He writes of the day when humans will be considered pets and useful for simple chores while the artificial intelligence (AI) creature rules.

The current Wired (July 2000) has a special section devoted to

Joy's article. You may want to get Wired and read the exchanges because it's the conversation we needs next have. I'm going to give you my take on it and include the email address Wired has set up for this exchange (*whythefuture@wired.com*) so we can talk not only with each other but with a wider audience.

Please don't let yourself be intimidated out of the conversation because the sharpest minds about these matters disagree. One of the things I love about this brave new world is that we acknowledge that intuition is a powerful part of human understanding. Let yours wander around this topic.

When I was in college, trying to make some sense of how we humans came to be such a big player in the world, I read Teilhard de Chardin's *The Phenomenon of Man* . Teilhard described evolution as a process moving from the simple to the complex. Inert matter, when it became sufficiently complex in its atomic structure, took on the quality we call life. When the internal structure (the nervous system) of the simple living organism became sufficiently complex, it could sustain a process we might call thought. And when the thinking being reached a certain level of complexity (the human central nervous system), it became aware of itself (human).

Now I've stayed clear of the question of how this process proceeds, but perhaps you get the picture. What about the next step, beyond awareness, beyond the human? Teilhard believed we were headed towards what he called the hominization of the earth in which each person is like a single atom in the one body of humankind. He envisioned something very like the Internet (he died in 1955) which he called the earth's central nervous system.

There are two issues I'd like to raise with you. The first is whether you think hardware, hard wiring made by us, can be so complex as to exceed the intelligence and creative imagination of the creature that made it? And the second is whether you believe we can or should make some sort of intervention and, if so, what sort?

Some have responded to the article by saying that Joy is a hand wringer, that we haven't the capacity to make something more creative than we. Others have compared his article to the letter Einstein wrote to Roosevelt in 1939 alerting him to the possibility of a nuclear bomb.

I am as yet agnostic about the first question; I'm amazed at what we've proven ourselves capable of, but I'm doubtful that we are able to create a truly original anything. No doubt building on the foundation of what has been previously discovered (atomic structure, splitting the atom followed by splitting the hydrogen atom, followed by the neutron bomb) has been awesome but predictable. (Scientists around the world were simultaneously onto splitting the atom and if Hitler hadn't driven the Jewish intellectuals from Germany, he might well have had the weapon first).

The larger question is about whether we can or should put limits on the development of AI. I believe the answer to both questions is no. Since Adam and Eve tasted the fruit of the Tree of Knowledge, that genie has been out of its bottle. We are fascinated by what we can do, always restless to press ahead. And we never know what we're going to find, good or ill.

I suppose the dinosaur, in whatever way it perceived, regarded itself as having conquered the earth. We've now been here less time than the dinosaur and, because we seem maladapted to this planet, polluting and crowding, I'd guess we'll be here no longer than they were. (I know, most believe a comet hit the earth and created a dust storm that killed off everything . . . so who's to say

there won't another comet one of these aeons . . . go to the
movies much?)

It strikes me as hopelessly arrogant of us to think we're the
crown of creation, that we are what evolution has been pointing
towards since the big bang. If some AI that we had a hand in
making gains a creative imagination and ability to innovate
greater than ours, well of course that AI is going to take over the
world.

And if we think we can preserve our 'privileged' place in this
scheme by legislating against developments that have the
potential to threaten our global hegemony, we're deluding
ourselves. All we'll accomplish is the creation of a new brand of
cyber terrorist.

The irony is that, as our species, at war with itself since Cain
and Abel, discerns a looming threat, we will at last come
together as a species. Just in time to surrender.

DOCTOR DEATH

Notes From Zone 4

May 2001

I had noticed him sitting in the third pew staring up at me with a beatific smile as I was preaching. Three Sundays in a row, same pew, same smile. Made me uneasy. Either he was seeing something I wasn't, or he was simple minded, or maybe he thought I was. He even laughed at my jokes, startling my solemn congregation.

I hadn't caught his name when he shook my hand at the door following the service, so when my secretary said Douglas Dixon had called for an appointment, I didn't know who it was and asked her to put him off.

"He's insistent," she said, "Can't I just put him in that Tuesday afternoon slot you leave open for emergencies?"

When he came into my office I recognized him. Chiseled features, cheeks flushed, his sparkling blue eyes seemed sunken. He was smartly dressed in a brown tweed suit, electric blue shirt and wide colorful tie. The suit hung on him a little loosely as if he had recently lost weight. His shoulders were square, his waist narrow. I guessed he worked out. He smiled warmly as we shook hands, then turned away from me and, before I could offer, as I normally did to show I was in charge, dropped into the overstuffed chair and got right down to business.

"My name's Douglas. I'm 41 years old, a forensic pathologist, have just become the assistant coroner for San Diego County. I moved here from another city where I was head coroner when I refused to sign the death certificate saying the Mayor's girlfriend who died of an overdose was a suicide." I wanted him to pause for a breath but he rushed ahead.

"I'm a devout Episcopalian, I'm gay, I have AIDS, will be dead two years from now, have a partner, Sam, who last tested negative for the virus. I'm as fascinated watching myself die as I have been investigating others' deaths for the past 15 years. Now, tell me, do you think I'll find a home for myself here at St. James?"

St. James is a 100 year old parish in an upscale coastal town in Southern California. When I arrived as Rector from a colonial New England church, I imagined I was going to be the surfing Rector of a light-hearted swinging congregation. What I hadn't reckoned on was that in boundary-less southern California, people would look to the church as the finger in the dyke holding back moral anarchy.

"I sure hope so, Douglas. I'm pretty new here myself and I haven't figured out how to read this crowd that well yet."

"O.K. Fair enough, we'll find our way together on this one. Now, when does the group meet that I'll use for moral support?"

I swallowed hard again, blushing, feeling sheepish.

"I see," Douglas said, "so we have to start one. How about this time every Tuesday afternoon, from 2 to 4pm?"

The Blessed Group (Blessed are those who mourn, for they shall be comforted) began with Douglas and me, and a man in his

80s who over the previous 20 years had survived cancer in every bone and organ in his body. He was on watch for anyone who hadn't heard about his orchiectomy. When they asked what an orchiectomy was, Al would lower his chin, regard the person over the top of his glasses for a long moment, and in exaggerated falsetto, explain, "They cut your balls off."

AZT was new and Douglas, an adventuresome physician, used it, successfully, for a spell, before side effects caused him to give it up. He held the group spellbound with his detached clinical descriptions of symptoms, anecdotes of the progress of his disease. He was our chief recruiter, editing the description of the group from Those Living With Terminal Illness, to Those Touched By Terminal Illness, to Those Touched By Challenging Illness, the last finally broad enough to attract every lonely voyeur in the parish. The loneliness that a dying person feels about talking with people would first draw them to the group. Douglas kept them coming back.

"I've started practicing my dying," he announced one afternoon. He had dropped 20 pounds in the past few weeks and developed an angry purple Kaposi's sarcoma on his left cheek. The inside of his mouth was sore with thrush and he couldn't eat much solid food. He'd taken disability leave from his job, so instead of his suit and tie, he came to our meetings in shorts, Hawaiian shirt and thong sandals. He always collapsed into the same overstuffed chair as he had that first day, and if a newcomer sat there before Douglas arrived, they were waved off.

"How the hell do you practice dying?" Al wondered.

"I'm trying something I learned in yoga. I lie on my back and surrender my body, an inch at a time with each breath, beginning at the soles of my feet. So far I've gotten to my knees.

I can tell, it's going to be ecstasy when I get to the top of my head and let it all go with one final breath.

"My goal is to become so good at relaxing that I won't freak out when death comes for me. I want to be conscious and aware as long as I can, right up to that last breath if possible."

Whenever Douglas revealed another dimension of his pilgrimage, he would lie back in his chair, silently. For a long time I thought he had exhausted himself emotionally. I eventually understood that he was studying our reactions, sizing each of us up, clinically, to judge which of us was up to the task he was going to assign.

Though none of us knew it at the time, our final exam came the day Douglas was too sick to come to the meeting and had Sam call to ask if any of us might be willing to go meet in Douglas' bedroom. I said I would ask the others.

"Sure," Al responded, "Why not?" Sally, who was recovering from brain surgery that had removed about half of her aggressive tumor, thought it would be a gas to go over to Douglas'.

"I bet he sleeps in silk sheets."

The others demurred, so Al, Sally and I went.

He did sleep in silk sheets. And silk pajamas. With his two fox terriers. Sam met us at the door, formally ushered us into Douglas' bedroom, as if for a royal audience, and disappeared. I now saw the urgency of Douglas's search for friends on his way through these uncharted waters.

Despite being too weak to sit, his face flushed with fever, he greeted us with a broad smile. His voice hoarse, he introduced his terriers.

"This is Muffin and this is Terrence. Muffin is Terrence's mom, you'll find Terrence more outgoing. Muffin's kind of shy, like her Daddy." Douglas's laughter sent him into a paroxysm of coughing that seemed life threatening. We must have looked alarmed. When Douglas could finally speak, he smiled. "You look like you're scared I'm going to die. I am, but not today. Maybe a couple of weeks."

He pulled up his pajama top to show us another lesion on his chest. "It's all breaking down now," he said, betraying no emotion. "I think Jesus is getting me ready. I got all the way to my shoulders letting my body go last night. I'm hoping to do a dress rehearsal tonight, get right up into my head."

We talked for a few minutes, then Douglas revealed his agenda. "I could lapse into coma any time. I can't eat or drink much and I'm not going to do an IV. But don't assume, if I can't respond, that I'm not aware you're here. Talk to me. Pray with me. Encourage me. Even after my heart has stopped, please treat me as if I'm still with you. And when I get to the other side, I'll pray for you. I don't mind if you cry or feel freaked out, but I want you to help me leave this life and this body."

We promised we'd do our best. He said he'd try to die on a Tuesday, at our regular meeting time. We thanked him for his thoughtfulness, provoking another near fatal laughing/coughing spell.

The following Monday Sam called to say he thought Douglas was near the end. I went over and spent an hour with him. He could no longer open his eyes but he could still speak. He said he had begun to hear voices he thought were from people he knew who were dead. He told me about a few people he'd seen who he was pretty sure weren't still on earth. He seemed to fall asleep, then would stir and ask if he had been talking. I asked him if he wanted the others to come tomorrow.

"Yes; I think I'll still be here. I'm gonna try. This is going good."

The next afternoon, Sally, who was now on a walker, and Al, who, aside from no balls was fit as a fiddle, and I went. Douglas was comatose though we all thought he smiled when I asked him if he was ready.

At first we were awkward talking to him, self-conscious, as if we were reading from a script he had written for us.

"Douglas, it's us, The Blesseds. We know you hear us and we're going to stay with you." Muffin was on the bed, her head next to Douglas', never lifting from the silk sheet, her eyes following us. Terrence was in the kitchen with Sam. After a half hour they both appeared. Sam carried a tray with cheese nachos and three glasses of iced tea. He put the tray on a table next to the bed and he and Terrence left the room.

I nibbled on a nacho. I was famished. I ate six before I paused for a sip of tea. Muffin whined, she probably wanted a nacho. Douglas always fed her from his own plate.

"I think he's gone," Sally said.

Douglas's head was turned in an odd position, his eyelids half open but no pupil showed. I put my ear next to his mouth, nothing. Muffin whimpered again. I touched Douglas' carotid, nothing, then his wrist I thought I might sense something, realized it was my own pulse. I marked the sign of a cross on his forehead with my thumb.

"Douglas," I said, feeling light-headed, "you've been our guide, our teacher, and now we commend you to God with thanks to you for showing us the way. If we can trust God with our life half as much as you trusted Him with your dying, we will be blessed. Blessed are you."

Muffin, her head down next to Douglas's, tracked us with her eyes as we each leaned over and kissed our friend good bye.

THE YOUNG MAN
IN THE TOMB

Notes From Zone 10 Easter 2000

A friend pointed out that the women who went to the tomb to anoint Jesus' body (how did they think they were going to move the boulder?) actually went inside the tomb and so they met the young man. Probably most of us would have stayed outside moaning and bitching about life's unfairness, but they went in, risking an encounter with the stench of death and with the destruction of their best hopes. And that rearranged their whole lives.

Easter hope is not about being rescued from our fears or even from death, but about walking into the certain, necessary death of all we have pinned our hopes on, and being told that the one we were seeking is alive, changed and somewhere else.

Our friends in Zimbabwe are living out our worst nightmares right now, challenging the Easter claim in a way I've never before met in the flesh. I suspect every rich white person from the Northern Hemisphere knows this dread, however subtly, consciously or not.

I grew up in the segregated south in the 1940s, lived years in the Philippines in colonial splendor and spent a sublime sabbatical in Zimbabwe in 1984 after their independence but when the old Rhodesians still largely held sway. I have a recurring nightmare from as early as I can recall, of our home being overrun by angry blacks overturning the old order. In 1968 in Watts, in Hough, I thought it was happening. In Zimbabwe, where the racial mix is the reverse of here, (only the whites make up 1/10th what the blacks here do) it is happening. No one knows whether any whites will be able to remain or who or how many may be killed.

When I was in Zimbabwe I was reminded of my childhood in North Carolina. The benevolent racism of the whites reminded of our ways. I felt rather removed, having been through the racial revolution in our country, and proud when black Zimbabweans told me how impressed they were that Jesse Jackson was taken seriously in the US as a presidential contender.

But I lived the life of an old colonial Rhodesian. I was conscious enough to know that my fear of blacks was largely a projection of the feelings I imagined I'd have if our racial reality was reversed, as was the case in Zimbabwe even though the overwhelming black majority still deferred to the white minority.

Now Zimbabwe friends are looking out their window and seeing armed blacks coming up their driveway. A little turn of events here or there and that could be me in Charlotte or in Manila or La Jolla, watching Mexicans or Native Americans coming to claim what they believe was stolen from them.

I once heard Jesse Jackson describe an incident in which he was walking on an urban street late at night and heard footsteps coming up behind him. He tensed, readied himself and, as the person walked by him he saw that he was white and Jackson was relieved. It was in that moment that Jackson said he understood just how pervasive racism in this country is.

In the 70s, when John Hines was Presiding Bishop of the
Episcopal Church, the church responded to the angry black
revolution with money and transfer of significant authority.
Some accused Hines of caving in to threats and his guilt; I
thought he acted on prophetic reality. Those days seem long
ago. We now all agree free enterprise is the panacea for creating
opportunity. But the open sores that soiled the American Dream
continue to fester.

Some part of every white American stands alongside those white
Zimbabweans watching in horror as our worst fears come true.
We know we have too much at the expense of too many but we
are not creative or courageous enough to set it right. So this is
the way it sorts itself out, in bloody retribution.

Our friends in Zimbabwe are walking into the tomb. They've
known for some time it would be like this. For none of them is
the stench of death theoretical and for some not even
metaphorical. Though they seem heroic to me the reality is that
they have no choice, none of us does. Our euphoria over our
soaring stock market and fantastic wealth has only partially
distracted us; we, too, have known this was a house built on
sand.

No one knows what to do. No one has a solution. We have only
the Easter choice. We can stand just outside the tomb
lamenting, complaining, tut tutting, grieving for the good old
days, waiting for reality to swallow us. Or we can walk in, knees
shaking, knowing only that we're courting the death we've
dreaded and hoped to avoid. Resurrection is not about having
things put back as they were, but about what lies ahead once
we've let go of how we thought and wished it might be. For
people who have had as much as we have, it looks fearfully like
nothing. The Easter promise is not that we will be rescued from
death or our fears, but that once the worst is realized, the unknown

young man will meet us. He will point us to where the new life for us lies, a way we would never have willingly walked.

Easter has been a sentimental solstice celebration for many of us for some time. This year for some, soon enough for us all, it is a full-bodied walk into the tomb.

ENERGY WONDER

Notes From Zone 10

Ides Of February 2001

I

If California were a nation
she would be a member of the
G7   though we
can't keep the lights burning.

Each time
one of these Notes decides to
deliver itself
of me,
it generates an energy
storm
that feels likely to drain me
dry.

Remember
that early physics lesson,
No energy ever lost, just
changed
exchanged?

40 million of us
wonder
when the lights blink whether we'll
extinct
now.   Nope, not
today, not ever. Those migrating
electrons
may mutate, but never
dissipate.

Turns out it's not the void we dread, not the forever
nothingness
But the transformation, the
evolution
we didn't vote for, never saw hiding out around the
bend.

That long beaked beach bird working the surf's edge for
sand crabs
descended, so they say, from the
dinosaur
Boffo bio/evolution/trick
that monster awkward energy
inferno
repacked into the fiercely efficient finely formed flying
fisher/wader gull
consuming calories
at a clip to even awe
Three Mile Isle or
Gold's Gym.

II

So if those lumbering giant serpent
cells
raging, immoderate, over-the-edge eaters
have morphed into
delicate catch-the-breeze, floating, soaring seemingly
care-less
birds,

What wonder might my end-of-the-rainbow
California
straddling San Andreas no fault of its own
soon perhaps to float itself as rival
continent
come to be?
Some paradise perhaps for cousins yet hidden in
our marrow?

And this horrendous
hemorrhage
of my disassembling energy
discharging
into cyber space,
while your computer considers, translates
transfers
tenuous tentacles of inscrutable information,
binary bytes
to some new hue
I never
conceived,

You have to wonder
about this
energy,
where will it never end?

NOTES FROM ZONE 10

Epiphany Prayer 2000

The night before we flew from Vermont back to La Jolla, Lacey and I were driving on Route 100 by Mt. Snow just after sunset. The long afternoon winter shadows quickly turn to deep darkness in the mountains, and an ominous wind was blowing so hard that the already freezing temperature felt much colder. I couldn't seem to ratchet up the Pathfinder heater fast enough to keep up with the falling thermometer.

As we approached the convenience store at a particularly dark spot on the road we could just make out some sort of commotion, several cars and people milling about. I slowed down and a man ran across the road into my path motioning to me to pull over. When I did and rolled down my window, he shouted, "We need your jack to get the car off this guy!"

I stopped the car barely off the road in the parking lot and jumped out, flinging open the back door to find the jack. Though I've driven the car over 50,000 miles I'd never used the jack and couldn't remember, in that frantic moment, where it was. Lacey and I ran around the car several times opening doors and compartments, flipping seats forward, looking, while the man who had flagged us down kindly reassured us that no one knows where their jack is anymore. All the while I was aware of a car stopped at a weird angle across the street and a growing number of people crowding around it.

Finally we found the jack, half under one back seat and half under the other, and I yanked it free and ran across the street. When I got on the other side of the car I could see its front windshield had been smashed. Two feet, utterly still, toes down, were sticking out from under the car. My heart leapt into my throat. I felt slightly nauseous.

I handed my jack to a man who was hunkered down beside the legs of the person beneath the car. Barely visible was what looked like a man, maybe in his twenties judging from his clothes, pinned beneath the right rear wheel of what my memory says was an SUV, maybe a Ford Bronco. I wished he would stir or make some sound, moan maybe, but nothing. A lean, hard jean-clad man wearing a heavy work jacket was lying on the ground beside the trapped man, alternately speaking to him and barking orders to the rest of us. Another jack had arrived just ahead of mine and someone began jacking up the offending wheel.

"Easy," the man beside the injured man ordered. "Everyone else get the fuck out of here!" he shouted. I was standing right next to him, remembering I'm a priest, remembering the numbers of times I've been in situations like this, feeling lost, commanded, terrified.

"Unto God's gracious mercy and protection we commit you," I intoned the ancient Aaronic blessing, holding up my hand over the injured man and the one directing the rescue. No one heard me, I don't think. The icy wind was blowing hard; two people were holding a tarp in back of the car trying to save the pinned man from freezing. Someone put a blanket on him. "The Lord bless you and keep you. The Lord make His face to shine upon you and be gracious unto you. The Lord lift up the light of His face upon you and give you peace, hope, healing, for this night and forever more."

"O.K., he's free," the man shouted. "When I count three I want you to pull him, just six inches, slowly, carefully." Then, to the injured man, as if he was listening attentively, "We're going to pull you free. Don't move." There seemed little chance of that; he was totally unresponsive.

They pulled at the count of three and he was fully visible. Blood was seeping from his ear. Several people crowded around him. I walked back across the street and found Lacey. We drove to our friends Louis and Wendy's, neither speaking. Lacey broke the silence once to say she wished she could make a conference call to all our kids to make sure they were all right. I felt on the edge of tears all night. Wendy and Louis' house was warm and felt safe. I wished the night at their table might last forever. I wished I never had to drive out in that forbidding frozen dark again.

The next day, as we flew across the country, we became aware that Jasmine, our Siamese cat, hadn't eaten since she'd been anaesthetized four days earlier to have her teeth attended to. We began to fret, hoped maybe her gums were sore and she would come around once we got settled in La Jolla.

But she didn't so we took her to the vet. He did blood work and called Lacey at work. "She's in acute renal failure," he said, "her lab numbers as bad as I've ever seen." She's a young cat, not yet six, successor to Chiredzi, our last Siamese who was killed by coyotes in a canyon next to where we used to live in La Jolla. The vet didn't give us much hope. He said putting her down was a legitimate option, but he did offer us the choice of hydrating her for five days with intravenous fluid to see if it might jolt her kidneys back into operation. He said he'd seen it work occasionally.

Of course we've taken that course. She came home last night with her right front paw tightly bound to protect the IV lead in her vein. She worried it so we were afraid she might tear it loose and hemorrhage. We went back to the vet and got one of those plastic cones to put over her head so she couldn't get at her paw. Or her food or water, or pretty much anything anywhere. We spent the night worrying and fussing over her, waking after a couple of hours' sleep ragged and exhausted, wondering if we're doing her any good or just prolonging the inevitable. Taking her to the vet each morning feels a lot like saying that prayer over the guy pinned beneath the Bronco, flimsy and necessary.

"I just don't know if I can take more loss right now," Lacey said this morning, "and I guess I don't get to choose."

EVERYBODY TALKS ABOUT IT

Notes From Zone 10

January 2002

Fifteen years ago when we were moving from Boston to San Diego a friend warned, "You're going to hate southern California; all anyone ever talks about there is the weather." Today, cloudless, 71°, the ocean sparkling like a diamond, is the sort of day we yield to the weird impulse to brag about living here. Of course we secretly believe those of you slogging through slush in Chicago have more character.

That's what I'm writing you about, the weather.

You may have seen Elizabeth Kolbert's article (Ice Memory) in the January 7 New Yorker. It seems for the past forty years scientists have been drilling into the ice pack in Greenland because it gives them a clear picture of the earth's climate for more than the past hundred thousand years. According to Kolbert, in the past decade climatologists have come to agreement, an agreement that has changed everything about the way they view the history of the planet and of human tenure here.

The two main features of this consensus are: for the past hundred thousand years the earth's climate has been in flux, changing not gradually, but violently and without warning; and our own relatively benign experience of the climate is not the norm. If the past pattern continues, we are due for a dramatic cooling, in fact another ice age, perhaps within decades.

This discovery has come as a surprise to scientists who have only what they regard as irrefutable overwhelming empirical evidence; they have come up with no theory for why this is so.

Paleontologists and anthropologists have wondered why human civilization seems to have abruptly flourished beginning 10,000 years ago. Now it seems it may be because 10,000 years ago, quite suddenly, the climate that would support life as we knew it began. And the ice record suggests we are at the end of a 10,000 year warm period and about to shift, suddenly, into a cold period that will not support human civilization and will last 125,000 years.

I'm not sure why it has always cheered me up to think the earth will be here long after our species is gone. So much of our picture of things is focused, understandably, on ourselves, as if we were the crowning achievement of evolution and on our continued future hangs the fate of the everything . Looked at in geologic terms that seems a silly parochial view. We have been here a very short time and may turn out to have been an interesting if brief experiment. That we are, so far as we can tell, the only ones who reflect on these matters doesn't change the fact that we are here at the sufferance of the climate. (Did you read that they just discovered a month ago that there was a meteor large enough to do in Europe, that narrowly missed us?)

Fossils in the ice cap show there are species that can hunker down through those extended freezes and emerge during the shorter warm times. I suppose we are the heirs of the last batch. Wouldn't it be something to know what the next creature to emerge in 150,000 years will look like?

Nothing about any of this seems to diminish our resolve to keep going, do what we can as long as we can. But it can only do us good to understand that everything, even our place on the earth is, as the Shakers say, a gift for a season.

EVERYTHING

Notes From Zone 10

Late Sunday I went to look up a date in my date book/telephone book. Not on my desk. Troubling the seemingly smooth surface of my consciousness.

"Lacey," I called accusingly, "do you know where my date book is?" Naturally she didn't even though I knew she had just looked up a number in it. "You sure? You had it last." I then noisily with much sighing, rummaged around the apartment ineffectively scattering piles of paper.

"You know," Lacey said helpfully, "you just took out a lot of trash; maybe your date book was with it." I dismissed the insulting suggestion with a huff, until, having exhausted every crevice in our small apartment, I waited until Lacey was distracted and sneaked down the back stairs and out to the street where I had just rolled the bin for the morning trash pick up. I lifted the lid and the date book was on top of everything, my gold leafed initials plainly visible. When I returned with the book in my hand, Lacey was as gracious as it is in her to be.

I mark the beginning of the episode as Friday afternoon when I played singles against a visitor from Phoenix. I was, as they say, in the zone, played like a teenager for two amazing sets, prevailing 6-2, 6-2. "Got another in you?" he asked. Who knows if I'll ever get in that groove again, so I agreed. I got down 5-2, consoled myself that I'd really already won the match, then thought maybe I'd give it a big go and see what happened. My game picked up a whole level and I won the third set 7-5. Hard to describe the pleasure it gave this aging warrior.

Despite the wonders of Vioxx, most of my blood volume the next 48 hours went to rescuing oxygen starved muscles, leaving my brain to suck hind teat. I napped from 5 to 8:30pm, rising long enough to watch a movie and take a cup of tea, then back to bed at 11 until 8am. Despite still reveling in my reprieve from gerontology tennis, I felt mildly depressed, distracted, semi-conscious. After a long walk on Sunday, I again took to my bed until dawn Monday when I rose ill-tempered to feed and walk the dog.

After breakfast I began packing my backpack for my walk up the hill. "Lacey, have you seen my journal?" She didn't need to and somehow resisted making the obvious suggestion. I again waited until she was otherwise engaged and tiptoed down to the street to check the recycle bin, from which the red and white Mead Composition notebook glared up at me accusingly. When I walked through the front door, Lacey smiled, not a really friendly smile.

"You think it's early Alzheimer's?" she wondered helpfully.

When she left for work I signed onto Matt Drudge's daily political gossip web site, which I do to distract and offer myself numbing solace. I linked to a site built by fired CNN workers (Tedsturnovers.com) that trashed a woman TV actress CNN just hired to anchor one of its news shows. They gloated that she had previously posed nude, helpfully providing a link to the offending photo. I have never dared visit a porn site for fear the Feds might be on the other end or I could get addicted or something. But this was a sort of CNN site, and I could use a little pick me up, so I clicked.

And my computer froze, then crashed. Gone. Blank. Nothing.

I've outgrown the God who rewards and punishes. But letting go of all hope of diversion, of distracting myself, has proved more challenging. I was put in mind of something a wise and dear friend, a discalced Carmelite Nun who has spent the past half century in enclosure once said to me. I was distressed about what felt to me like a huge cost I had to be prepared to pay for making a move in my life I wanted to make. She smiled a smile I had come to associate with the grin of a fox.

"Blayney," she asked, "What do you think God wants from you?"

It felt like the hardest, most obscure question I had ever been asked, and I was not only without an answer, but blank, clueless. I must have looked miserable, like an 8th grader caught without his homework. After a long silence she laughed, loud, raucously, as if she'd just told a risqué joke.

"Blayney, you know what God wants from you; God wants everything."

YOU THINK I'M A FREAK?

Notes From Zone 4

August Dog Days 2001

Ill-suited. The notion had darted through my mind, like a sparrow skillfully, swiftly flying into a dense bramble bush without so much as brushing a thorn. I wondered why, where did that come from? And how did it navigate around those billions of neurons, landing intact, prettily perched so I could watch it, unobstructed, in the tangle? Not that it's unusual, this seemingly random fleeting thought, but this time I marked it. Maybe because I was sitting down to make a journal entry and I usually wonder what's going to emerge from the snarl.

Last night, after a trip to Wahoos for a burger and fries, and a root beer (Lacey's in California working this week), I settled down on the couch to watch "The Sixth Sense" featuring Bruce Willis. I don't think I've ever seen a Bruce Willis movie before because I don't like horror; it's too like my mind and my dreams. But one of our kids had told me it was good, and the conversation among the dog and cat and I was getting stale.

Ill-suited. That's Bruce Willis'. You pick it up the first time he appears on screen. He plays a man who has been killed and takes the whole movie and the direction of an intuitive little boy to discover that he's dead, a device to hook into that sense we all seem to have, that we don't quite belong here. That we wandered into someone else's reality, where the rules are theirs, not ours.

The thought, ill-suited, raced through me this morning, not last night as I watched Bruce, but maybe Bruce triggered it? Really, that's the point here; I suspect nothing triggered it. It just happened by.

The bar just beneath the page I'm writing right now, sometimes shows the page number, paragraph number, even the line and space number. It makes me feel oriented, safe. Then it disappears, goes blank, for no reason I can discern, and my frantic attempts to get it back come to nothing. It really matters to me. I can't think of a single time when I changed anything because of what it told me, but that's like saying I've never changed my spending habits after checking my net worth. Why do we feel the need to justify our obsessions?

Two years ago we got street signs at all the intersections in our town, even the most remote dirt roads. 911 came to rural Vermont and insisted that each road have a name so they would know where to answer the calls. No problem, I thought, these roads have had names for at least the twenty years I've been around. But it turns out they not only were known by different names to different people, but sections of them were known as one name, other sections others, depending on who had lived there long enough for the house to be known, like our house, as Minnie Stetson's.

For the past two years, town meetings in Vermont have been battle scenes. Most people think it's because of Act 60, our state's attempt to refigure school budgets since the Supreme Court said they couldn't be based only on property taxes. No doubt the Yankee venom aimed at Governor Dean, a Connecticut flatlander, is in part inspired by requiring towns to send the tax money to Montpelier instead of keeping it to spend on the schools as we see fit. But the street name battle is the real issue. It's one thing to mess with my money; telling me I have to surrender to your name of my road is another.

I can't come up with a name, any name, street, drug, animal, my own or my wife's, if the moment requires it. If it hadn't happened all my life I'd attribute it to senility. What I make of it is my lifelong inability to keep anyone or anything in neat order. They're all in there and so long as it's unimportant, I can usually retrieve them. But my catalogue system . . . well, I don't have one.

What's pretty interesting is that I do At Random with Olympic skill. And Lacey, who has never felt any need to order her conversation, lets her synapses fire at will. She just assumes that whatever makes its way in and out of her conscious is either doing the same in you, or you will see how it's going in her. I long for her assurance that you'll either catch up or not. It's not important.

Order is overrated. "Chaos," wrote Henry Adams, "is the law of nature, order the dream of man."

So what? So plenty. I think we're haunted in this culture by worry that we're the only one who's like this. The little boy in "The Sixth Sense" who could see and communicate with dead people, feared his mother's judgement more than he feared the dead people. "You think I'm a freak," he whined to her.

No doubt we have to come to some agreement so we can arrive at the right place in an emergency. But that doesn't mean we have to torture ourselves over our secret, that so much of what we notice doesn't fit the street signs. Or to deny what we see to make ourselves fit.

Hey, I just figured out how to make that bar at the bottom of
the screen tell me where I am on the page. I've been fretting over
that for three years. Now I can go back to wondering whether
you're going to think I'm a freak for having brought this up.

DISNEY AT REED HILL

Notes From Zone 4

Summer 2001

Ok, here's the scoop. We'd both had a full day of exercise, Lacey 35% more than I, and were exhausted by 9, got into bed around 9:3o and were finally both asleep by maybe 10:15.

Eeyow! There something in this bed! Shouts Lacey, waking me, throwing sheets everywhere. I roll out of bed onto the floor as if someone was shooting at us through the window. When I can collect my wits, I rise, turn on the light and begin shaking the bed clothes.

Nothing. I'm pretty pissed about being wakened so violently at my advanced age, by Lacey's unfounded hysteria. I no doubt show that. We look around some more. Nothing.

Just as I'm about to turn off the light and get back to bed, I see Jasmine emerge from under my bureau, led by a small gray field mouse. The mouse she had moments before held lightly in her mouth, so as not to bruise it, and hopped onto the bed.

A certain amount of chaos ensues. It quickly becomes clear that Jasmine's interest in the matter is keeping herself entertained, no killer in her. She chases the mouse around the room, stopping each time she corners it, hunkering down, watching patiently until the mouse makes another desperate bid for freedom and off they both go.

I get the waste basket and chase after the two of them, hoping I may be able to pop the basket on top of the mouse, though I have no idea what I'll do after that, maybe just have the thing in one place. But forget that, I can't come within a foot of the mouse, though Jasmine seems to enjoy watching me try.

We've now closed the doors to the hall and the closet to keep the mouse from going to another part of the house, and this being our first real summer night, we're both pouring sweat and wondering if this is how we'll be spending this night. We discuss leaving the two of them to work it out while we go downstairs and spend the night in the guest room, but we'd be directly beneath them listening to their tiny toenails scurrying across the floor all night and then be right back where we now were in the morning.

The cat lost the mouse a half dozen times and hunkered down beneath the bed while Lacey and I shook dust ruffles and moved furniture. Each time the mouse would eventually make a break for it and we'd go through another heat.

Finally, in desperation, Lacey went across the hall and pulled Alyssum from her cage (she wasn't keen about having her night's sleep interrupted either) and brought her into the room. We wondered if, at her advanced age (92, I reckon, in our years), deaf and with a faulty heart valve, she would be up to this one more time.

We needn't have fretted. As soon as she entered our room she picked up the scent and began frantically running the room's perimeter, her nose to the floor, whimpering excitedly. She flushed the mouse four or five times, once slamming her own head hard into one corner as she lunged for it and the mouse ran right under her to the other side of the room. Again, we lost the mouse several times, while it must have been desperately clinging to the underside of some piece of furniture, and each time it would finally let go and run and Alyssum would run after it, her nails slipping and sliding on the wood floor.

After ten or fifteen minutes the mouse made a fatal wrong turn; and Alyssum cornered it over by the closet. She jerked her head forward and had the thing in her mouth in a move too fast for me to track. She chomped down on it a couple of times and then, jerking her head back and forth, swallowed the thing.

Alyssum was reluctant to go back to bed, and Lacey and I had some trouble settling down, too. Jasmine took it all in stride. Tough little terrier with unbeatable instinct.

THE COUNT

Notes From Zone 10

Election Day 2000 + 2

Last I looked they were separated by fewer than 800 votes. My friend and financial advisor, who believes Clinton/Gore is (near as I can tell, he thinks it's really one guy) not so secretly attached to the satanic hip, was fidgeting in his chair as if it were hot-wired when I stopped by his office this morning.

My visits are a trial for him. He discovered long ago that I not only am a yellow-dog Democrat but that I actually like Bill Clinton. When Alan King said America's dirty little secret is that, even though we know we're not supposed to, and even though we don't think oral sex in the oval office is a good idea, we like the guy, he was talking about me. He's the uncle who sidles up to us at the family party, puts his arm around our shoulder and asks, "How's your love life?" And then actually seems to listen as if he's interested.

My financial advisor and I have somehow managed to stay friends and genuinely enjoy each other. I've been his client for many years and he's the one I credit with my being able to quit work, confirming my theory that a friend is anyone who makes our life better.

Our conversation took an even more circuitous route than usual

this morning on its inevitable route to the question of whether
Bush and the Republicans are more morally upright than
Clinton/Gore and the Democrats. Financial offices are a
fascinating array of theories built on the mountain of arcane data
they collect about everything from the net worth of angels
dancing on the head of a pin, to the consumption of bitter in
London's pubs as a measure of the pound's performance against
the lire. Today he trotted out a map of the US to show that Gore
had carried the perimeter states where the immoral elite live,
while Bush had carried the great moral middle.

I find these theories dazzling if immaterial.

His point this morning was driven by his conviction that Gore
was challenging some of the Florida vote count because he was
behind. I allowed as how that was no doubt true and would be
going on if Bush was behind. After all, their friends have
invested something over $1 billion in having their chum in
the White House and, as Everett Dirckson once said, "A
billion here, a billion there, and pretty soon you're talking
about real money."

Quickly our conversation moved to our usual critical difference,
about whether it is possible to discern morality. I've discovered
that George W. evokes the sort of visceral response in me that
Clinton/Gore evokes in my financial advisor. I'm tempted to
assume that's because my moral radar has detected his true
character. But I'm afraid it's because he reminds me of the guy
in my second grade class at Eastover School whom I envied because
he seemed so sure of himself. I once challenged his claim that
Butch Butler was a better running back for the Charlotte Clippers
than Rocky Spataccini. He punched me in the nose and the girl I
loved laughed. I think that's what I have against George W. Bush.

But do I care which one wins? Passionately. Do I think it will make a huge difference in how life unfolds? I do. But I have no idea how. Reagan ran up the largest deficits in our nation's history and Clinton balanced the budget; run that through your litmus tester.

The reason we have morals and commandments and rules is because there is no code of conduct built into the order of things and we humans are capable of anything given the right circumstances. I have invented many sound reasons over the past fifty years for my allegiance to the Democratic Party, especially the commitment to work toward economic equality, however impossible and vague. But had the Republicans offered as elegant and articulate a candidate as Adlai Stevenson in 1952 when I was 12, I might count myself a Republican today.

It may be that what first attracted me to Christianity was the outrageous idea of Grace, that God, before and without our doing anything, loves and forgives us, no chooses us with helpless, scandalous passion. Like a cuckold, a scorned suitor who keeps coming back to his unfaithful lover because, against all better judgment, he can't stay away.

Strikes me that Clinton (not so much Gore on this one) knows that either God loves without any conditions or Clinton's cooked. Bush seems to think he's repented enough to have earned God's love.

In my book anyone who believes they're safe with God is scary. The unnerving thing about God, and about being God's creature, is there's nothing we can do to escape God's love. The only reason we are instead of aren't (after all, there's a lot more nothing in time and space than something) is because of love overpowering the abyss. It's a weird, unlikely, against-all-odds deal that we did nothing to win and yet we now inhabit forever.

So the count goes on and one of those guys is going to end up in the big chair for the next four years. I'm rooting for the heir to Adlai, who may still have sufficient irony to wake up on January 21st, roll over and say to Tipper, the way Bill did 8 years ago to Hilary, and many of us do many days: "Can you believe this shit?" But if it's the heir to Reagan, I'll live with it, and bet on his waking up, maybe sometime later than January 21st and saying to Laura, "I had no freaking idea when I got us into this . . ."

2002 OVER THE TOP

Notes From Zone 10

New Year's 2002

Good Judgment comes from experience; experience comes from bad judgment. Jim Horning

Who would ever want to live to be 90? Everyone who is 89. Winston Churchill

Ted Hughes, the British poet laureate who died recently, shortly after publishing distressing accounts of his life with his long ago divorced late wife, Sylvia Plath, once wrote of the "simple animal courage of accepting the odds."

Strikes me that's what many of us are up to these days. Our Christmas cards and letters seem not so much distressed or depressed, as maybe sobered. The odds have not changed, we have. And though we Americans have long prized optimism above most other habits for screening the world, perhaps any chance we get to honestly recalculate the odds is worth taking. The conviction is that reality is always worth more than illusion.

Sometime around 1970, when I turned 30, I began being aware of the coming close of the century and the millennium. For whatever reason the possibility of my reaching 60, and of seeing the new era, seemed remote. I couldn't wrap my mind around speaking the year as two thousand and one. I didn't think I could adjust. The statisticians (I guess that's who figures these things) tell us that if you reach 60, your chances for 80 are something like 70%. Now that I am past 60, I find myself figuring the odds more often than I used to. And two thousand and two, less than a week away, feels as simple as letting yourself slip into water that is slightly colder than the air.

How quickly we grow used to what so recently seemed exotic.

A few years ago I had one of those conversations with one of my children, the kind you imagine before they visit, but almost never seem to have. We talked about what we imagine it's like to die. I must have sounded calmer than she felt about it.

"But aren't you scared, Dad? I mean what if it turns out to be nothing?"

"I was when I was your age, when it seemed gross that I might cease to be. But somehow it doesn't seem like such a big issue now."

The metaphor that I like best is: God's love, the source for anything, everything, is irrevocable. The mere fact that you are instead of are not, is evidence enough of the rich dependability of reality. Like the astonishing odds-against life-giving warmth of this morning's sun, the manner in which you came to be is trustworthy.

Of course trying to cling to that happy surprise, define it, pause it in process, refashion it, causes suffering. But even that suffering is no match for the miraculous arrangement of matter we know as you.

Where religion seems to go wrong is in trying to claim special status for its own metaphors. Whether Jew, Christian, Muslim, or agnostic, we forget that the most metaphor any of us can make is for the part of the elephant we can sense in the shadows.

I like the metaphor of God's love because it concedes the unexpectedness of reality. It strikes us as routine after the fact, but which of us could have imagined it?

Amidst the absurdity, a man trying to light off his shoe in a plane, a Zimbabwean patriot gone wrong and wrecking a nation, a baby starving in Afghanistan, my sweet terrier gracefully losing her grasp on life, remains the sublime mystery; out here in the vastness of the universe, where for aeons there was nothing and will be again one day, today there is this startling dance, so complex as to defy description, to which we have been invited.

To expect more than that we be amazed, delighted to be included, seems, in two thousand and two, maybe a little over the top.

HITTING THE ZEN WALL

Notes From Zone 4

October 4, 1999

For more than a year I've been anticipating a training weekend at Zen Mountain Monastery in Mt. Tremper's, New York, a tiny village near notorious Woodstock in the Catskills. As I write, I've been back from the weekend less than 24 hours. It was the most terrible and clarifying retreat I've ever done.

Zen Buddhism has become a trendy avocation for American spirit junkies among whom I number myself. I subscribe to Tricycle Magazine and follow the exploits of Richard Gere, the high profile Zen disciple and confidant of the beguiling Julia Roberts. So a year ago I signed up to do the introductory weekend at the monastery.

It was a terrible weekend because I wasn't up to it. It was a wonderful, clarifying weekend because I saw crystal clear and without self-recrimination my limits. The reason I'm writing this to you now is because I think many of us have exalted notions of our spiritual aspirations and are secretly ashamed of how lazy or afraid we are of pursuing them. As a parish priest for thirty years, I lent to that shaming, maybe even to a few of you. Now that I find myself on the other side of the aisle, I want to make some amends.

"During this intensive and demanding retreat, we will study some of the most important aspects of Zen training. Because each part of the schedule is essential to your experience of Zen practice, we ask that you come prepared to participate in all of the weekend's activities, and to stay until the retreat concludes at 1:30pm on Sunday."

I remember trembling a little when I read that, then reflecting on the countless weekend retreats I've been to and led. There were several times during the weekend when I wanted to flee. During meditation sitting from 7:30-9pm when my folded knees threatened to blow apart. At midnight the first night, in a room with nine other men, seven of us snoring, all sucking up more oxygen than the room held.

At 4:15am when the rising bell sounded. In the morning meditation from 4:55 to 7, the evening meditation from 7:30-9 and Sunday's sitting meditation, and teaching from 9-12. It was the sitting meditation that got to me most. I dreaded it, not only because of the physical pain of sitting, but even more for the psychic pain from my rebellious distracting mind.

I remember years ago, at a vestry retreat, the wife of a vestry member coming to me before we began our second meditation and saying she was going to excuse herself because she got so angry during the first mediation she didn't want to go through it again. I felt slightly superior to her in that moment. That person receives these Zone Notes. I feel kin to you today.

I thought there were no limits to my hunger to go inward and learn. I found my limits this weekend. I do a simple meditation, sing parts of Morning Prayer and read scripture most mornings in my studio before I begin writing. I figured I would be a hardened veteran at the Zen training weekend.

When I left on Sunday afternoon, I felt exhilarated. On the three hour drive I was filled with energy (even though I hadn't slept more than a total of six hours the two nights) and sang my way up the NY Thruway and across Route 7, through Bennington, over the mountain to home. At first I thought my burst of energy was due to being let out, but the more I reflected on it the more it seemed from a different source.

For the first time I faced the limits to my hunger and willingness to sacrifice on behalf of the kingdom of God. And, thanks to the compassion of the Zen Way, I saw those limits not as judgement on my lack of commitment or sincerity, but simply as a measure of where I really am in my life. I suspect I've known for a long time that I'm not the evolved Buddha I like to pose as, but this weekend gave me a hard look at that reality in a way that was so demanding and so generous, posturing seemed pointless.

The chief insight of Buddhism is, "You're perfect. Just the way you are. All the idols you chase in search of perfecting yourself are unnecessary, illusions that will collapse. Eventually you will be left with what you started with, yourself, made perfectly."

I suppose that can't help but sound nihilistic to our overachieving ears. But I have long believed Jesus was saying the same thing. I just never thought it was for me, that I was all right the way I am. Until this weekend at Zen Mountain Monastery, when I came face to face with the spiritual infant I am.

As I fidgeted and stole glances at my watch, praying for the meditation to be over, I asked myself what I was prepared to do to deepen my resolve, to enlarge the swath of reality I engage. The answer is, not an awful lot. I was clear that the community at Zen Mountain Monastery has set aside most of what I consider normal life on behalf of that quest. They showed me clearly, without apology, what it's like to make that choice. I do understand that the choice will one day be made fully, clearly, no matter what I do now, illusion will fall away and I will cease to cling. And I'm getting close to that time. But the monks showed me a clear apostolic way to get started now.

No doubt I will focus my practice because of what I learned from the monks. But no more pretending that I am a spiritual giant tuned like a great Buddha. I have been given a clear, compassionate look at myself, and the first shock of embarrassment has given way to an incredible lightness of being.

STOP THE PRESSES

Notes From Zone 10

November 2000

The paper of record reported this week a
stunning study
suggesting that when men look at
beautiful women
the same part of our brain
lights up
as when we are hungry and offered a
good meal.
The study also shows that [heterosexual] men press
harder, longer on the lever
that keeps a picture on the screen when the picture is of a
beautiful woman
than when it is of a man, even an attractive man.
Stop the presses.

Our aging terrier, female, laboring under congestive
heart failure
has new energy since we returned to California where she meets
another fox terrier
and an English bull terrier
on her morning walk. She's mostly aloof, ignoring other dogs,
but
these two set her tail in frantic motion and she

flags them, brazenly
backs into them.
"Your dog fixed?" the bull terrier's handler asked me one morning.
"Uh huh, right after she had a litter."
"He's not," he gestured to his drooling dog, "looks like your
dog knows."

The NY Times said the study didn't run similar tests with
women;
their cycle presents so many variables they couldn't write a
computer code complex enough to take them all
into account.

Unless our terrier finds some way to tell us, I guess
we'll never know
about women.

I RECENTLY HIT THE WALL AGAIN

Notes From Zone 4

September 14, 1999

I recently hit the wall again. Again. The wall. Hit the wall. Again. Hit. Again. The wall. The wall.
WILL YOU SAVE ME?
Dreams of salvation. Of being good, useful, admired. Loved?

The burr under this saddle is Buddhist meditation, cultivator of dis-ease. Breathe ten long easy relaxed breaths. Notice what you notice. What is it you're working on?

Enough. I'm working on enough. I am enough. I have enough. It is enough. I've been holding out, out for you. I figured you'd eventually come through. It's been nearly sixty years but I haven't given up. Haven't outgrown it. Hoping. Wishing. Praying. Begging. (A rabbi once told me that Jewish foreplay is two hours of begging. I asked him if he'd translated that from the WASP.)

I've still got a few tricks up my sleeve.
Like dying. I could die and then you'd see it my way. That was the wall I hit recently. There was blood; I didn't recognize it right away, did my denial thing. Then I felt a smile creep across my face. This is it. The big One, Elizabeth.

Ten easy breaths. What did you notice? The blood? Not really. More you. I noticed you. Well, did you notice anything in yourself? Well, yes. I noticed my head was very heavy (my favorite birthday card, or was it a get-well card? Was the one that asked on the front, "Want to lose ten ugly pounds?" When you opened the card, it read, "Cut off your head.") My neck felt tired. I saw the color red, deep blood(!) red. Watch the breath come in. Feel your body expand to accommodate it. The rich red oxygenated blood rushes through your system, warming your extremities. (Despite the humid hot days, the Vermont mornings have fall in them already.)

But it was mostly you I noticed. I watched carefully to see if you were holding out. But I couldn't be sure. WILL YOU SAVE ME? You would if you understood how anxious I am for you to do that. Unless you sense how willing I am to hide me and trick you to get you to do that. How fearful that you might see inside and, knowing whatever it is I've always kept hidden, turn me down. Pissed.

I have a sure fire Geiger counter for measuring your willingness to save me. When the little bugger begins to click and whine, warning me that you're using your nuclear arsenal to get from me what I want from you, my transmission switches instantly automatically into reverse. Fast reverse. I remember that first signal from you, the one that said you're willing to set yourself aside on behalf of my hunger. When the alarm sounds, warning me that you're at Defcon 4, ready to fire your destructive firepower at my insatiable soul, I fire my retro-rockets. MAD.

Surely you don't think I can save you? You can't want me to do that. You don't even need saving.

The wall. So I hit the wall, like the black fly buzzing frantically around my study. Banging, flinging itself against the windowpane, going berserk until it lights, exhausted, on the hemlock beam beside my desk. Wondering "where do I go from here? And where will this come out? Will this be where it ends?" This morning I found the fly that had been buzzing around my head yesterday, dead on the beam. I wondered how it died. Did it exhaust itself. Do flies have heart attacks? Cholesterol? And the Canada Geese denuding our field, exchanging grass and bugs for crescent-shaped green and black turds. They mate for life, I'm told. For what? Salvation? Do they fall in love? They've become a plague, these life maters. They are no longer Disney romantic. There'll be a season on them this fall. Tracey, the dairy farmer, says only geese and cows can consistently shit more volume than they eat. We all do it from time to time. But we homo sapiens(?) don't do it for long before we die. The reason the dog and I chase the geese back into the pond is because they do it all the time and seem the healthier for it. A field slick with goose shit has no spot in our plan of salvation.

Tuesday morning we were startled awake by gunfire, shotgun, behind the house, echoing across the pond. We rushed downstairs and onto the screen porch. Two young men in battle fatigues, firing at the Canada geese. I'd heard the geese are hard to kill, that you have to hit them in the head because their bodies are so thick with feathers. I couldn't tell at first whether they'd hit any. Then I saw two birds sitting on the water, seemingly swimming normally, and wondered why they hadn't flown away. The men rowed across the pond towards them and they flapped their wings pathetically. Wounded. They swam into the heavy brush on the pond's edge. The boat pursued. BLAM! BLAM!

I'd agreed they could hunt on our land. I was so pissed at the geese polluting our place. You'd think, after nearly sixty years I'd have accepted that the solutions to these problems aren't neat, sometimes are about as sinister as the problem. I've sanitized life. I felt sick to my stomach as I saw the fire leap from the barrel of the shotguns. As the two men jumped out and pulled the birds out by their necks, they talked excitedly. They exchanged high fives. I wanted to scream at them. But they were doing my bidding, ridding my personal property of a nuisance, a living marrying nuisance that was here before I was.

The blood in the toilet brought me brought me to full attention. As in Emily's solemn description, "After pain a formal feeling comes."

I acknowledge you, my blood from the deep interior. I've felt, or was it imagined, you coursing, gurgling brook, sometimes encouraged by my deep, measured meditation breath, mostly on your own hook, making your way smartly into capillaries, warming, reassuring. How many new tributaries have you cut, the Snake gorging through aeons of plaque-encrusted schist and shale? Can you find enough yielding places to keep the flow, oxygenating streams of unexpected microorganisms, stirring life-giving and life-threatening bacteria?

In the morning I take the anti-oxidents, C, E, Zinc, staving off the free radicals, cheering on the white cells in their battle against rogue cells forming a gang, a chaotic mound of would-be assassins. Host, I am their inhospitable host. I want the oxygen that grows and cures, but not too much, not random, giving life to my death.

The cat and the terrier suddenly on the chase at 3am. In the bathroom, down the hall, into our bedroom, terrier screaming full cry, cat dancing a crazy pirouette. It's a cold night, below 40°, and the rodents seek a warmer, friendlier home. Ours.

The cat's at play, the dog's in search of a meal. Cat's faster, cleverer, catches the frantic brown field mouse and tosses it into the air. Terrier goes nuts. The free radical has made its way into the unwelcoming host, our humble castle. Like my bleeding body, it warms its invited guests and hunts its unwelcome intruders. Let the warming, healing diners belly up to the table; surround, starve, devour those that have their own notion of what to feast on.

The terrier shocks us, in one sudden shake of her head the mouse disappears, it's scurrying little feet and tail sucked, as if by a huge vacuum, from the terrier mouth into the terrier stomach. Primitive, genetically perfected moment, the ratter swallowing the rat. Whole.
My stomach lurches. I've yet to face the full reality of this symbiosis. When my terrier smells a rat, my best interests merge with hers but not the rat's.

AL GORE &
BRIGETTE BARDOT

Notes From Zone 4

Labor Day 2000

If you liked Brigette Bardot you're going to love Al Gore. If there's anyone out there too young to remember Brigette Bardot, she was the French sex kitten who sizzled the big screen in the 60s. Those of you who remember her as I do, with heart palpitations, (mine not hers), will likely not immediately see how she reminds me of Al Gore. Here's how.

Last October Lacey and I went on a walking tour of the Amalfi coast of Italy. The day we walked Capri we came around a bend on the sheer rocky coast and looked down on an extraordinary stone pyramid house that seemed to have been part of the geologic formation when the rocks around it were thrust to the surface. Something about the bold statement the house makes, and the unlikely setting peaked our curiosity. Stories about the house were confused, someone said it was associated with a British movie star early in the last century.

Several months later I was leafing through an art magazine and came across a picture of the house with an article about it. It seems the house was built in the years between 1938 and 1944 by the enigmatic writer, Curzio Malaparte (he adopted the name to contrast with Bonaparte) and he considered his "House Like Me" his life's greatest achievement, greater than any of his writing. The article mentioned a movie, "Contempt", starring Birgette Bardot and Jack Palance (that's right, Jack Palance), written and directed by Jean-Luc Goddard and filmed in 1964. The article said the best way to see the house was to watch the movie, the last third of which was filmed at the house.

After several false starts I found the movie on a web site. The box it came in showed a picture in faded colors of Bardot and described it as having been made by France's controversial filmmaker, Jean-Luc Goddard, his first big-budgeted American film. "One of Brigette Bardot's earlier, most exciting roles . . . she literally pulsates with sexuality."

You can imagine the excitement at our house when the kids came home and showed us how to run the VCR. The excitement lasted about 15 minutes when, one by one, everyone except for me drifted off to other things, then up to bed leaving me alone on a chilly Vermont night to watch what Martin Scorsese called "brilliant, romantic and genuinely tragic . . . It's also one of the greatest films ever made about the actual process of filmmaking."

I fought sleep, determined to see, not only the wonderful views of the Casa Malaparte that had captured our imagination on our walk on Capri, but this movie that had caused such a stir among critics 36 years ago.

Here's the part about Bardot and Gore; they make you do much more of the work than we have become accustomed to doing in the past several decades. I've watched the movie three times now, each time seeing much I missed before. But even so I have to curb my annoyance that nothing is happening, that the actors are wandering randomly before the camera saying whatever comes into their minds. The movie jacket tells us that Bardot has an affair with Palance but all we see are two kisses so tame they wouldn't earn a Disney film a PG today.

When was the last film clip you saw of JFK, our first media idol President who died the year before this movie was made? I was startled listening to his voice recently speaking at American University when he called for the Test Ban Treaty. It sounded tinny, lacking inflection and his Boston Irish accent had an unsophisticated parochial ring I hadn't remembered.

I get annoyed with Al Gore for not doing more to keep me interested. Until I remember people voting with their feet when I preached, and how mad I got, even righteous sometimes, that people want to be entertained. I wasn't too pure to try it, once brought my portable leather bar from college days as a prop in a sermon about the prodigal son (one couple left the church over that sermon, saying they were going to find a church that still had some sense of dignity). But those electrifying moments were few and labored. Mostly I was the proverbial talking head laying out ideas that hardly anyone except me (and sometimes not even me) cared about.

But now I read old sermons and am amazed at how packed they are with rich nourishment. If I can stay awake. On my third viewing of "Contempt" I began to love the movie and see it as one of the most amazing, best I've ever seen. I expect to watch it several more times before we leave Vermont and winter and our VCR, for southern California where we have neither.

There is no moral to this story, no cajoling or persuading you that if you would only regain your discipline and sensibilities of 40 years ago you might actually find Al Gore's speeches fascinating, easy to listen to. What is, is and the media have moved us to a new place. No one can change the manifest culture. It is fascinating to see Brigette Bardot after all this time, the woman who made my breath go away when I was 24, and here she is filmed nude but in such a way that seems as if she was posing for a life drawing class. Less animated and no more provocative than Tipper Gore.

Somebody should get a copy of this video for Vice President Gore. It probably wouldn't teach him anything new, but it might make him feel a lot better, maybe even help him like himself better, seeing how sexy and alluring he could be if either he was running a long time ago or we were a retro bunch of citizens.

INVOKING JESUS

Notes From Zone 4

Fall 2000

Lacey questioned me sharply the other day because she noticed a difference in the blessing I said when all our kids were here for my birthday and the one I said when asked by former parishioners to say Grace at a beach picnic. In the first I didn't invoke Jesus' name, in the second I did.

"Do you speak of Jesus only when you have to for PR reasons? Or did you omit Jesus to pander to your daughter's Buddhist leanings?" she asked with her usual gentle curiosity.

It used to frost me when my wife turned out to share the sensibilities of parishioners, when she told me she found the sermon arcane, or she thought I cared more about the sound and cadence of words than I did about making a coherent point. When I responded that trying to express the ineffable was tricky, she'd allow as how I never seemed reluctant to give it a whirl. Many's the Sunday she wondered if people left church with anything comforting. I told her I thought church-going was to prepare people for a disruptive encounter with God. She would point out that I usually took a kinder, gentler position in the fall when we were raising the church budget.

Then our conversation took a more generous turn, towards the subject of marriage and true love. Even though she's five years younger than I, Lacey shares my sense that passion evolves and relationships go deep into old bedrock when marriage survives the whitewater of its early days. She no longer bristles at my saying that we've got love all wrong in this culture, that it's not only about how quickly or how often someone can arouse your libido, but about recognizing when you are inextricably bound to that person.

For better, for worse, for richer, for poorer, sickness and health, until we are parted by death; not exactly a formula for a skin flick. The arousal is one authentic dimension, and it takes the form not only of great sex but of scary conflict. Nothing is more sobering than discovering that someone has this hold on you, forever, and most of us spend at least some of our energy resenting and resisting.

This takes me back to Jesus and God. I find invoking Jesus much like the early, heady days of a new relationship, in this case with God. Jesus is God's skin, which we can touch and smell, a source of arousal. Not for nothing do we refer to Jesus as God incarnate, God in the flesh.

I remember a prayer group in Africa, all women, whose praying sounded to me like the soundtrack of a blue movie. Breathy invocations, "Oh, Jesus, I adore you. Yes, Lord." My Yankee anxiety was on red alert. I asked Lacey to come with me the next time, both out of fear for my own ability to manage the energy in the room, and to get a second opinion.

"It's genuine," she judged later, "That's really the way they experience their life with Jesus."

I have found that, as with my sense of sex, love and marriage, my relationship to God has evolved, particularly the place of Jesus. I wouldn't trade in my adolescent fleshy sexual excitement, nor would I have given up the thrill of encountering God's flesh in Jesus. There are still moments when those things push their way to the center. But I'm grateful that both of those energies have flowed into the more murky waters of old age where sharp definition gives way to mystery and uncertainty.

It's not so surprising that now that I'm nearly thirty years older than Jesus was when he died, my appetite is more for sitting loose with the unknown than for a formula to unravel the mystery. My obsession with death has even begun to relax into a some sort of trusting that, whatever it is, it is. Most days.

I don't mind invoking Jesus when I pray, but it doesn't seem as urgent or necessary as it once did. Best of all, I'm certain it's fine however one does it. Our relationship to God is a marriage, for better, for worse, in sickness and in health, for richer, for poorer, and, unlike marriage, I suspect, imperishable by death. Utterly trustworthy, dependable.

JUDGE NOT
ASHES, ASHES,
WE ALL FALL DOWN.

NOTES FROM ZONE 10.

February, 1998

I wrote this to try to explain to Lacey (and myself) what motivates the characters in my fiction. Bad enough, she'd said, That you quit work, but now your characters are doing the same thing. I decided to send it to you because it might trigger some debate about what's real.

Judging. When I wrote my last Notes From Zone 10, sort of defending Clinton, or at least hoping to address self-righteousness, one person said he'd never taken to this "Judge-not-lest-you-be-judged," business because he believes our kind is a naturally judging creature, and we do it for survival, for good reasons and with good effect.

Makes sense to me. I certainly have few moments when that tape isn't running in my head. You know the one: my, she's put on some weight; he's certainly acting like an asshole; God, I've sat here next to this person for ten minutes and can't think of a thing to say; let's just kill Saddam Hussein; can you believe that adolescent jerk went and got himself a red Porsche?; omigod do

you s'pose my love handles look that big to everyone else?
Judging seems as natural as breathing.

I don't think the Jesus saying means exorcising that instinct. It
means understanding it in a new way. The Jesus ethic at first
blush looks self-defeating, the reverse of most of what we're
taught, maybe even come to by instinct, which is why it's always
been considered utopian, not possible in the real world. And I
think, because it requires a discipline which runs counter to
virtually all others we're taught, only a tiny minority ever try it
seriously. But that tiny minority make up a pretty significant
group. Start with Ghandi and Martin Luther King. And Jesus.
The fact that none of them died in their beds may also account
for their ethic not having been given a serious look by the
majority.

Though my quarrel is not with the Christian Church (or at least
that quarrel is not what this piece is about), you ought not to
look to the church to see this ethic at work. Of course there are
minority movements within the Christian Church, as there are
in Judaism and Islam, which commit themselves to this
discipline. The Brethren come to mind in the Christian
community.

The discipline is marked by a few assumptions.

1.   Life is precious, unexpected and proximate. Not ultimate.

Though I don't know if a two-celled fetus has the capacity for
astonishment, a natural response to discovering one's Being is
astonishment. If we were not so well guarded by layers of
unconsciousness, I'm sure we'd be continually amazed to be.
How did it happen that, in the face of incalculable contrary
odds, in a universe made up 99+% of nothing, we are instead of
aren't? With that astonishment comes the understanding that

this life, like everything else, isn't of our own making and isn't forever. No doubt there's some sort of dimension after death, but this life is for a while.

For a long time we weren't, and pretty soon we won't be again, and for a long time. I suppose that could be the basis for despair, but for those who discover it, it seems to elicit wonder, and even gratitude. For being.

2. There is no inflation in God's economy. Everything gets used.

I remember a book I read as a kid when I lived in the Philippines, about a group of men who had a PT Boat they ran behind Japanese lines during the Japanese occupation of the Philippines. The title of the book was *They Were Expendable* and the point was that these men, some of whom were killed, were willing to die because they believed something bigger than themselves was at stake. But I knew one of these men, he was my friend's father, and he was fun and exciting, full of life force, and good to me. I knew that even though he might be willing to sacrifice himself, he wasn't expendable. No one is.

Saddam Hussein isn't expendable. When I was first involved in the civil rights movement I went through a training organized by the Fellowship Of Reconciliation. I still have the pamphlet they gave us. The point which remains imbedded in me is: "In the solution you envision to this injustice, is there a place for your enemy? If not, it's not a solution, but the perpetuation of new injustice."

Bill Clinton's not expendable. When we shame another person into exile, into hiding for their moral transgressions, we exile, drive into hiding, essential parts of ourselves which we have cast onto the transgressor.

Mind you, this isn't an endorsement of the status quo, leaving things as they are. But it does assume that whatever solution we come to will include those we now perceive as perpetrators of the problem we're trying to resolve. If not, count on the problem reemerging.

Gandhi wasn't being sentimental when he took care not to step on ants. He was being consistent and scrupulous. There is no inflation, nothing to be thrown away, in God's economy. Though we're not able to live this out in all its implications (I step on ants and eat meat), there is no wasted motion in the universe, no action without reaction.

Whether bad weather, a plunging economy or my failing health, it is of a piece, all moving inexorably toward Grace. There is finally, for everyone, a moment in which they relax fully into the embrace of Absolute Love. I may have my face lifted or excise a tumor, sign up to fast freeze my body at the moment of my death, but my goal is finally to welcome and embrace the fullness of reality, what is. And I will. Embracing the fullness of reality is a working definition of dying. We're going to do it. It's built into the design.

3. Grace is the fundamental nature of reality.

Every religion tells of an event which underscores this. For Christians it's the story of Jesus. For Jews the covenant with Abraham and the Exodus. Those stories are about God calling into being something which wasn't. Deuteronomy 26:5, "A wandering Aramean was my father . . ." tells the story of how a nobody became, by God's grace, a somebody.

Each of us was once nobody. We came to be somebody by Grace, not through any effort or achievement of our own. The fear of being abandoned is fear of once again being a nobody. We spend a lot of our life energy seeking to earn this gift of being. And we know our efforts are futile. Being, it seems, is preferable to not being. Most days.

(Somewhere I read an account of one of our most gifted writers, Samuel Beckett?, a profound melancholy. He was watching a cricket match on one of those rare cloudless, cool English days. His companion said to him, "What a day! Makes you glad to be alive." "Oh," He replied, "I'm not sure I'd go that far.")

Grace is the name we give to a treasured gift given to us which we did nothing to earn. We did nothing to earn our being, but we have it. That is the basic nature of reality. The fact that it feels ephemeral, that we can't indemnify it, freeze it in time or be certain how it evolves over eternity, is a mystery. The mystery can offend us, because we can't earn it and we can't hang onto it. It's a mystery we'd like to master, and most religions make some claim to have solved that riddle. But we all know the mystery remains. The fact of my being infuses reality with Grace. Even the most pessimistic view, that this is a veil of tears finally interrupted by a black abyss, must begin with Grace, the surprising gift of being out of nothingness.

That surprise, at the discovery of being, is the religious impulse.

4. No matter is ever either created or lost.

Sounds like elementary physics, and it is. From this one could infer some sort of continuum from before birth to after death, or the stability of matter in history. This doesn't mean everything stays the same, but that evolution reuses atoms and molecules, again and again. This understanding could lead one to speculate about reincarnation. Or maybe reordering of one's atoms and molecules.

This is another perspective on there being no inflation in God's economy. It could confirm the existence of ghosts and make the waging of war seem futile. Ghosts are the remnant of what our five senses tell us seems to be gone, and war the attempt to rearrange reality.

One of the attributes assigned to God alone by the pious is the power to create ex nihilo. To actually create matter, from nothing. And I believe even the pious think God does not do that routinely. One interpretation of the creation story in Genesis is that God did creation by working on a preexistent chaos, not by making something from nothing. No one thinks the creation of novelty, of something from nothing, is usual.

In other words it's a rare, miraculous event when anything is added to the universe, and we can't do that. Rearrange maybe, create, no.

What this understanding contributes to ethics (how to act) is that surgical excision, whether of a feeling, a person, maybe even a tumor, not only doesn't achieve the hoped for result, but inevitably leads to unforeseen and unintended consequences. I suspect it may be this insight which has lead some people to embrace Christian Science, a useful if unbalanced picture of reality. This is a hard one because it seems to counsel total passivity. I don't know what happens to the atoms and molecules which are cut out of a malignant process in the prostate, nor can I grieve honestly for Hitler's suicide, but we shouldn't habitually choose such solutions because they inevitably lead to places we can't anticipate and wouldn't choose. The Psalmist warns against putting our trust in horses or in men's legs.

We have to act, and our actions aren't futile, but they are less and more than we understand. That's because we haven't the power to do other than rearrange atoms and molecules, not create or destroy them. Our inability to see the consequences of our choices is the fabric from which tragedy is woven. This alone would, it seems to me, dampen any tendency towards hubris, and make us cautious about heavy surgical intervention as a means to resolving frustration.

5. Compassion and empathy are the wisest and most effective strategies for coping with one's enemies.

Empathy is the insight that what we hate in another is present also in us. When we find ourselves in the face of intractable opposition, especially when it's focused in a particular person, we'll come out best when we assume we have met in that person a part of ourselves which is unresolved. Maybe even unexamined. Or unknown. This, I believe, is the root meaning of Judge Not. It's not that we don't, or even that we shouldn't have an attitude, but that we'd do well to understand that that attitude is never solely about the other. A wise friend once taught me that we only ever have contempt for ourselves. A Christian saint has said that whenever the church affirms something or someone it's almost always proved right by history, and when it condemns, history almost always proves it wrong.

So when we kill Saddam Hussein or disrespect an opponent, we're perpetuating an unaddressed process in ourselves. It's a failed strategy. I have heard the objection that compassion and empathy in the face of implacable evil plays into the hands of wicked people, giving them carte blanche to carry out their malicious intentions. James Earl Ray and Pontius Pilate would seem to be proof enough. Yet, aside from conferring martyrdom, and maybe confirming the power of King's and Jesus' convictions, it's hard to see what the assassins accomplished. Certainly not what they intended.

Here's a very hard part. There's no such thing as an evil person. There's evil in each of us, maybe to greater or lesser extent, but the world isn't divided between good and bad people. This doesn't mean no one ever needs to be restrained from carrying out evil intentions. It does mean giving up our wish to eradicate evil by getting rid of evil people.

Even though I may be able to restrain myself from doing evil through self-discipline, I will never be able to eradicate evil from within myself. And an inescapable irony is that the more strenuous my attempts to rid myself of evil, the more likely I am to want to lash out against evil I see in others.

In other words it is the world's most fiercely pure who become most vindictive. Be wary of those who have cleansed themselves of bad habits, or lost a lot of weight.

In summary:

1. I'm glad, blessed to be, though I find this Being precarious.

2. I'm awed by the efficiency of creation.

3. Basically, it's all a gift, given from pure love. Beyond my understanding.

4. I'm gaining confidence that I can count on this gift even though I don't deserve it and can't control it.

5. When I trust that my being given this gift was no mistake, I can believe the same about you.

6. Though I hardly ever know what to do with them, I increasingly believe my passion and my feelings.

In my fiction, I long to create protagonists who are convicted by these insights, even if they can't live them consistently. One of their biggest struggles is to forgive themselves for their violations of their most profoundly held beliefs. Much of the mischief they find themselves bogged down in stems from their dogged determination to carry out those beliefs.

Before you begin fretting about whether all this rings true to you or not, understand that this writing is an exercise in bringing to awareness what lies beneath the surface of consciousness. Thus, virtually all of the time, when these characters are breathing and moving around, it's with no awareness of all of the above.

If, upon reflection, people subscribe to this general picture of reality, a few things might turn out to be true about them.

1. They will want to worship in some form, surrender their impulse to control, and give expression to the wonder of being.

2. They will find it easier to forgive themselves, which, in turn, makes them more generous in their acceptance of others.

3. Their work may become more free of compulsion.

4. Their death and abandonment anxiety may evolve into a lively curiosity.

5. The fact that none of these good insights become consistent or even frequent, and that even those who come to them continue to suffer the slings and arrows of normal life . . . well, sorry. Shit happens.

LAST THINGS
EVELYN UNDERHILL DAY

Notes From Zone Four

Ides of June 2001

"If I go to hell I'm going to have a lot of company."
Timothy McVeigh

Two visions of the end of
time
One mine, one heard years ago from Madeline L'Engle
first hers:
Standing behind God's throne, she sees two men, facing the throne
arms around each others
shoulders
like happy boys
buddies.
Somehow she recognizes Michael the Archangel, right where she'd
expect, but the other, more shabby, who is
he?
Madeline strains to stretch around to get a better look
(she said she felt nervous about being discovered), and
finally
from a full profile, recognizes
Lucifer!

What's Lucifer, Satan, for God's sakes, doing in heaven, standing
    before the throne of
God
arm around the mighty righteous shoulder of
Michael?
A flash of recognition; I get it, it's the Last Day, End of
Time
and Lucifer, fallen angel, Michael's best friend before the Holy
War
must be restored to the place for which he had been Made.
Last Things.

Now Mine:
Adolph Hitler stands before God's throne, shaking his
fist
at God, shouting,
Send me to hell, I'm ready, I'm not scared, I lived my whole life for
hell
so let's get on with it.
Well, Adolph, God responds, It's not that simple, first we have
    some work to do.
There's no work needed, Adolph yells, the veins on his forehead
pulsate,
Just send me to hell, Now.
God turns slightly left and nods
from behind the throne comes Tadeusz, the first
human
to die in a Nazi death camp, a Polish
tailor
nattily dressed in striped trousers, morning coat, shoes highly
    polished. Hitler
recoils
Tadeusz approaches him and
speaks:
Hello, Adolph, yes it's me, Tadeusz, I forgive

you.
No! Hitler shouts, frozen in place as Tadeusz embraces him,
No! No more, just send me to hell, now."
We'll see, says God, We've got 5,999,999 more to go, then we'll
see.

Later, I asked Madeline's son-in-law
Alan Jones, Dean of Grace Cathedral in San Francisco,
What do you think of these two visions?
He looked serious, stroked his bearded chin, paused and said,
I think, to call yourself an orthodox Christian,
you have to believe in
Hell
But I don't think you have to believe anyone is there for
eternity.

THE MERCEDES COUNT

Notes From Zone 10

The Ides of March 2001

Everyone is seeking some sign that this market plunge has hit bottom. I think I have one. Remember, you heard it first on Notes From Zone 10.

It's the Mercedes count, La Jolla's leading indicator.

I began this count a couple of years ago; it's a kind of mantra. On my mile and a half walk home from the Museum of Contemporary Art where I go each day to write, I count the Mercedes. I walk the main streets of the village, down Torrey Pines, the only road in and out of town, into La Jolla Shores. So of an afternoon I see many of the heavily trafficked roads.

I started counting out of curiosity. I grew up in North Carolina in the 1940s, where the Chevy was the volks car. The Mercedes is the standard here. In rural Vermont where we spend the gentle half of the year, you can go weeks without seeing a Mercedes. I don't know a single person who owns one there.

When we first moved to California in 1987, the abundance of exotic cars struck me as much as the ocean views. Not long after we arrived, a Lamborghini, with a price tag nearing $300K, missed the turn from Torrey Pines onto La Jolla Shores Drive and crumpled itself into a fire hydrant. Having driven past the wreck became a marker, like having passed North Bundy in Brentwood after the murders. A few days ago I walked by the Marine Room, a restaurant that at high tide takes breaking waves across its big glass windows, and there were three Corniche Rolls Royces in the parking lot.

Mercedes may be an exotic in Vermont (no longer in Charlotte); in La Jolla it is assumed. I might have had one if I'd had the money and it hadn't seemed indecorous for the local vicar.

Warning: the following may contain material unsuitable for children and Mercedes owners.

I knew one person in the town southwest of Boston where I was Rector before La Jolla, who bought a Mercedes. He was a retired banker, a Yankee who eschewed luxury. I expressed astonishment that he had traded in his Ford Fairlane for a foreign extravagance. He told me he had done so only after he became convinced that, considering the maintenance and the way it held its value, the Mercedes would prove more economical than the Ford.

I asked him if he knew what Mercedes and hemorrhoids have in common. He didn't. I've been told that sooner of later every asshole gets one. To his credit, he laughed. Maybe because he knew I would have killed to have one. A Mercedes, that is.

I have a friend who has stepped up her search for a larger house because she just got a Mercedes roadster with interchangeable soft and hard tops. She loves the car but the garage is too small to house both the roadster and the alternate top. She stores it in the guest room. She hates having to choose between her car's soft top and her grandchildren, so she's seriously house hunting.

My record count is 88 Mercedes, made on a sunny Friday

afternoon last year in March when Torrey Pines was stop-and-go in both directions. That was the day the NASDAQ briefly passed 5,000.

The lowest count was a little over a week ago when I counted a measly 34 Mercedes and the NASDQ first dropped below 2,000.

Yesterday, when all markets tanked, again, I counted 75 Mercedes. Today the dawn sky was a cloudless blue and pink, for the first time in weeks. Though it may be a while before CNBC picks it up, and the other indicators may lag, yesterday's Mercedes count signals the turn around.

Buy, if not a Mercedes, a share of Microsoft.

[Today, early February of 2002, The Dow is struggling to regain 10.000, the NASDAQ would kill to clear 2,000, and a few days ago I counted 114 Mercedes on my walk home.]

LOVE YOUR ENEMY?

Notes From Zone 10

Epiphanytide 1999

For many years I dreamed a combat dream. I haven't had one in a decade or more. It terrified me. I went to my share of war movies during WWII and Korea. We all saw jungle warfare in Viet Nam in our living rooms (though we threw out our TV during those years). But I've never been in the military and have always thought myself ill suited for that life. (Yet another reason I identify with Clinton instead of hating him).

The dream always followed a sort of formula. I am dug in a foxhole. The terrain seems borrowed from our backyard in Charlotte. I am behind one rocky mound and the enemy is behind another on the far side of the yard. (Those mounds produced huge juicy strawberries some years, some years nothing.) The enemy (come to think of it, the enemy is usually white European, looks more like me than the Japanese or Chinese I might have expected) is also dug in about a hundred yards away. I'm sighting through the scope on my M1 as my enemy sticks his head up above his bunker. I have a perfect easy shot. I begin to sweat and tremble. Even though I'm shaking, his head remains in the crosshairs of my sight for several seconds. I want to fire but my finger won't squeeze the trigger. It's dream paralysis.

I hear a noise behind me, look up and see the man who has been in my sight, standing on the rim of my bunker. His rifle is fixed with bayonet and he's pointing it at my head. His face is expressionless.

Again I'm paralyzed, staring up at him wondering whether I'll feel the bullet or hear the rifle fire. Then comes the moment, the dénouement. I've been shot, though there's no sensation. I have neither felt nor heard anything, but I understand I have been shot dead.

Now, am I or am I not?

Here I wake and immediately have two intense feelings: fear and frustration. Fear at being killed and frustration at not being able to stay asleep and in the dream long enough to have a good look at what it's like to be dead. The fear is fed in part by my wondering if I perhaps did in fact stay long enough, saw what it was to be dead and either erased it from my memory, or saw clearly that it was what I remember, nothing.

Because of the dream I was for years a pacifist of the Jesus/Ghandi stripe. Violence in any form, even self-defense, is self-defeating, ends up causing more problems than it solves. (Remember Stokeley Carmichael taunting? "President Johnson, he say 'don't do violence; violence don't solve nothin'. He say that while he bombing the hell out of Viet Nam. Who he think he's kiddin?'") It was while being trained for civil rights demonstrations by The Fellowship of Reconciliation ("Envision a place for your opponent in your solution to the injustice you're opposing," they taught us. "If you cannot see your opponent in the solution, it's not a solution but just replacing his injustice with yours.") that I realized I hadn't the moral discipline to call myself a true pacifist. I would surely lose my clear resolve when things got hot enough.

And I was suspicious of my motives. Maybe this wasn't principled; maybe I was merely a garden-variety coward.

How come I was unable in the dream to fire my weapon when I had the enemy in my sight? I'd love to believe it was my willingness to die rather than to kill, but I know myself too well to swallow that.

I think the man I had in my sight looks like me because that's who he is. And that's why I couldn't kill him. He is the part of me that needs to stay out of sight, dug into his foxhole. If he rears his head, not only is he likely to be shot, he's going to be seen, exposed. But if I kill him, I'm going to kill some essential part of me. A tougher dilemma is whether, if I l don't kill him, he's going to sneak up behind me and kill me.

You'd like to know what part of me that might be. Before I venture there, I want you to understand this is a universal exercise. In the Manichean struggle most recently made manifest in the Senate trial, [the impeachment trial of President Clinton] one can pick out those who would fire at their enemy-selves and those who would not. Even the bitterly partisan nature of the drama doesn't hide those, on both sides of the aisle, who believe it is safer, smarter and more moral to eradicate problem parts of themselves than to risk having them see light.

Let's get the basic premise on the table, another pesky Jesus paradox: **there is no person or deed so foreign or heinous that we haven't within us the same impulse we deplore in them.** Remember Pogo's cry: We have met the enemy and he is us.

From responses I have received from previous Zone Notes I know there are both sorts among you. And I learned from Pat Grant that it is never a fair fight between what we used to call liberals and conservatives. A piece of the liberal agenda is to include everyone, even those who hold different views. (The Fellowship of Reconciliation position) The conservative goal is to reach the Truth even when that requires pitching some non-believers over the side.

It's not about whether to annihilate our enemy; that turns out to be a practical impossibility. Jesus warned that when we sweep one of our demons from the room we make room for seven new ones. (Beware the dry drunk.) It's about how to live with our enemy so (s)he doesn't sneak up behind us and destroy us. I've learned the bedrock reality that I cannot squeeze the trigger when my enemy is in my sights for the same reason I cannot take out my eyeballs and stare at myself.

And who is my enemy? Every wish, impulse, compulsion, appetite in me that does violence to the picture I want you to have of me. And to the picture I want to have of myself.

The reason it looks so hostile, alien and threatening when I see it in Saddam Hussein or Bill Clinton or even Adolph Hitler is because I haven't been able to look at the desires in me that they are now putting in my face.

Though none of us is serene enough to live without enemies, the admonition to judge not, let God be the judge, turns out to be the only practical way to keep from destroying ourselves. We are notoriously poor judges of what about us is wheat and what chaff. Virtually always our persona, that part of ourselves we put out for the world's review, includes much that is not our essence. And hides much that is.

I'm tempted to try to list what is and what isn't essence, but I don't know. What I do know, and maybe it's why I don't dream the dream any more, is anytime I set out to destroy someone or something I hate, I end up with it all over me. (Ref. the tar baby. You know what I'm saying?)

NOTES FROM ZONE 10

Martin Luther King 2001

Struggling to remember
what about him
stirred more in me than I could
manage

He minded me of
Jesus
who was murdered on a garbage dump
Martin got gunned
down in a Memphis motel
where he'd gone to support the
garbage
collectors

And he
made me think of
me
a son of the south
longing for release from the prison of prim
pride and prejudice
I'd once thought the patrician's prize

So what
I wondered
had his passionate plea for people poor pigmented and dis
possessed
to do with lily
white
st grottlesexed ivied church of england old
boy?
why did the sight and sound of
Dr. King
race my racist heart and wake an
ache
in me to loose the bonds of so-called
privilege
in favor of an extravagant energy I'd only ever
fantasized?

I've got it now
I think
all these years later

J
Edgar
Hoover, hero of the tightly twined
his whoring hidden homo
erotic
shaming tormenting him
had hovered about King's
bed
staining, so
Hoover hoped,
his hero's halo.

It worked
the other Way for me.
I saw the
danger/hope
now not only that
revolution
might break boundaries color, money, class, race
but that
Fear
of me, of the passionate pursuit of you in me
could be
ravished
in the scandalous ecstatic embrace of
Jesus and the
smelly Samaritan woman at the well, in
Martin Luther King's
extravagant invitation to taste,
dine sumptuously at the banquet
of full-bodied
Freedom.

OSCAR & MAUDIE
KAMEHAMEHA AND EMMA
OF HAWAII DAY

Notes From Zone 10

November 28, 2001

Checking back into my novel after a few months away
and now I love it.
This morning I picked up my new glasses on my way to my writing
station.
I'm considering the novel through new
progressive lenses.
The words waver on the screen; at first I thought the computer
     wasn't sitting flat on its four corners. It is. It's my perspective
     that's
wavering.
I'm not going to tell you the novel's stirring story, on the off chance
     it just might be completed in my
lifetime. Or yours.

I will tell you the story would make a great movie. It's got everything
international intrigue
memorable sex that crosses national and racial boundaries
power politics enlisting both hemispheres and first and third
world nations,

friction between personal fulfillment, appetites for power, hunger
    for justice.

The focus is on a young African woman and young American man,
    both beautiful
smart, ambitious, idealistic
and drawn inexorably into realpolitik. Where reality trumps ideal.

Here's my dilemma, if it really is a dilemma:
Over the past three years I've gotten to know these two people,
what they look like
how they think
their habits
their unconscious prejudices and passions
their religious impulses
what they like to eat and how they're apt to dress
what scares them into hiding and what gives them creative energy
how their bodies smell when they're aroused.

The man (OK, he's Oscar) seriously wishes reality to fit his
desires
and mostly, until he encounters her (Maudie), it's worked out fine
    for him.
I've now been with these people enough to see that Oscar's going
    to
have to suck some serious wind, a fairly foreign feat for him.
Maudie doesn't do that; she'll settle for nothing less than
everything
whatever the cost.

I haven't told you my dilemma yet, though you may think I
have.
It's pretty simple
or it was until I looked at it through these enigmatic new lenses.
It's that, for all the flesh I've savored on these two, and

on several others along the way,
I haven't a passionate stake in how it all works
out for them. Or for me.
I like them, sometimes even romantically love her,
feel absorbing compassion for him.
I once assumed the privilege of writing the novel was to
make it come out the way I wanted.
I've discovered there is no certain way I want it to come out.

That was keeping me from finishing the thing,
that Maudie and Oscar might merely be
living their lives, riding reality, like I
do.

As those wavering words fall, finally, into
focus,
I see that they
are.

NERVOUS NELLIES

Notes From Zone 10

Veteran's Day 2001

So now we've traveled, flown cross-country, seen the young men and women in camouflage, looking awkward but reassuring, eyeballing us as we check in. The pilot came on the intercom after takeoff and said he hoped he'd had a chance to greet each of us as we boarded. I read somewhere that the airlines have reminded the pilots that they are the captains of their ships and if they don't like the look of someone, they have the right, even the obligation, to refuse to take them. I suppose that could result in a doozey of a lawsuit, but maybe we're all willing to face that now.

The issue of civil liberties is getting dicey. In the end it's a pragmatic choice, like all American choices have always been. We have strong ideas about how we want things to be . . . we hold these truths to be self-evident, but there are moments. It's just, how can you be sure when it's one of those moments in which circumstances render the rights no longer self-evident?

I read a fascinating review of a couple of recent books written about the Supreme Court decision that, everyone now agrees, elected Bush President. The reviewer was agnostic about the decision, believes we are still too close to say whether it was a good or bad decision. But he was appalled by some of the legal experts who slammed the decision, not on any legal basis, but on a vitriolic, partisan basis.

I was surprised, not having thought about it for a few months, that I am relieved that the Court made the decision it did when it did, even though I am a partisan Democrat and believe the Court may have prevented the man who won Florida's electors from claiming them. I want the Supreme Court to deliberate dispassionately, on the basis of their most carefully considered legal precedents and understanding of the Constitution. But, with some embarrassment I realize I want those nine justices, when they get behind closed doors, to worry and wonder what the practical result of their decision might be.

And to some degree my willingness to admit that may come from the terrorist attacks. More and more I see this, as Andrew Sullivan wrote in the New York Times a few Sundays ago, as a religious war. Not, however, of Muslims against Christians, or even the undeveloped east against the wealthier west (though that issue must be faced before there can ever be lasting peace). The real issue is between True Believers, Fundamentalists, those who believe their cause is Absolute and from God, and secularists, relativists, equivocators, nervous Nellies.

Yes, I purposely used pejorative words to describe the side I think I am on, because I've had to face criticism, most harshly my own, of my lack of certainty and conviction. You think only Islamic extremists would fly a loaded airliner into a crowded building? Timothy McVay was an American in the John Brown tradition, who believed that making his statement was well worth 'collateral damage'.

The really tough part is how to wage a war between those who believe the means totally justify the ends, and those who think there are limits. And the troubling irony is that once the relativists drop their doubts, it becomes a holy war between true believers.

Here is something I was taught nearly forty years ago, as I was being trained by the Fellowship of Reconciliation for the first civil rights demonstration I ever took part in. This was in Boston after a federal judge ordered busing across ethnic and racial lines. Louise Day Hicks was head of the School Board and vowed to defy the court order. I was 23, from the pristine suburbs, and righteous.

"When you are faced with an angry, cursing, shouting, threatening person," our trainer insisted, "picture where that person fits into the solution you see to this problem. If there is no place for them in your solution, then it's not a solution. It's only replacing their bastards with ours, setting up the basis for the next battle."

I don't pretend to know how Osama bin laden might fit into a solution to the scary situation we're in, but I'm pretty sure killing him won't make it go away. I'm not principled enough to be a pacifist; I think some military response is required to the challenge we face. But the moment we see that response as more than a strategic necessity, with limits, we join the holy war.

God bless planet earth, this tiny, unlikely green/blue dot of living, breathing organic beauty in the vast grayness of space.

NEW PHYSICS

Notes From Zone 10

Shrove Tuesday 2001

How is it we experience the same thing, movie, music, storm or person, and come away with different perceptions/opinions?

This piece is inspired by an article in yesterday's NY Times Magazine about a teenage boy (Jonathon Lebed?) who locked horns with the SEC for his online shenanigans as an amateur stock picker, and a review in the same paper of The Bit And The Pendulum, a book about the new physics by Tom Siegfried, a science reporter.

The book's thesis, on which I have only the most fragile intuitive hold, is that our old metaphor for reality, that everything is some form of energy, is giving way to a new metaphor. No energy is ever lost, but because of entropy, ever since the Big Bang, the energy in the universe is becoming less organized, scattered.

To personalize the metaphor, we were conceived as two tightly bundled cells that have been becoming more diffuse (thus the cellulite in our thighs) ever since. At some point they will be so loosely organized that they cannot sustain the transaction we call consciousness. Then we will be dead and our cells . . . well, that's one of the puzzles we're working on.

Siegfried describes the basic unit, not as energy but as information. The simplest bit of information is an either-or state, 0 or 1, on or off, yea or nay, a protein either active or inactive. Information is not a formal way of analyzing systems; information is real, physical.

Jonathon Lebed ran afoul of the SEC because he put opinions on chat room bulletin boards about stocks he'd bought, and when the stock rose he sold it. He started at 13 with $8000 from a savings bond his parents bought when he was born. By the time the SEC stepped in (they called him in for questioning when he was 14, then took action when he was 16), his stock was worth around $1 million.

The SEC said he was engaged in stock manipulation and threatened to prosecute him. He couldn't see how anything he was doing was different from what Merrill Lynch analysts were doing. He gained his information from reading, talking with other investors and intuition. He wrote what he believed. His lawyer cut a deal in which the boy paid a fine equal to the proceeds from what the SEC said were illegal transactions, leaving him with something over $800,000.

When the reporter asked the people at the SEC why they went after him, they were never able to say precisely, except that a teenage boy offering opinions to that many people and making that kind of money, clearly upended their picture of the orderly world the SEC was created to ensure.

You read the boy's responses to the reporter's questions and you realize he's processing information differently from the way the SEC enforcers were processing seemingly the same information. It registered 1s in him, 0s in them.

Newly discovered rock in the Asian desert suggests that asteroids hit the earth and cause the disappearance and origin of species.

They make the earth unsuitable for species that have been here (dinosaur) and create new conditions (volcanoes cooking a new soup) that begin the process from which new species (humans) emerge.

In other words, the bytes of information (DNA codes?) get translated, rearranged. The Internet is such a collision in the evolution of our species. A 14 year old boy challenging the Wall Street Gray Beards is a shot across the bow of the old dispensation in which hierarchy could appear to manage the flow of information.

What if we adopt a new metaphor for uncovering what we're doing here? Suppose instead of struggling to reach a common mind, on religion, economics, politics, ideal weight, we assume that the information bytes in each of us supports a profusion of differing, accurate and necessary insight. Instead of persuading you of my view, I stand in awe of yours.

Looks like George W. Bush may have carried Florida after all.

GOING DOWN
ON THE PRESIDENT.
NO GOOD DEED
GOES UNPUNISHED.

Notes From Zone 10.

Valentine's Day 1998.

La Jolla. Huge surf. Whales.

*   *   *

Why, it has been wondered, do cats lick themselves in their private parts? The eminent Swiss behavioral biologist Hans Fuhrer has postulated that cats do that, "because they can."

These are reflections on President Clinton's sexuality, both his own proclivities, and our reaction. Though I am not neutral about how this may affect his tenure (I hope he stays until the end of his term), these comments are about why he would do such things and why we would care so passionately. I'm pretty certain an honest look at both those things would have a profound impact on our judgment about the man, but I'll leave that for the more formal commentators. Truth be told, I see some early signs that we're looking at all this in some ways other than mere moralizing and public temper tantrums, maybe the first thoughtful response to a President's foibles since Watergate.

Michael Ignatieff, in an essay in his new collection, *The Warrior's Honor*, (Metropolitan Books $24.95) describes his attempt to get a Serbian militiaman in a command post in eastern Croatia, to tell him what he has against his former Croatian neighbors. The man "looks scornful and takes a cigarette pack out of his khaki jacket. 'See this? These are Serbian cigarettes. Over there,' he says, gesturing out the window, 'they smoke Croatian cigarettes.'" So now you understand.

These comments are about motivation, Clinton's and ours, and they begin with the assumption that we often haven't the foggiest idea why we do things. And we *never* understand fully why we do anything, especially those things which engage our passion. Not only are we all driven by compulsions and obsessions, biological urges programmed into us from before we climbed up onto the dry land, but even those choices we make consciously are filled with motives we haven't identified or examined.

Add to that a phenomenon which I think is quite new in human experience, the blurring of fantasy and reality. Television and the Big Screen, instant electronic communication, Virtual Reality. It has made what was once science fiction into the commonplace, causing the most grounded of us to wonder what's real.

Some were horrified to read that the morning after His Inauguration, Bill Clinton and Hillary woke (did they spend that first night in the Lincoln bedroom?), looked at each other and began laughing. One woman commentator said, "We've got Bonnie and Clyde in the White House." It reassures me. I take that laughter to mean they understood the absurdity of their being where they were. The new President and First Lady, that over-achieving ambitious philanderer from Arkansas and the street-smart wife with the scary modern credentials. God save us from a President who actually believes he deserves to be in the White House, or got there because of his virtue.

So why would Clinton risk all that for a tryst? The short answer is because he wanted to and thought he could. There are good reasons for privacy and reticence, they shelter us from our naked selves. What do you suppose it would be like to lose all your privacy, to have no sense any longer of boundaries between your public and private self? At least Clinton's latest frailty seems not to have been videotaped. Imagine George Bush watching himself on television countless times, vomiting on the Japanese Prime Minister's shoes.

A couple of weeks ago I heard Robert Olen Butler, author of *They Whisper* and *The Deep Green Sea*, explain that the way he draws his characters is to listen for their yearnings, their deepest desires, those things which, by long habit and good sense, most of us turn away from most of the time. He has his characters turn towards those yearnings rather than away from them. This may mark the essential difference between good fiction and real life, that because we do turn away from our desires, knowing what peril there is in them, we love to watch what happens to others who turn towards them.

It may be that being President of the United States blurs the lines which are normally drawn between fiction and real life. One need not be Sigmund Freud to notice that we live out in our dream life much of what we would never dare try in our waking life. What if we were to find ourselves in a daily existence which felt almost dreamlike?

David Halberstam records a moment in his classic, *The Best And The Brightest*, as Lyndon Johnson walks onto the tarmac at Andrews Air Force Base and heads towards the backup helicopter instead of the one which is going to take him.

"Mr. President," the young Marine guard at the gate gestures towards the other craft, "that's your helicopter over there."

"Son," Johnson responds, "They're all my helicopters."

And so it must seem. It would do us all some good to step back from our clucking and acknowledge that we, too, would love to have at least a moment in which our dreams and fantasies might merge with real life. Probably most of us would want to be quickly excused from that rich fare, not only because it would too severely test our mettle, but even more because every ounce of our conditioning has been designed to warn us of the consequences of life with the throttle at full.

Who knows what the reality of Clinton's sex life is, but all the rest of us are imagining that he has had access to as many exciting partners as he wants. Some of us envy him and some condemn him, but I assume both responses have the same origin, the sexual hunger in every human being. Sexual pleasure, affirmation, excitement, adventure, things we all enjoy when we think we can pay the heavy price tag attached to them. There are good reasons for disciplining ourselves, sparing ourselves the horrendous cost of following our passion. Yet, our pent-up frustration at such self-discipline feeds our condemnation of Clinton.

Jesus' take on this makes the most sense to me. He said that lusting after someone, even secretly, is close kin to committing adultery with them. Notice he didn't condemn either, though he knew the moral code did. (Remember the woman who was about to be stoned to death for having been caught committing adultery, and Jesus stepped in front of her and challenged, "Let the one among you who is without sin cast the first stone."?) Jimmy Carter earned derision for saying he didn't condemn adulterers because he had lusted after women in his heart. He was laughed at for being hopelessly naive. But was he? Or had he discovered the key to how compassion actually works in practice? By becoming aware of one's own honest inner life.

The feminists have taken a lot of criticism for their inconsistency on this one. Noted feminists have been silent about Clinton and Lewinsky and their motives have been criticized because, so it is said, they've made progress and have found allies in Clinton's presidency, and now they don't want to do him in even for violating their own code.

I see an opportunity here for all of us to back away from the power interpretation of sexual relationships. Yes, the personal is political, because we are all drawn up into the whole of life all the time. It's not possible for the President to stop being the President when a woman arouses him. It's not possible for a Secret Service Man to jettison his maleness when he sees the President obviously aroused by a woman. But President and Secret Service Man, are only partial descriptions.

We've chosen 21 (or in some cases 18) as the age at which we say a person is adult (conscious?) enough to take on the responsibilities of peer relationships, without protection. Though it is true that people, men and women, are often drawn sexually to those who wield great power, the two people, no matter how uneven their political power, are equally responsible for their choices if both are adults. To say other is to say two can virtually never meet as peers. And when the blood runs rich through their genitals, peers they are.

Larissa MacFarquhar, writing in a recent New Yorker, ("May-December Dept." Feb. 2, 1998) suggested that if there was any victim in the Clinton/Lewinsky encounter (which the writer believes there was not), surely it would have to be the President, not Ms. Lewinsky. Who, after all had the most to lose? It has to be true that most encounters of every sort between people, whether sexual or not (though I doubt there is any such thing as a non-sexual encounter between two human beings, ever) has a power component, since one person's will is often stronger than the other's It is not true that whose desire prevails is a complete or even adequate description of their encounter.

And we know it. The old adage that a man can have blood in his brain or in his penis, but never both at the same time, is a useful theory, but it no more means men are helpless before seductive women than vice versa. Except in cases of rape, there are no victims in a sexual encounter. Children and people who haven't the mental development of adults require protection, no one else. And *Lolita* is a reminder that there may be exceptions to even that.

The Jesus standard requires a lot of us. It asks us to examine what we often refer to as our unconscious, that seemingly huge part of our mind/imagination which lurks beneath the surface, not only of the person we show to the world, but the person we face in the mirror. It means believing our feelings, those pesky sensations which course through our brains and bodies, regulating everything from temperature and pain, to the urge to embrace and reproduce. That doesn't mean we must act on every urge, but neither can we deny their existence. The purpose of choosing to act in this unfamiliar way, examining and acknowledging our deepest desires, is to make us more aware of what is driving us, (presumably enlarging our range of choice) and more compassionate towards others when their urges burst into action.

The Jesus standard requires us to set aside judgment of anything another has done if we find any evidence in ourselves of ever having wished to do it. And clearly Jesus believes there is, somewhere in every one of us, the urge to do everything any human being has ever done, from incest to murder, from climbing Mt. Everest to farting at the Queen's banquet.

Mind you, we still might decide someone who seems to have too little control of his impulses is not suitable for President, but not because what he has done is so heinous that it is beyond our imagining. And we might decide someone who habitually steals or rapes needs to be restrained, but not because we can't imagine the impulse which leads him to act in that way.

I have no idea if the weird phenomenon of Clinton's performance ratings staying high through this latest scandal means that the country is more cynical or more tolerant. I well remember at the height of the Viet Nam War, being in a demonstration in Lafayette Park across the street from the White House. President Nixon was imprisoned in his mansion. Someone next to me spoke his conviction about what was at stake.

"If the President had to come out into this park every morning and sit on a bucket and do his business, the war would be over in a couple of days. No one who had to do that could sustain the arrogance needed to order other people's sons to go risk their lives."

In a real sense we have required every President since Nixon to do more and more of their private business out in public. Then we have trashed them for squandering the dignity of the office. It may be that we've finally been sobered by our own national hypocrisy. Maybe it's not only because we're prospering that we haven't gone for Clinton's throat on this one. Maybe we finally do see our own reflection when we watch this man, carrying out our bidding, fall headlong into a ditch as his reach stretches beyond his grasp.

So what difference does this make? Why should we discipline ourselves in this way, striving towards national compassion rather than our usual unrestrained chase of the fox? What's in it for us?

Everything. When we lock our sights on the President, we catch ourselves in the crosshairs. This impulse to destroy our President comes from our deep distrust of ourselves and those parts of us we neither know nor understand. Which of us feels comfortable with, let along understanding of our sexual urges? How many of us could cope with groupies, attractive, available, constant sexual invitations?

Most important of all, when we develop empathy for a person, we cease condemning ourselves. No doubt this is the biggest reason we are reluctant to do this, the worry that forgiving ourselves, having compassion for our own complex, contradictory selves, especially our sexuality, might unleash a monster we couldn't live with. It must be that in Clinton we see our deepest fears about what could happen to us, the chaos and betrayal, the lack of restraint.

I suspect Clinton is himself a deeply unconscious person, often surprised by his own actions. When we claim those parts of ourselves, desires, fantasies, dreads, which have lived beneath our surface, we become more able to choose, not less. And when we refuse to condemn those who have acted out our unconscious impulses, we befriend those impulses rather than driving them into unconscious exile where they can work their mischief without our awareness.

I recently read an article by a young man about how we teach our young people today about their sexual desires. He compared it to drivers education in which the rights and wrongs of the road, the opportunities and dangers of driving a two ton vehicle among others was stressed. But in the tiny amount of sex education he received, all he learned about was the terrible risk and danger. Nothing of the pleasure or even a possible biological purpose (procreation) was mentioned. He said that if drivers' Ed was taught like that, no one in their right mind would ever take the car out of the garage.

It is that self-defeating attitude which could be at stake in this moment with our randy young President. Try to imagine yourself in the Oval Office with Clinton as he begins pouring out his heart to you about all the women he's been involved with, and how frightened he is, not only by what this might do to him and the nation, but of those impulses he has thought so many times were under control, only to have them rise up (sic) in him with renewed urgency.

As he goes on and on, recounting incident upon incident, your mind wanders, not only to those occasions when you have violated others' trust, but your own best resolve. You can feel your ears redden with recognition of what he's talking about. You look up from your reverie and realize The President hasn't spoken for several moments. He's looking at you quizzically, wondering how long you haven't been listening to him.

"Sorry, Mr. President, I was just thinking about all the times in my own life when I've felt the way you're feeling right now."

LIVING COLOR

Notes From Zone 10

Vernal Equinox 2000

Some of what follows may be unsuitable for children and the faint of heart.

Yesterday I saw myself on TV in living color. It was a signal event. If you know what a flexible sigmoidascope is, you know what I saw. With the aid of modern technology I did what some have suspected I've done for years; I put my head up my rectum. For one who never quite got beyond the anal stage, it was fascinating.

When I was 7 or 8, my mother's father came to live with us in Charlotte. He'd retired young from a practice of allergic medicine in New York City, demoralized by the death of his wife from breast cancer, and the recent development of sulfa drugs and penicillin which he believed made allergic medicine unnecessary.

Maybe I asked him a lot of questions, but next thing I knew he'd ordered up a bunch of used medical texts which he gave to me with some ceremony one afternoon after school. The one I remember best was a Body Scope, a big black portfolio, like one carried by a model or an architect. When you opened it, on the left was a large drawing of a man and, on the right of a woman.

Each of their bodies was scooped out from chin to feet. You turned a wheel so you could see the nervous system or the reproductive or digestive or circulatory of skeletal system. I spent hours in my room studying it wondering if I looked like that inside.

Like many clergy of my vintage, part of my training was watching surgery. When I was a parish priest in Massachusetts, before the days of liability anxiety, a surgeon friend used to invite me to watch when he was doing a particularly interesting case. The body cracked open and undefended between the sterile drapes wasn't quite as orderly as the neat color-coded Body Scope, but it interested me just as much.

In the past couple of decades I've avoided any brushes with medical care myself. My fascination with others' health is a totem, an attempt to placate the gods about my own vulnerable gizzards. I keep myself in reasonable shape for a 60 year-old, exercised, mentally active, pretending I'm ready to die at any moment. But my friend who runs a medical clinic persuaded me there are rudimentary exams that could signal easily treatable problems.

Against my Samurai code, I went for blood tests and the big "up yours". My cholesterol is over 250 (shame!), but you should see my colon. I have a few places on me that could be either barnacles or melanoma, but you should see my colon. My pectorals have slipped down to my hips, so I'm now pear shaped, but my colon looks like the uncorrupted flesh of a newborn.

I once auditioned to be the host of a local TV show in a Boston station, but even I could see on the monitor that I had all the on camera interest of a bank clerk. The outside of me will never be a TV star. But you should see my colon.

INSIDE OUT

NOTES FROM ZONE 4

Autumnal Equinox 1998

My daughter Jen's boyfriend, Josh, called me one afternoon in August, excited about a book he had just finished. Ken Wilber's *The Marriage of Sense and Soul; Integrating Science and Religion.* Random House. 1998. Josh told me all my talk about the Enlightenment and the loss of confidence in western conversation about the inner dimension, had never computed with him until he read Wilber's book. Suddenly he felt as if he'd had a look inside so many things he'd long wondered, and wondered whether anyone else wondered as he did.

As soon as I hung up, I went to Amazon.com and ordered the book. You might want to do the same. If you don't know Wilber, one of the few New Age writers who has endured, you'd do well to pick up a copy of *The Essential Ken Wilber; An Introductory Reader.* Shambhala. 1998, which contains short passages from his many writings in a helpful, coherent collection.

Wilber believes that we have reached the point, in language and in understanding, at which we can affirm the contribution made by science, the inquiry into the outward, rational realm, and at the same time, lay claim with new confidence to the inner realm, the life of the spirit. This epoch's alchemy.

Wilber proposes a sort of scientific method for testing inner experience which he believes rescues it from its chief criticism, that it cannot be verified. I warn you, Wilber is going to ask you to trust and believe your own inner experience, to describe it just as you might a table you have seen, and to regard your intuition as an integral and legitimate part of reality. I warn you not because there's something ominous about it, but because we've all been conditioned to disregard and disbelieve our inner experience, and trusting your insight and feelings can be an odd, shaky business.

On the strength of my recent encounter with Wilber (which I've at times found boring and somnolent), I've returned to regular meditation, a discipline I once practiced and have done infrequently the past several years. With Wilber, I think sitting meditation is the Way to access inner reality. With the sixth sense, the inner eye.

There is a reason more people don't pursue the inner life. It's boring. We're so used to being stimulated, entertained and distracted by outward stimuli, that being still, attending to inner reality, feels flaccid, tedious. And what we discover there is sometimes confusing or even frightening. For what we eventually discern is that focusing our entire attention on outward reality has trapped us in what the Buddhists call *samsara,*, the endless cycle of desire and dissatisfaction.

Being utterly bereft of outward stimuli may be our greatest fear. That, I suspect, is at the core of our fear of death, that it's nothing.

Now there's a new novel by the English writer, William Trevor, *Death in Summer,* which I hope you'll read while tuned to your inside reality. The reviewers have praised the book, its restrained, elegant writing, and have commented on how the reader becomes almost mesmerized by these English gentry who seem to have ice—water in their veins. A man who laments his inability to love his very lovable wife, the bloodless account of the wife's untimely death, hit by a car while transporting chickens in a coop on the back of her bicycle, right after the birth of their daughter, and his quiet surprise at discovering that he actually does love the child. The story is so carefully and cautiously told that I nearly gave it up.

I'm so glad I didn't, but it took me until almost the end before reading the book provided any pleasure. Though impressed by Trevor's writing, even occasionally moved, I fought drowsiness and impatience through the first two-thirds, then was affected by the courage and discipline Trevor exercised in refusing to titillate the reader.

A large portion of my life as a parish priest was spent figuring how to market whatever it was we thought we were doing. How to excite and gain people's attention. Seduce people into an encounter with God. Marketing, searching for people's hot button, is as integral to being American as watching CNN. I never did it very well and always felt frustrated by my failure.

Now it occurs to me that the nature of what we had to offer, access to and confidence in inner reality, requires the sort of restraint with which Trevor has written *Death in Summer*. It is like a tiny step for us in the glandular west, toward weaning ourselves from our addiction to entertainment and stimulation. Trevor offers the reader contact with the dimension of reality which seems at first neither entertaining nor stimulating.

In a thoughtful article in The September Harper's, "Beyond Belief; A skeptic searches for an American Faith," Fenton Johnson suggests that as the formal monastic movement dwindles in our culture, a popular interest is being kindled in

the underlying intent of poverty, chastity and obedience. Fenton
points out that these vows, common to all monasticism, in the
east and in the west, address the three great obstacles to faith,
which are also the cornerstones of secular culture—money, sex
and power.

This is no parochial call for a return to church and creed. In fact
the author says the church has by and large forsaken her purpose
and chased the cultural idols common to all western
institutions. Johnson draws a critical distinction between faith
and belief. Read the article. Several people have told me they
found it boring and couldn't finish it. Stay with your restlessness
and boredom. Simply reading the article may provide you with a
first clue about how to listen to and trust your inner life. It will
stir dormant synapses.

Why should you bother? Think for a moment about that
samsara, the endless cycle of desire and dissatisfaction, the
method of what we call free-market capitalism. We are its
children. Your restlessness, your free floating anxiety, your
embarrassing narcissism, may not be character flaws or even
signals that you need a seratonin uptake inhibitor, a new spouse
or a new job. It may be your healthy immune system's signal
that you've been turning a blind eye to half the field of vision
needed to discern an authentic, undivided claim on your life.

Why am I sending this to you? Because I know you. Because of
some soul connection I have with you. Some clue I've picked up
that you're hungry for God. As I am. Because something told me
to.

DISEASTER; JESUS DECLARED INCOMPETENT

NOTES FROM ZONE 10.

EASTER 1998

Norman Mailer said no story teller can evade the story of Jesus. It's a story which must be told and retold. Each generation needs to cast it in the idiom of its moment. The Passion. Where Mailer went wrong in his recent effort was in trying, even while using his own colorful language, to keep to the story and its details as we have it in the Bible. Monday of Holy Week, fretting my way through morning meditation, I caught this much of a report on NPR:

> There is to be a competency hearing today for Joe Blow who is scheduled to be executed this week. He was declared competent to stand trail umpteen years ago, but because of bizarre behavior while in prison, new questions have been raised about his sanity. By law he must be sane, able to understand what they're going to do to him, or the execution cannot go forward.

The Dispassion narrative which follows, tracks the story in an end-of-the-millennium cast.

*   *   *

Judas and Peter are sipping wine in a little cafe on a side street in Jerusalem. They've come to the city with Jesus who rode into town in a staged demonstration, taking his cue from ancient prophecy (Jeremiah), riding the foal of a donkey. Every Jew understood the gesture, and added to its impact by tossing royal palms in front of him. The Romans are just beginning to sense the rising tide of revolutionary fervor among the Jews in Jerusalem. The Romans have suffered through such moments before and have learned that making a tough, shocking early response, works better than delaying.

Judas: "Goddamn, Peter, Jesus is never going to get off a dime. He's been talking revolution, all about how he's here to reestablish God's Holy Kingdom, for three years. And the fucking Romans are more entrenched in our land than ever. Don't you think it's time we forced his hand? He could go on like this for another three years."

"Judas, the guy's for real. I'm feeling impatient, too, but I really think he's about to make his move."

"Aside from the 12 of us and a handful of whores and lepers, who the hell does he have on his side to pull the thing off?"

"Yeah, that's worried me some, too. Maybe he thinks there'll be some sort of spontaneous uprising when he declares himself. Of course that's what the CIA said about Cuba before the Bay of Pigs."

"Spontaneous uprising? Get real, Peter. How many Jews are there in the whole Empire? Just about enough to provide entertainment in the Roman circus. When was the last time a big group rose up to join Jews in anything except a financial scheme? I'll tell you what I'm beginning to worry about, I think Jesus might be blowing smoke. Or crazy."

"Oh God, Judas, don't even think such a thing. What's to become of the rest of us? We've burned our bridges. I sold my boat, have no money to buy another."

"Peter, I'm serious about this. The time's come to piss or get off the pot. I'm going to the Praetorian Guard and tell them I'm willing to sell Jesus out for money. I'll say I've got proof he's working to overthrow the government. You know how jumpy Pilate gets around Passover. He'll probably pass him onto Herod to pronounce a death sentence. That ought to do it. I just know, when Jesus is up against it, he'll use that amazing God-power we've all seen in him. I mean, this is about throwing the Romans off God's holy land."

"Good Lord, Judas, that's pretty radical. What if he doesn't? I mean, what if he can't? And they take all that Kingdom talk seriously? What if he keeps up that nutty passive resistance stuff, and won't fight back? You've heard him; love your enemy, return no evil for evil, turn the other cheek Shit, Judas, they might just kill him! And he might just let it happen."

"If all that happened, it would be because he's crazy, Peter. Either he is who he says he is, and we've done the right thing by throwing everything else over the side to come with him these past three years, or he's crazy. And so are we. Fools. You ever hear of the Holocaust?"

"No."

"You will. It's what happens when Jews listen to this passive resistance shit, turn the other cheek towards a nasty, unprincipled enemy who's determined to prevail no matter the cost. That's what Jesus is asking for, whether he understands it or not. I keep my hopes up that, when he sees how little humanity these bastards have, he'll move. And it's clear he has some sort of other-worldly power. Like Moses. Or Joshua."

"I don't know, Judas, it's running a pretty big risk. But maybe you're right about how he'll react. It's probably too late for anything else. Oh God, I hope you're right. I don't know how I'd ever forgive myself if we pushed him like this and it backfired. But something's got to break this logjam. You've got to do what you've got to do. Go do it, brave friend. I'll back you."

They join their right hands, fiercely, like gladiators about to do combat, then embrace, and Judas leaves the cafe, striding rapidly down the way, with purpose. Peter watches him until he disappears around a corner. Peter feels a wave of dread pass through him.

"Maybe I should have tried to talk him out of it. Jesus is our master."

*   *   *

A room above another cafe. Jesus and his twelve closest lieutenants are stretched out on cushions by a long table, taking the Seder. They've completed the ritual prescribed by their tradition, ("How is this night different from all other nights?") remembering the Jews' miraculous escape from Egypt. Conversation has drifted to the similarities between their ancestors' captivity and their own political situation now, under the Romans.

Andrew: "I've never known whether to believe the story exactly the way it's been told, or whether it's symbolic, gathering a lot of stuff and making it into a good story. I mean, I believe God has a sense of humor, but frogs and hemorrhoids? That's a bit much. The part about the dead Egyptian children and the blood on the doors, now that sounds like real revolution. What do you think, Jesus?"

"I think those who have ears to hear, will hear."

It pisses off Judas, and Peter, and probably most of the others, though they won't show it, when Jesus does that, refuses to answer a perfectly straightforward question. Poses a riddle instead.

Matthew: "Hey, we're talking God here, not some two-bit Pharaoh or Emperor. What makes you think God can't give Israel's enemies nasty hemorrhoids if He chooses?"

Judas: "It's not that God couldn't, but what sort of asshole god would?"

Even Peter is shocked when Judas becomes outrageous about God. Judas is so pure about what he eats and with whom. He always performs the required rituals meticulously, has nothing to do with the ritually unclean, Samaritans or menstruating women. But when he gets pissed, there's no telling what he'll say. Or do.

Jesus roars with laughter. "Hemorrhoids! Asshole god. Very good, Judas." The others join in, tentatively at first, then the room erupts, an explosion of pent up frustration and fear. When the laughter recedes, a heavy silence falls, then Jesus speaks.

"I can tell you're all getting pretty tired of all this," Jesus says. "I don't think we're going to be able to hold it together much longer."

Murmuring around the table. Judas looks down the table at Jesus as if he's crazy.

"Master, what are you saying? Not be able to hold it together? What's that supposed to mean?"

"That you're going to run out of patience, Judas, and do something precipitous. I want you to know it's OK. I understand. Hard as these things are, they're necessary. So go ahead and do what you need to do. Just do it as swiftly and kindly as you can."

"Master, we've hung in through thick and thin. (Judas wonders if Peter has told Jesus about their conversation.) You're always telling us the Romans can't maintain their power here, because God's Kingdom will tumble their Empire. We believe you. We're with you. We're Jews, too. But we need some sign, some signal that you are who you say you are, from God, here to establish the Kingdom."

"My Kingdom is not of this world, Judas. The only sign this generation will see is the sign of Jonah," Jesus' voice is even, unruffled. But there's no mistaking his determination. He's not going to be bullied or panicked.

"Oh, for God's sweet sake, that's it for me," Judas shouts. "You and your stupid riddles. This is serious business. You just don't get it. You're a hopeless pussy. I'm outa' here!"

Judas rises and storms from the room. The color drains from Peter's face. The others study their feet. John, who falls apart at the first sign of conflict, and who never leaves Jesus' side, leans against him and sighs.

"I know how hard this is for you, Jesus," he whispers.

"Do you?" Jesus retorts abruptly, causing John to lift his head and look at Jesus quizzically.

"I'm feeling full of supper and pretty jumpy," Jesus says, "I'm gonna walk up to Gethsemane and get some fresh air. I need to go where it's quiet. Anyone who wants to come is welcome."

They all rise from the table and follow Jesus from the room. As they reach the street, Jesus and the ten turn to the right, towards Gethsemane, a mile down the road. Peter goes left, hoping to intercept Judas before he does what he's told Peter he's going to do.

When Jesus and the others arrive at Gethsemane, he turns to them and says, "I'm going in to pray. I'm feeling horrible. My gut's convulsed, I feel like I might throw up. I'm terrified and feel totally alone. I'd really appreciate it if you guys stayed nearby and prayed with me. If that's not asking too much." They've heard him angry and sarcastic like this occasionally, with the Pharisees, but rarely with them.

"Sure. Absolutely. Count on us. Sorry you're having such a hard time. We're with you all the way. You bet. No problem." After Jesus is some distance from them, they turn to each other. "Boy, he's sure got a hair across. Judas shouldn't've done that. Jesus's gotten himself over tired, that session with Lazarus did him in."

Jesus walks to the middle of the garden, a couple of hundred yards from where he left the others. He stands stock still, breathing long, deliberate inhales, followed by even longer exhales. The furrows on his brow smoothes, his shoulders sag. He holds out his hands palms up as if he's begging. He squnches his toes into the dust beneath his feet, asking the earth to reach up and embrace him.

"I think I'm going crazy," he prays. "Sometimes I feel so clear and confident. The next minute nothing makes any sense. I don't even know if I'm talking to You right now or just blowing random thoughts into thin air. I don't even know if You are. If You are, how about doing something useful? Like getting me out of this mess."

He feels horrible, listening to the dead silence. He's suddenly convulsed, drops to his knees. He vomits his supper onto the ground. Beads of sweat pop out on his forehead. His stomach cramps again, doubling him over so his head touches his knees. He wretches a second time.

"God, you don't s'pose I've been poisoned? Judas had a weird look when he handed me the wine goblet. Listen, I don't want to die, OK? How about a break from all this?" He rises laboriously and staggers to where he left the others. As he approaches them, he can vaguely make out shapes in the dark. It looks like they're all lying down. Oh no, the assholes are asleep!

"You pigs!" he shouts, immediately sorry, as they wake with a start, looking up at him, terror in their faces.

"Jesus, we're so sorry. We didn't mean to fall asleep. It's just that we're all exhausted."

"Yeah, well what do you think I am? Would it be too much to ask of you to just stay with me an hour?"

The sarcasm again. "No, of course not. We'll gladly do that. Count on us. Are you OK?"

"No, not really. Back there I had such convulsions I thought I might've been poisoned."

"Poisoned? By whom? Who'd want to do something like that to you?"

Jesus goes back into the garden and the others promptly fall back fast asleep. This time he can't pray at all, can only focus on the argument raging inside his own head.

"You knew it was going to be like this."

"Bull, I'd never have done it if I'd known this."

"Hey, there's still time to back out. Just walk away. Now. Before this thing gets any worse."

"Walk away? After all this?"

"I s'pose you're going to tell me this is God's bidding, that you're doing this under some sort of divine direction?"

"Yeah, well, right, why else would I do it?"

"You know what they call people who hear God telling them what they're s'posed to do? They call them insane. Crazy, fucking assholes."

Jesus begins to sob. He finally drops into a fitful sleep. Dreaming.

He's with Mary Magdalene, his beloved. He left her to do this work. He's heard awful things about what's become of her since. But now, in his dream, they're together again. They've stomped on the glass goblet in the traditional marriage ceremony, feasted and drunk the special wine, and they're retiring into the nuptial bed chamber. Mary turns to Jesus, opening her arms. He feels his groin stir. He realizes how much he's missed that smile. She makes him feel safe, alive. Why did he ever leave? Thank God they're back together. He reaches for her, can feel her breath, the warmth of her flesh, when he's wakened.

"Master, wake up, it's me."

"Judas, what are you doing here?" Jesus can't quite yet remember where he is. He sees the others coming through the grove of olive trees. He stands. Judas embraces him passionately, as if they haven't seen each other in a long while. From the other direction, the Romans, a full complement, moving slowly towards him from over the hill. In battle regalia. Silver helmets, breast plates, carrying spears.

"You cowardly son of a bitch. You had to bring the Roman guard." Jesus holds his hands out to the captain of the guards, a gesture of surrender. The captain roughly binds his hands with twine. Two other members of the guard take Jesus by the elbows and begin marching him out of the garden.

Judas looks on in despair.

Things move rapidly now. They take Jesus to Pilate's house, a guard wakes Pilate and tells him he must sit right away. It's a capital case. Involves blasphemy, a violation of Jewish Law which calls for execution. And sedition, which the Romans punish with the same sentence.

Pilate's not happy to be wakened, but he knows what can happen if Herod hears he's refused to take one of these cases which turns out to be a threat against Caesar. He's heard stories of this provincial Rabbi, this is the first time he's seen him. He'd expected him to be more impressive. The man's quite slight, his legs bowed as if he was malnourished as a child. He's obviously been beaten up by the guards. They've whipped his back, it's bloody, covered with angry raised welts.

"He's probably another of those nuts claiming to be God's special agent," Pilate thinks. They've put a purple toga on him, making fun of his claim to be a royal person. And to inflame Roman fears. Pilate hates these things, they require all his political wiles. Requiring him to walk a tightrope between Jews and Romans. Any one of these could be ignite the whole thing.

"So," he addresses Jesus after they've stood him in front of Pilate's chair, "you're the Nazarene they're calling the Son of God?"

Jesus stares silently at Pilate. Pilate sees his cheek is terribly bruised, his right eye black and blue. They've really knocked the shit out of this guy. Jesus stands still. Doesn't speak.

"Well, are you the Son of God?"

Nothing. A guard prods Jesus with the point of his spear. "Answer him!"

"If you say so."

"Look, pal, maybe you don't get it. They've routed me out of a sound sleep for this. They've raised some pretty serious charges against you. In fact you could die if you're convicted. So maybe you want to cooperate here. Get my drift?

"Now, let's try again. Are you the Messiah?"

"Some have said so."

"What about you? What do you say?"

"The Son Of Man has no place to lie his head."

"Riddles aren't going to do it, friend. You're going to have to give me some straight answers if you want to save yourself.

"Now I'm going to give you one last chance. Are you The Son of God?"

Jesus stands utterly still, as if he hasn't heard Pilate, looking at him like he's some sort of curiosity. The two of them hold each other's gaze for a long moment. All the others in the room become mesmerized. The room is dead still.

"Yes."

The room erupts. "See? He said it! You've got no choice. He's dead meat. String the bastard up!"

"Quiet!" Pilate shouts. "I find this man guilty of the charge of blasphemy. The penalty under our Law for this charge is death by stoning. But there are two further issues which must be decided by a higher court. I do not have the authority to do more than recommend that he be executed.

"And I believe he may be mad. Under both Jewish and Roman Law, if he is ruled insane, he cannot be executed. I'm sending him on to Herod for judgment in those two matters. Now take him away and let me get some sleep."

When he appears in Herod's court the following morning, only two of his band of followers are nearby, Peter and John. The others have fled the city, fearing retribution against them. There's a rumor that Judas has committed suicide.

John melds into the crowd as they push into Herod's courtroom. He's desperate to see what happens, but terrified of being known as one of his followers. Peter stays outside in the courtyard, warming himself by a fire. One of Herod's servants, coming to tend the fire, looks at Peter who is hunkering down.

"See that nose?" she calls to her friend. "There's no mistaking those Galileans. They all look alike." Then, speaking to Peter, "You're with the guy in there, the one on trial, aren't you?"

"What? Who? With him? No. I just happened to come in here to get warm. I've never seen him before."

Herod's court is grander, more ornate than Pilate's. Herod has grown weary of minor insurrectionists, but two Roman guards have been ambushed in the streets of Jerusalem in the past month, both disemboweled in ritual unmistakably Maccabean. Herod has doubled the guard around his own palace, feeling increasingly alien in this provincial dead-end. He takes this skinny provincial more seriously than he might once have.

The guards have taken turns taunting Jesus through the night, keeping him awake, and crowds outside the cell have shouted taunts.

"If you're the Messiah, why don't you make the walls of your cell fall down and leave. Joshua knocked down the walls of the whole city, and he wasn't even the Son of God."

One of them lifted himself up to the cell window and spit in. Jesus felt the spray on his shoulder as he lay in the straw on the hard floor. "If you're a prophet, tell me who just lungered into your cell."

Herod sees the man is spent, completely done in.

"Tell me," he addresses Jesus, "how you plead to the charge of sedition? Guilty or not guilty? Are you a king, here to replace Caesar?"

Jesus considers him in silence, staring at him as he had at Pilate.

"Did you hear my question?"

"Yes."

"Well, how do you plead?"

"I don't plead before the Roman court. I plead only to God."

"But I thought you *were* God. Or the Son of God. Or the Messiah. I can't keep all you people's titles straight. Which is it? Are you God? Or God's Son?"

Jesus smiles wearily. "I am who I am," he says. A shocked murmur runs through the Jews in the crowd.

"Did you hear what he just said? Herod Antipas," they shout, "he's just convicted himself."

"I don't get it," Herod protests, "what did he say? Sounds like a riddle to me, not sedition."

"You have to put him to death now," one of them shouts, "You've got no choice."

"Oh yes I do," Herod insists, "I've got the authority to decide this man's fate, and I intend to use it." He turns his attention back to Jesus. "Have you heard what they've said? That you've convicted yourself with this weird answer? 'I am who I am.'?"

"Yes."

"And have you convicted yourself?"

"Yes."

"Do you understand the penalty?"

"Yes."

"What have you to say in your defense?"

"I am who I am."

"Won't you even plead for your own life?"

"I am who I am."

Herod sits in silence for several minutes. Jesus body seems to be sagging under its own weight. He hasn't slept for 48 hours, nor has he had anything to eat or drink except some sour wine.

"I've decided," Herod finally breaks the silence. "This Nazarene is insane. Incompetent. Roman law forbids executing him. You may hate him and think he's a blasphemer, but his steadfast refusal to speak a word in his own defense persuades me that he's mad. He's harmless. Look who he's got for his minions. Nobody. Not a single soul capable of making trouble. He's harmless.

"I want you out of Jerusalem." Herod addresses Jesus again, "Today. Go back to Nazareth or wherever it is you're from. We're giving neither your enemies nor your fellow fanatics the satisfaction of making you the latest martyr. You people love this sort of thing. Well, we're getting sick of it. We've got some really scary folks, like Barabbas in custody, and we're going to crucify those bastards before they do some real harm.

But this guy's no threat to anyone. Let him go back to the provinces and live out his life in obscurity. The rest of you go home. Go back to work. Get a life. Case dismissed."

Easter is canceled.

OKLAHOMA CITY SAMARITAN

Notes From Zone 10

Easter Week 2001

The biggest row I ever caused was with a sermon I preached
about the Good Samaritan
Familiar story, old hat
Guy gets robbed and beaten nearly to death
some upstanding types don't want to get involved, get their
hands dirty, mixed up in
messy legal troubles, so they
cross the street, keep moving.
Another guy comes along, stops, tends the guy's
wounds, takes him to an inn, gives the innkeeper
money to care for him.

Jesus asks his hearers,
So who was neighbor to the guy who was robbed?
Duh. Dumb story. Obvious popular pious point.

Only, Jesus was talking to upstanding people,
Pharisees, like Jesus was,
who weren't supposed to touch a wounded or maybe
dead guy because then they couldn't do their sacred work,
temple ritual, they were unclean.

And the good guy, the one who acted like a neighbor,
was a bad guy, a Samaritan, scumbag, and Pharisees weren't even
supposed to touch them.

So I'm wracking my brain to figure out how to help people
understand how shocking Jesus' story would have been. As I'm
wondering, the Federal Building in Oklahoma City gets
blown up and a whole lot of innocent people,
including some babies in day care
are killed.

I said it would be like someone telling the story of a guy who
gets robbed, and George Bush, Colin Powell, Alan Greenspan,
Billy Graham and Hilary Clinton all cross the street so they
won't get drawn in.
Finally a scumbag comes along and he stops and helps the guy,
takes him to the hospital and pays for his care. Suppose the
scum who helped, I said, was the Oklahoma City bomber?
He's the hero of the story.
A woman in the congregation got the point. She knew someone
who had been killed in the explosion. She wanted me fired.
We didn't know then who the bomber was. Now we do. Know
his name, what he looks like, that he's not sorry.

We're going to kill him in a few weeks. Someone's petitioning
the
Supreme Court for the right to carry the execution 'live' on
the Internet.

You know he's going to figure in our lives the way the
Good Samaritan did for those who heard Jesus' story.
Puncture our pieties,
flip us off as he dies.
Maybe it should be shown on network, the
whole country spellbound as Tim sighs and

dies. Probably bring the country together
until the thrill chills,
we turn off the TV, get ready for bed and have to watch who's
brushing
our teeth.

OVEN MITTS

Notes From Zone 4

The Eve of All Hallowed Saints 2001

9/11 + 7 Weeks

What could we say is different about us, or the
world
these past seven weeks?
And is it a matter of how we're going to settle the score
or will we change?
Probably no one ever changes willingly. The wisdom of
Mercer Beasley, legendary tennis coach,
Never change a winning game, always change a losing one,
rules.
So the issue is, do we have to change, or can we wait this one out?

I know the pious answer,
we've been changed already, nothing is the same after
September 11.
Really? I still hold my breath for the daily stock market report.
My foreboding about flying has honed but is not of a different
   order. The script I conceive for what may derail my life, has
   manifold
new images, but I forget to worry about opening the mail or eating
   raw vegetables.

The actuarial number of my friends have received grave diagnoses
    or died
since some unknown number were buried in the twin trade towers.
I've learned to sleep again, as well as one
sleeps
having passed 60. I go for my daily designer
coffee. I send you Zone Notes.

My wonder has expanded since September 11.
Language is the oven mitts with which we handle reality. I find
    words
clumsy, deadening, not up to the task.

Knowledge is a veil over the known.
Each attempt to gain a glimpse, a coherent
reflection
of what has happened and what to make of it, assembles instead
    another uninvited overlay of obscurity
separating us further from what we
know
but believe we cannot bear.

Attorney General Ashcroft
announcing anonymous amorphous annihilation
prospects
and our earnest President deputizing each of us
soldiers
in this weird war
injure our old illusion of
American might
sheltering us so we could go about our acquiring with
impunity, immunity
from the winds that lean the frail scaffold we thought would never
topple underneath
us.

And though I would certainly sell my
soul
for some even modest rebirth of that
illusion,
the kinship I now know
undeniably
with the Israeli or Palestinian in the pizza parlor, enraging
unwelcome intrusion,
bin laden labeling me the evil
one, mirroring my president
has answered the prayer I never bargained on
God
taking seriously
That we all may be One.

BEAM ME UP

Notes From Zone 10

Ascension Less a Week 2001

What can we know, really?

In a review of a book (Gender and Desire: Uncursing Pandora, by Polly Young-Eisendrath. Texas A&M 1997) sent to me by Michael Dwinell, I came across this pithy parable providing insight into a conversation in which we all take part, usually without knowing it. The conversation is about what's real and how we know. The shifting understanding of how we know is often depicted as having evolved through three historical periods; pre-modern, modern and post-modern. Here's the parable:

Three baseball umpires are talking about how they call balls and strikes and which of them is best at it. The first says, "I calls em as I sees em." The second claims, "I calls em as they are." And the third, "They ain't nothing till I calls em."

Three versions of the truth, reality. The first, pre-modern, bases truth solely on observation without any consideration (or maybe awareness) of how the observer may relate to the truth. What you see is what you get.

The second is modern, a product of the rational, scientific age. While acknowledging the human mind may block or illuminate truth, he has confidence that there is a knowable objective reality; with sufficient self-discipline he can know exactly how things are.

The third umpire is post-modern; he believes truth consists of what we name it, that any version of truth depends on the person who is observing and is affected by their assumptions, perceptions and feelings.

Because it is the potion in which we swim, we are usually no more aware of this debate than we are of the oxygen molecules rushing into our nostrils as we inhale.

And to further confuse us, at any given moment, in each of us, all three perspectives will be represented.

I sometimes hang in the back of groups touring the San Diego Contemporary Art Museum where I do my writing, listening to their reactions to the art pieces which, by definition in a contemporary collection, lure viewers into post-modern perceiving.

"That's not art," complains a third grader, looking at a large canvass with several squares displaying the many skin colors of the members of the museum trustees.

Once when I had preached what a colleague perceived as a challenging if not heretical sermon, he begged me to say publicly that I believed the Ten Commandments. I said that since Jesus seemed willing to finesse them when they stood between people and full life, I hardly thought I had the authority to reinstate them.

A fundamentalist Baptist asked a friend of mine if he really believed in infant baptism. "Believe in it?" my friend responded, "I've seen it!"

In San Diego we watch the western horizon as the sun disappears into the ocean, hoping to see the Green Flash. Lacey has seen it many times; some never have. Someone rudely suggested her perception is Margarita driven.

I regard my computer as a partner in my work, sometimes a help, sometimes my tormentor. Despite my physicist brother-in-laws insistence that it is merely mimicking my instructions, I believe it can act capriciously.

When my newly born first child came home from the hospital, I discovered that I could cause her to wake and wail by worrying and wondering when she would. What if I had learned to meditate before bringing her home?

That same first child, when she was 30, asked me if I wasn't afraid of dying. What, she asked, if it turns out there's nothing? I told her that had worried me when I was 30; now it causes calm in me.

You know about Information Theory, the understanding that each bit of reality, the smallest particle, is made up of information? Like DNA, information that encodes genetic structure. As your mind winds around an ancient enigma, like dying, consider those billions of encoded bits that have organized themselves into that tight integrity you consider your self. Chances are, of course, that the lot of them have come and gone quite a bit over the decades. Ever wonder where they'll go next?

Next Thursday, May 24, is Ascension Day. Forty days after Jesus was raised on Easter, his ascension to heaven is celebrated. Pilgrims from the west are often entertained on trips to the Holy Land when the guide points to the indentation in the rock from which Jesus is said to have pushed off. I'd guess at such a moment a western believer would have pre-modern, modern and post-modern bits in him, swimming around each other like a school of guppies.

On the year anniversary of my mother's death, as I was sitting on the edge of my bed on a sweltering afternoon in Zimbabwe, she stood next to me and smiled, then told me she was going to be all right. Someone later explained that of course she came while we were in Africa, because Africa is welcoming to the other more indirect dimension of reality. I was pleased that she was dressed in the slacks and blouse she'd bought from a catalogue, a lot of oranges in them. She thought they were cheerful.

John Updike, we're talking the randy post-modern writer here, not Pope John Paul, wrote a poem in which he said either every cell in Jesus' dead body was alive on Easter or Christianity is a fraud. He didn't say which he believed.

This is a lot of fun, this trying on new dimensions with you. Which umpire would you choose to have calling strikes if you were the pitcher? Or the batter?

We'll be just newly arrived back in Vermont (Zone 4) on Ascension Day. I still can't get used to flying out over the Pacific in the morning and over the Atlantic before dark. Beam me up, Scottie.

SHOULD WE FUCK URSELVES?

Notes From Zone 4.

January 15, 1998

(4th Quarter Taxes Due Today.)

It's sometimes less elegantly referred to as cloning, though the issue is much bigger. The question is, should we? The answer is, we do, and we will.

In a review of a book on bio-engineering in the Sunday New York Times (January 10, 1998), the issue of cloning was raised. It seems President Clinton is about to sign some sort of international accord calling for the banning of human cloning, and calling on biologists to set limits on their human genetic tinkering.

The review refers to the fear that we might one day engineer headless humans to provide a harvest of organs for transplantation. (He also discusses the fascinating possibility of rich people doing such elaborate genetic tinkering that they eventually evolve into a species so exotic they can reproduce only with each other. Thus the old issue of the gap between rich and poor becomes either absolute or disappears.) The reviewer says that the author, one after another, raises all the scary possibilities, and one by one, claims that the technology already exists and in fact we're already using it.

A few years ago a couple with a teen age daughter who had myleogenous leukemia, went on a fruitless nationwide search for a suitable donor for bone marrow, their daughter's only hope for survival. When they could find none, they decided to conceive a child of their own (the mother was 42 years old), in hopes that she might be a suitable donor. The odds were one in four. An amniocentesis showed that the fetus was the right type. No mention was made of what they might have done had the fetus not been a match.

When the baby was 19 months old, they harvested her bone marrow, injected it into her sister, and it worked. The sister has been tumor free for four years. The reviewer claimed that the baby was the first human known to have been conceived for the purpose of becoming an organ donor.

We are horrified by the possibilities. The writer makes the point that, when it comes to the emotionally explosive issue of reproducing ourselves, nothing will be able to stand in our way. (A fiction book reviewed in the same issue, is about New York, when, because of tinkering with reproduction and the increasingly toxic environment, the birth rate has dropped so low that only 2 or 3 babies a day are born in the city. Au pairs carry loaded guns when they walk the babies in Central Park.) With the worship of children (a biological expression of our dashed dreams of immortality?) a present reality (been to a fine restaurant or movie lately?), do you think we're going to pass up the chance to shape them as we wish? To make of them the perfect beings we'd wished for ourselves?

The reality is that we posses the ability to engineer genetic outcomes now and we're going ahead with it no matter what laws may be passed. The debate sounds much like the debate (after the fact) triggered by the Manhattan Project. Some principled scientists quit once they discovered the project's true aim, some became spies after Hiroshima, believing that exclusive possession of the nuclear secret created an intolerable power imbalance among the nations, especially between the haves and the have-nots. (Fascinating now to think that, with the nuclear genie nearly as readily accesible as the personal computer, it may be a have-not nation which could bring our species down.) The human drive to discover and shape, especially our genetic heritage, is insatiable and unstoppable.

The writer believes we cannot and we ought not try to outlaw genetic engineering. (He's not sanctioning using people as unwitting guinea pigs) His reasoning is sublime. He reckons that human reproduction and development, while an interesting piece of the unfolding of life in our biosphere, is by no means the centerpiece, and we need not behave as if it is.

Bravo!

Aside from our habitual narcissistic inclination to read the history of the planet (if not the universe) as a scheme for achieving human life, what thoughtful basis do we have for regarding our own kind as either the highest form yet reached, or as pointing the direction of future evolution?

None. We're fascinated with cerebral development, even though war and pollution, over-population and internecine animosity would lead a more objective observer to question the long term usefulness of more complex brains.

Spiritual development, awareness of a more subtle realm apart from conscious five-sense reality which has hogged our attention since the Enlightenment, is often cited as evidence of our special place in the hierarchy. But our grasp of this realm is tenuous and vague, and our knowledge of how other creatures (rocks, whales, schizophrenics) may be tuned to this reality, is practically non-existent.

Let us go ahead with our experiments, he argues, because, not only is outlawing them another futile prohibition, (resulting almost certainly in another ugly chapter of cops and robbers) but in the long haul, what becomes of us is not all that important.

What he doesn't say, but I will, is that, though it is surely instinctive for us to seek our own survival (though humankind shows the strongest inclination of any species yet, to work against its own best interests), the evidence viewed objectively points to a brief tenure for Homo Sapiens (Sapiens? says who?) on earth.

The first clue that these debates about bioethics are mostly posturing, not measured, is their lack of humor. The solemnity with which we gather the "best minds" in some tropical resort in dead of winter, to discuss whether to pursue technology which can destroy human life, or whether to give the green light to geneticists who have discovered ways to affect the human genome, is laughable. And an exercise is futility.

We're going to do it if we can, no matter what rules we adopt. And, aside from our natural fear of the unknown, we have no basis for making rules because we can't fill out the myriad details of the picture that is so much larger than our involvement.

A professor of bioethics at Penn asked his students what they thought about genetic manipulation of a fetus in utero. More than 90% of them were opposed. He then asked, "Well, what if you could alter their genetic code so they would be immune to AIDS?" All but a tiny fraction changed their minds. They weren't hypocrites, they hadn't thought about all the possibilities.

Nor can we. What we can do, we will, we always have. One of these experiments may well contain the elements of our own demise. We won't know that until the demise. It may be that we have already engineered our exit vehicle.

Important though my own survival seems to me, nothing I can do will insure it for long. And this simple understanding holds the clue to human freedom. It may be that much of the world (rocks, whales, schizophrenics) already enjoys this freedom.

The ego self which clings and grasps, adopting creeds, programming its offspring for Harvard Medical School, is in thrall to its illusions of personal power. And the same is true for our species as a whole. Our benighted longing to program our future out into infinity is making us not merely too solemn to be good company for the rest of the species who share this place with us, but a bore to ourselves.

We will grow beyond our wish to replicate ourselves, lose interest in the tricks aimed at cheating death, as the old formulas lose their potency, no longer providing solace. Our deepest hunger is finally not for certainty, not even for reassurance, but for transformation. We long to be changed from self-preoccupied and anxious, to daring adventurers, eager to spend our creative energies.

Ken Wilber writes of transformation in Shambhala Publications' Web Site.

" . . . authentic transformation is not a matter of belief but of the death of the believer; not a matter of translating the world but of transforming the world; not a matter of finding solace but of finding infinity on the other side of death. The self is not made content; the self is made toast."

Whether this comes as good or bad news, fills us with hope or foreboding, indicates where we are in our pilgrimage. It is neither a moral issue nor a test of character, not an issue we can work on. The emotions attached to this discovery might be relief and pleasure. Relief that we can't wreck the creation, and pleasure that we can play with our dreams and imaginings even though we don't know how the play will come out.

"Sufficient unto the day is the evil thereof," a compassionate jester once suggested. Don't sweat the small stuff.

Should we fuck ourselves? Sure, we always have. And when we tire of it, not because it's immoral or dangerous, but because it lacks the power to transform, we become free, to live, spending ourselves extravagantly, free to die.

[Since writing this piece I've been to see Amistad, which shook some of my mystic confidence. The horrendous suffering of particular groups, blacks, Jews, Armenians, momentarily shakes my confidence in a vision of a creation which can't be knocked off its axis, but I believe it is my confidence which is shaken, not the ability of the universe to grow new life in rotting flesh.]

SITTING AS SALVATION

Notes From Zone 10

Chinese New Year 4699 Year of the Snake

January 23, 2001

After burying two more, nearly the last of my parents' generation, I've been thinking again about one of the limits of western Christian practice. I'll keep this as simple as I can, though it's implications are subtle and complex.

I mean the tendency of Christian practice, for those who are regular and devout and for those who practice little or not at all, to point to a reality we're not sure is real. But Christian practice gives us virtually no means, no technique or discipline by which we might glimpse or encounter that reality.

Call it heaven, the Kingdom, the unconscious, nirvana, bliss, the other, it is often portrayed as being in contrast to the material world.

The reasons we in the west are suspicious of and lack of access to the other realm of reality, are many, coming from the truth of "incarnation" religion, the idea that God not only creates and loves the material world, but inhabits it with us.

I suppose it may be something of a cliché to say that while we in the west had been journeying into outer space, those in the east have been on an equally complex and sophisticated journey into inner space. Each culture has developed impressive disciplines to achieve equally impressive ends.

In the west we have developed complex, abstract systems of higher math and physics. In the east the focus has been on meditation.

The time is now ripe for grafting the two branches onto a single trunk. It is already much underway and marks, I believe, the next great step beyond the parochialism that still threatens to lead our race to species suicide.

Sitting meditation is the Way to an encounter with that other realm of reality, the means to weaning ourselves from love of illusion and addiction to distraction. Though meditation has always been a part of more rigorous forms of western Christian practice, notably monasticism, it has been regarded as too esoteric, too exotic for normal lay people going about busy working lives.

I am an amateur at sitting. I am easily distracted, easily dissuaded from doing my daily half hour. Here is how I have been taught: If you are flexible enough, sit on the ground or floor with your legs crossed, your hands in your lap so the fingers of your left hand overlap those of your right and your left thumb is barely over your right thumb. I usually sit in a chair or a knee chair because my back is puny. Keep your eyes open with a soft focus. Breathe normally. I count my breaths, an inhale and an exhale count as one, counting to ten, watching my stomach expand as I inhale, contract as I exhale. The purpose of counting breaths and watching the belly is to keep your focus from fixing on the endless distractions.

I usually do ten breaths of ten and that takes me about a half hour. I am constantly distracted, often think it's going so badly I may as well quit. Don't battle the distractions and the judgements, watch them as you might watch the ball at a tennis match going back and forth across the net, with compassionate interest but letting them pass lightly through your consciousness and then leave.

Ken Wilbur says, "That which is not present in deep dreamless sleep is not real." A Zen teacher says that what attracted her to the practice was that they asked her to believe nothing.

And there's the problem for most of us. We want results. And content. I experience sitting meditation as offering me access to a realm I have often imagined, occasionally experienced intuitively, usually doubt. I have done meditation in various forms for thirty years and feel no more advanced at it than when I began. I still find it boring.

I now experience most Christian worship as busy and noisy. I like ceremony and symbol, communal singing and the Eucharist. On the odd occasion when I find a church that observes silence during worship, I am grateful.

Though I am suspicious of most New Age How To religion, I regard sitting meditation as a key to the transformation we all are hungry for. The reason we don't practice it is simple; it faces us with what we use all those distractions to keep us from, ourselves, God, reality.

All suffering, so goes a Zen saying, results from wishing things were different than they are. Since we tend to measure power and success in our culture by the extent to which we can change, ourselves, others, the shape of the world, this is hard cheese. Vast energy and money in our commercial culture is dedicated to distracting us from reality.

I have no wish to persuade or argue this point. I do believe the happiness of our restless species rests on this simple, difficult discipline, so I dare to suggest it to you while I continue my own infant practice.

SUPER BOWL XXXV

Notes From Zone 10

January 2001

Pursuing the proper
name for
that carping voice that refuses to
settle
Not just the divorce, the law
suit
or the case for
God
but the
wholefuckingthing. Won't settle

Perhaps you saw the story in the far
left column as you watched the Super
Bowl
20,000 Indian people buried beneath Ahmedabad
rubble
earth's capricious crust

The paper of
record
selected a smashed school
high school kids
crushed

on a holiday
when other kids stayed
home.
They went because they wanted to be
doctors
lawyers
.comers
so they needed to show up when
other kids stayed
home
Our kind of kids
crushed.

Diverting
how fast we accommodate
or at least get back to the
game

But that goddamn voice
though thrilled with
back to back
kickoff returns for scores, a Super
Bowl record
and truly tickled
by Bob
Dole's prurient Pepsi
ad
won't settle.

SURGICAL STRIKE

Notes From Zone 10

Epiphany 2002

We've streamlined this procedure
significantly since you had your last one
done
he said as he jammed his finger into my
groin
while I turned my head and coughed.

Putting me in mind of George II
refining surgery some said his father never quite
finished
before faltering finances finished him.

All those years before they'd knocked me
out cold
sent me home with massive pain
killers
that posed more problem than the
pain.
No more. A little mood elevator, local
deadener
quick slice, insert screen, sew it back
together
voila, home again, jiggidy jig.

No news about civilian casualties
the editor
counseled his reporters. It weakens support
at home.

Less than an hour
after I'd kissed Lacey a hurried good bye
the surgeon sought her
to tell her it had gone perfectly,
I was already rejoicing in recovery
feeling fine.

On my own at home, prone, swallowed by the
down couch
my private parts painful, pulsating and
black
reality, an opened abdomen pulling me into fetal
fecklessness,
I considered the encouraging news
rival routed
evil excised
the Dow again topping ten thousand
hernia repaired.

No wonder we whitewash whatever we wish we would win in
a walk.
So, ok, maybe it has to be done
but spare me the dirty details of how it's going to
look later
down
there.

GOD AND THE AGNOSTIC; PIETY FOR A NEW MILLENNIUM

Notes From Zone 10

November 22, 1999

36th Anniversary of President

Kennedy's Assassination

That which is not present in deep dreamless sleep is not real. (Ken Wilbur.) *The fox knows many things; the hedgehog knows one big thing.* (Isaiah Berlin)

With the approach of the new millennium, questions about our species' fortunes seem to press on us more than at other times. Like the conundrum of the boundary between being and non-being. And what to do with our longing to worship now that the medieval synthesis that provided the object of our worship has collapsed.

How about the odds-against fact of our being here on this lush green planet in the vast gray emptiness of space, our understanding, usually unexamined, that we're a freak, like the dinosaur? And, like the dinosaur, likely to become a blip in cosmic history. Many have exhausted their efforts, biological, technological, religious, to hold off our coming non-being. My intent is to describe another choice.

I was ten years old in 1950, century half full, when I first considered the new millennium and my 60th birthday. I doubted I'd ever see that distant time. I thought that if I did, I would be so different from the boy imagining it, I would hardly recognize my older self. I was right.

In the fall of 1999, just after my 59th birthday, I did a meditation weekend at Zen Mountain Monastery in Mt. Tremper, New York. During one of the welcome breaks from sitting meditation, I fell into conversation with a young woman I had noticed the first morning of our retreat. Lean, her carriage ramrod straight, she seemed of royal bearing. Her gray-blue eyes burned with intensity. Her high cheekbones and deep set eyes, small mouth and thin lips, her aspect of serenity aroused familiar longings in me. Her skin was fair, clear, her close cropped, tousled auburn hair framed her patrician face. She sat apart from others at meals and I had gathered my courage to put my tray down beside her.

"My name's Blayney."

"I'm Sarah."

In that brief formal exchange I recognized the near total absence of the energy that marks a breeding man's encounter with a fecund woman. Yes, there was a vestigial remnant, but it was quiescent and we both knew it. I saw she was the age of my middle daughter. With relief and sadness I understood we were not going to act out, in even the subtlest, safest, most oblique way, any of the dances assigned to the mating ritual. Whatever passed between us would want for reverie of curbing our mortality.

Surrendering our dreams of immortality is the heart of
Millennial piety, of worshipping God whom we cannot know.

Countless writings explore the energy between men and women,
portraying the strongest drive in both genders as being to
perpetuate one's DNA, an ersatz immortality. The seed planter
and the child-bearer work out a compromise since neither has a
self-sufficient role. Feeding this drive is our awareness of
mortality and our desire to be distracted from, if not spared its
power to annihilate us.

The fever of ritual with which we greet the new millennium
betrays the depth of our longing to neutralize entropy and the
lethal passage of time.

Religion, nationalism, magic and ambition are aimed at
claiming for ourselves some virtue or power that earned our
existence and that will win immortality for us. Yet one day's tour
of Pompeii uncovers our dreadful knowledge of what awaits us.
And which of us is so vain as to believe in the moral necessity of
our being at all?

As I finish my sixth decade, my millennial meditation is marked
by a new stance towards the knowledge of my not being. For the
vast majority of time there was no me. And soon again there
won't be, for the rest of eternity. My unconscious energy for
most of my life has been directed towards eclipsing that reality.
In my introduction to Sarah I admitted a glacial shift. Like my
birth, this shift came unexpectedly, by grace, through no virtue
or effort of mine.

When you consider the vastness of time and space, and that all
but an inexpressibly tiny fraction is nothing, empty, the fact
that you and I are instead of aren't, is against odds so
overwhelming they are impossible to compute. Your birth is at

least as unbalancing as your death. But we cannot prize the wonder of having become, without also considering the certainty of dying and its power to take our being from us.

So what choices remain, beside despair, cynicism or hedonism, to those of us who want more than creeds promising immortality, or the seductions of commercial culture?

Our hope is built, paradoxically, on our hopelessness. Having exhausted our efforts to explain or justify our existence, we acknowledge that we have done nothing to earn our being. Whether random event or gracious gift, my being provokes responses in me that replace my efforts to justify my existence or to perpetuate it.

Awe, gratefulness, wonder, life held lightly, like a small fragile creature, not tightly grasped.

In my encounter with Sarah I saw my drive to insure my genetic immortality wane. Though every living being seems instinctively driven to perpetuate itself, the perception of grace, life as pure gift, provides a choice beyond instinct.

And it is a conscious choice, one that requires us to face down the instinct that drives our efforts to dull the sharp edges of mortality. And when we choose grace, instinct will challenge our choice.

What is this choice that is beyond instinct and faces down our unconscious? It is what is left when we admit we cannot outwit the power of non-being, whether by replicating our DNA or by driving a Porsche.

The choice is surrender, in awe, to worship. Surrender not to a hierarchy that defines the terms of our surrender, but to mystery that eschews definition. Symbolic worship, ceremony that points beyond itself to the ineffable and provides no explanation.

We have done nothing to cause our being and we can do nothing to perpetuate it. Cynicism would make sense if we had worked out our own existence and now find it was not worth the effort. Despair would be appropriate if some new threat was undermining the conditions of our existence.

But we have always lived by grace, each breath a miracle of unfathomable origin. I cannot pinpoint the moment when I became conscious of my being nor when I knew I could not grasp or perpetuate it. I can track the growing awe in me that led to worship.

Some marks of Millennial piety for those who choose grace with no promise of either God or eternal being:

Awe. That I am.

Esteem. For your being.

Gratitude. For being I neither grasp nor replicate nor perpetuate. (I believe it is more than diminishing hormones that cause a relaxing of sexual urgency in older people, especially since older people often report an increase in sexual pleasure with longtime partners.)

Reverence. In the face of the life force I bow, acknowledging a process of which I am a part, yet which is beyond me.

Hope. I dare to hope that whatever mystery has resulted in my being is no doubt richer than I can sense. And though there is much about how I use this existence that might make me feel unworthy of it, whatever force is at work here clearly is not bound by my ethic.

Repentance. Not so much for having violated life's rules, (though I have. I don't own the means to life and I am subject to rules I didn't make) but for having squandered vital energy trying to control that to which I am subject.

Surrender. I investigate this mystery but I give up hoping to control, understand or manage it. I am utterly dependent and it's active partner. I surrender to the paradox.

Worship. That which is totally other inspires deference and elicits ceremony.

What prevents me from choosing despair or hedonism? The possibility that grace, the inexplicable free gift of being, is the origin and destiny of life. I'm open to the rich possibility that this odds-against enterprise in which I find myself is a primer. The choice for wonder, awe and hope holds the future open. Despair shuts down the possibilities, a futile strategy for control.

Worship (whether of nature, power or Porsche) seems innate in us. But what can legitimately claim our worship? A commercial culture provides countless idols, none with the power to address our imminent non-being.

Virtually all religion begins with the requirement that we surrender. We surrender our hope of justifying our existence or winning immortality, but not our awe and gratitude at receiving this gift. When religion claims power to understand or control life and death, it becomes an idol alongside the Porsche. Those of us who have hit the wall of our mortality can worship in virtually any tradition, though we may have to pick and choose among the its symbols. Our obedience is to the open-ended wonder of this unexpected, unearned gift and our reverence in the face of it.

Abandon hope all ye who enter here. A counsel not of despair but of promise. The Apostle Paul calls death the final enemy, but perhaps death is not the enemy. Perhaps death is the only reality that gives life its due. So long as we place hope in any of our strategies to outwit death, we court despair. The mystery, impenetrable by human effort or intellect, drives us to the worship that resonates with our hope that beyond our anger, fears and cynicism, grace can be trusted.

[I am indebted to Jerome Miller and his seminal work, "The Way of Suffering", Georgetown U. Press. 1988, for this line of inquiry.]

THE OTHER SIDE OF 9/11

Notes From Zone 4

Francis of Assisi, October 4, 2001

So now it seems time to look at the other side. My sleep is still uncertain, I find I have some of the survivor's uneasiness, feeling maybe I shouldn't be sleeping well when 6,000 of us sleep forever.

But I've been thinking about those phone calls, the ones from the towers and the ones from the airplanes. The e-mails. Because of the circumstances under which they were made, the caller now certain survival was impossible, I regard them as a reliable measure of how those people met the worst we could imagine.

A large part of my emotional response has, I think, been what I feel I owe those people who were burned, crushed, dashed to death. But it is the phone calls that now persuade me I have had it all wrong. I thought I owed them my anguish and maybe anger, despair, fear. Strikes me now that this is a mistake we living almost always make about the dead, especially those who have died in a particularly fearsome way.

I love you. Have a good life. Thank you for being in my life. Look after the children.

They might even sound banal if spoken under different

circumstances. But these people were in no position to posture. They had only a little time to say whatever was most important to them. It may be that the messages too terrible for us to bear have been kept quiet. Never mind. The ones we have heard are plenty enough for me.

I've wondered, who hasn't, what it would (will, if I'm lucky) be like to know I'm about to die. I imagine all sorts of heroic things I might say or do, but I have a strong Walter Mitty streak in me and I doubted my fantasies were related to reality. I fear I'd probably cry, throw up, curl into a fetal position, think only of myself.

Or maybe I'd take the chance, if I had it, to call home and tell Lacey and the kids (they aren't home any more, but you get the point) that I love them, that they don't have to worry about me because I'm not worried, that it's been wonderful to love and be loved by them. Maybe I'd even want to hold someone nearby and comfort them.

I have been preoccupied with the awful thought that the terrorists had succeeded. That's because those of us who didn't die are now afraid something like that may happen again and we'll be there next time. But we're still considering this abstractly. That's terror.

If we want some concrete expression of how people, ordinary people like us, at work, on the phone, doing e-mail, taking a coffee break, might actually act, those phone calls and e-mails are about the most vivid evidence we could ask for.

What goes through a person's mind when they know they're about to die? Apparently a lot of people really do think, gratefully, with pleasure, about the people whom they have loved, and want to thank them, let them know.

Wednesday night, the day after the horror, a woman said to me that she would like on her tombstone, "Thanks for everything." I laughed, thought it was clever, then thought about those calls.

If it's true that what one cares most about in the minutes or seconds before dying, is those whom one has loved, and that once the terror triggered by the survival instinct has yielded to the certainty of death, being grateful is the dominant emotion then the terrorists have succeeded only in showing us something wonderful about ourselves we would never have dared believe.

THE VISION THING

Notes From Zone 10

April Fool 2000

There's this young woman in our neighborhood and she's losing it. I'd put her age at around 37. She rides by our friend's house on her bicycle shouting obscenities. She's settled into a 10:30pm and 7:30am routine. Here's what it sounds like from our bedroom:

"Fuck you, all you rich people! Fuck you, Alex, you miserable sonofabitch! Eat shit, you asshole! Yeooooweh!" When she's on her rounds, our normally bustling neighborhood goes eerily silent. The pizza guys across the street and the Surf Systems salesman, who usually are on the corner chatting, disappear.

She's attractive, red haired, trim, dressed in a white warm up suit. Lacey and I had a conversation with her a few weeks ago when we stopped in at a local pub after supper for an Irish whiskey. Lacey admired her cap and she immediately took it off and gave it to Lacey. Beguiling though she was, after my years in the parish brushing against what we called "borderlines", or "manic depressives", she set off an old warning signal in me.

The way I can usually detect such a person is that I'm drawn to them. There was a woman in one parish who, in her manic phase, would hop airplanes all over the country and shop. She

was a talented newspaper journalist and managed to keep just
enough of a handle on things to persuade the paper, for a while,
that she was on the trail of a story. I once received a pair of
"Super Bowl XXII" athletic socks she'd mailed from New
Orleans. I watched the Super Bowl that year hoping to see her
on the field at halftime.

Once, between marriages, I had a roommate, not because I
wanted or needed one but because the guy who had rented the
apartment before me was too busy to move out. He graciously
slept on the couch in the living room and left me the bedroom.
If only I had needed no sleep those couple of weeks it might
have been one of the most fun times of my life. He, too, was in
the midst of a divorce and remarriage. In addition to
covering New England for whatever gidget he was repping,
he spent his considerable energy wooing both his estranged
wife and his upcoming wife with flowers, expensive gifts,
telegrams and phone calls from phone booths along route 95.
When they unplugged their phones, he'd show up at our
apartment, usually between 2 and 4am and regale me with
stories of what he'd been up to since I last saw him. He was
funny and clever, endlessly entertaining if your battery had
been recently charged.

My first brush with manic energy was when I was 24 years old
and a chaplain intern in the acute schizophrenic women's ward
at Worcester State Hospital in Massachusetts.

Arlene, who was a few years older than I, could chew up and
swallow a lighted cigarette while she carried on a conversation.
She was just over five feet tall, plump, her hair the color of
whatever rinse she'd gotten hold of. She tied her hair in a
ponytail that stood straight up on top of her head, and dressed
in the telltale warm up suit. She paced the ward's hall like a
caged cougar.

I'd watched the psychiatric resident berate her, treat her like a criminal, humiliate her. I decided God's love and mine would cure her. I spent the better part of three days talking with her. The first day she stopped eating the ash off her cigarette and began speaking in complete sentences. The third day she was calm, no twitches, and told me the whole sordid story of growing up in her abusive family.

Before I went home that day I wrote extensive notes in her record about our conversation, explaining that I may have been the first person to take the time to listen to her and take her story seriously. I described how she went from agitated and acting out the first day to calm and coherent the third day. She had even joined a group in the day room playing Monopoly, a breakthrough. I recommended that, if she continued to receive caring attention (I barely managed to keep from writing "from me") she be considered for a day pass the following week.

When I arrived the next morning, Jo Anne, the voluptuous and compassionate blond charge nurse whose approval and affection I hoped to awaken with my sensitive and skilled pastoral care, motioned to me to join her in the nursing station.

"I see you spent a lot of time with Arlene the past three days," she said, motioning to her chart. I tried to look humble and matter of fact as I allowed as how I had. "Looks like you made a real breakthrough," Jo Anne went on.

"You really think so?" Be still my heart.

"No doubt. Last night Arlene set her mattress on fire and attacked the night attendant. The Chief Resident would like you to go visit her in the back ward where they've locked her up. But be careful. It took four of our strongest attendants to subdue her last night. And she's pissed."

I went to see her, terrified as I walked through the tiled corridor with the linoleum floor slanting towards a drain in the center. They'd just hosed down the ward and the floor was wet and slippery. I found Arlene straitjacketed in a high-backed chair. She frowned, then spit at me.

"Leave me alone, asshole; you're the reason I'm here."

Chemicals calm these people down. But I wonder what it is they see without the chemicals. Because sometimes I think I may have seen it, too. "American Beauty", the movie that got so many Oscars, made me feel the way I imagine those people may feel. It's like having filters removed.

We call them crazy, I suspect, so we can reassure ourselves we aren't. I'm not the first to wonder about the connection between crazy and talented. Reading a piece in a recent New Yorker about Martin Scorsese, Mary Pat Kelly, a colleague of Scorsese, spoke of asking him where he got the vision to do a particular scene in "The Last Temptation of Christ." In it Jesus, out of focus, watches Mary Magdalene make love to three men. An Indian man also sits in lotus position watching. The focus shifts from Mary Magdalene to what the viewer is certain will be Jesus' face. Instead the screen is suddenly filled with the Indian's eye, a brilliant, unsettling Scorsese moment.

Scorsese told her that he woke in the middle of the night four years before and saw the scene. She realized he had been preparing for this film his whole life. She reflects:

"Who knows what talent is? I don't think talent is as rare as the need to express it or the strength to handle the rejection. I don't think Marty can help it; there's nothing else he can do with his life."

Perhaps we keep our distance with borderline people for the same reason we go to the movies; they show us what we normally filter out, the passion and the talent in us, the vision we have managed to keep quiet. It can be titillating to look through the director's lens with some of the filters removed, at least until the lights come up. When confronted with an immediate fleshy unfiltered person, we're not sure we're going to be able to keep the talent and passion, especially ours, in manageable bounds.

The truth, the man said, will set you free. Right, but what's it going to set me back?

WHAT GOES AROUND

Notes From Zone 4

Summer Solstice 2001

After two years of corporate jousting over recalls of tires and accusations of unsafe vehicles, Firestone Tire and Ford Motor severed their relationship that goes back to their founders, Henry Ford and Harvey Firestone.

{Take a wheel and put it round, round, round, as it goes along with a happy sound, along the ground, ground, ground, till it leads you to the one you love. In the night you see the oval moon, going round and round in a tune; and the ball of sun in the day, makes a girl and a boy want to say, Take a wheel, and put it round, round, round . . . till it leads you to the one you love. Pop tune from the 1950s.}

Your head must be spinning, Harvey, I mean with all the news in the papers about your tires being pulled off nearly every axle on one of our best selling models. Who'd have ever thought we'd come to such a turn?

When you think, Henry, how tight was the circle in which you and I traveled, it brakes your heart, to see this great wheel of good fortune, which has taken so many so far, grind to a halt. Not to mention the overturning of a century of corporate loyalty.

I'd tread a little lightly on that overturn metaphor, Harvey. And as for those virtues we once lionized; around our shop we no longer look to the wheels of justice to turn as they once did, smoothly, providing a level course on which the competitive race could be fairly run.

Quite right, Henry, you could be left at the starting gate waiting for the wheels of justice to turn. Have you considered the universe recently, its randomness? Why, some say it isn't even round, maybe flat as a Wilderness tire on an Explorer. Wheel of justice? Wheel of fickle fortune, spinning, stopping at random, red, black, who knows, leaving the loser in a ditch, sucked inexorably into a black hole.

But my dear friend, is there no way round this depressing conundrum? Am I to put my precious eggs, century eggs by now, into this one cruel basket, only to see my best energy come to zero? My torque miring me deeper in the mud, my wheels spinning pathetically? Is all this, as some have said, merely a cynical circle? In my beginning is my end? Thank you, God, for nothing. I'm left looking at that tiny prick of light I first saw from my mother's birth canal, that now they say is bent round infinity, comes back to my end, the light at the end of the tunnel, the light I first saw . . .

You bet my head is spinning, Henry, turning furiously, sloshing the fluid in my middle ear like a rolling surf, disorienting, or maybe orienting, ringing my ears, my balance failing, falling.

Do you remember, Harvey, telling me about vulcanizing, about the coming revolution in tires and thus in motoring, that was going to turn the American dream to reality? No more round trips to remote rubber plantations, wheels in every garage, put the American family on the road to prosperity? Do you remember what I said to you then, when we were on such a roll, so high it seemed like we might inflate a tube without a pump?

I remember well, Henry. You said, Slow down, dear friend; don't let it turn your head. What goes around comes around.

NOTES FROM ZONE 4

Labor Day 1999

One Friday afternoon in July 15 years ago, when we were living in Zimbabwe, I got a call to do a funeral at the morgue. A young woman had died of malaria. We were to do the service at the morgue because her body was then to be transferred by lorry back to her homelands where she would be buried among her own people. Lacey and I were supposed to be running a track and field event for the children at the local government school at the same time. Lacey wasn't eager to do it by herself.

I called George Sadomba, the lay President of the local Anglican congregation and explained my timing dilemma. My part was of predictable length, but I had learned that the Africans, who have elaborate customs for such occasions, didn't rush these matters.

"Oh Baba," George reassured me, using the honorific title 'father', "the body must reach her homelands before sundown because the lorry has no headlamps. You can be free to go within the hour."

I was reassured. Lacey and I agreed I would go buy some soft drinks at the kiosk and she would have refreshments first. By the time the events were to begin, I could be back at the school.

I arrived at the morgue promptly at 2pm as George and I agreed. There was no one there except a man building a coffin.

He and I conversed about the woman who had died, about how devastated her family must be. I watched as he constructed the simple, rather elegant plain wood box. I remembered a family back in Massachusetts whose young daughter had died of meningitis. They wanted to bury her in an unfinished pine coffin.

"They're not available," the undertaker explained. "They haven't made them for thirty years."

"So why couldn't we make it ourselves?" the distraught father asked.

"The cemetery has to approve all containers," the undertaker insisted They won't let you use material that will decompose rapidly. Makes the ground over the grave sink, even with a vault."

George Sadomba arrived at 2:20. The coffin was ready and the friend who was to drive the body the three hours north to Manicaland arrived, too. By now Lacey had been with her young charges for twenty minutes and none of the mourners had showed for the funeral. I was beginning to get anxious.

"George," I asked, struggling to sound unconcerned, "how many people do you think will be coming?"

"Maybe 300, Baba. They'll be here very shortly." He smiled broadly. I hadn't fooled George.

The coffin builder tried putting the coffin in the back of the lorry; the hatch wouldn't close. My blood pressure shot up. Neither George nor the builder seemed concerned. The builder made a mark on the coffin, took it back to where his tools were, checked his notes to be sure of the woman's height, and began sawing off the end of the coffin. Before he had finished closing in the foot, the body arrived, shrouded, on the flat bed of a truck. He hammered in the finish nails and the four of us lifted the body from the truck and placed it in the coffin. After some firm but gentle pushing down on the shoulders, her body fit snugly into the box.

My panic had begun to settle into resignation. Nearly six months in Zimbabwe and I still couldn't do African time. I was imagining the fight Lacey and I would have when I finally showed up at the school.
Mourners began drifting in, in two and threes. George, sensing my discomfort, attempted to divert me.

"Baba, perhaps you can explain; we don't understand this term 'sabbatical'. We have no such word in Shona."

I suspected he understood all right. I sensed I was being set up. But I explained it to him as if I believed he really didn't know.

"Does this mean," George pressed, "that when the sabbatical ends you will be leaving us?" He spit out the word sabbatical as if it were profanity.

"Yes, George," I explained patiently (I hoped), "I am on leave from my parish in the U.S. and must return."

"But Baba, you know we have no priest to replace you. We will be sheep without a shepherd," he said, in case I'd missed the biblical implication.

"George," I was feeling cornered, "they're paying my salary to be here with you. They've now paid me thousands of dollars and another priest is doing my work. I'm obligated to go back." It sounded hollow and mercenary even to me. George pressed his advantage.

"Baba, we have heard there are so many priests in America that some of them are pumping petrol because there is no work for them in the church." He stepped back and looked at me, eyes wide, waiting for a response to this monstrous rumor.

"Well, there's truth to that," I acknowledged, "but I still . . ."

"Then you must stay, Baba," George interrupted. He'd never interrupted me. "They will understand. They can simply go to the petrol station and get one of those priests. They don't really need you; we do."

Desperate, I changed the subject, and unwittingly led myself into even deeper water. "George, this coffin is so beautiful. We don't have coffins like this back in America." I wasn't being disingenuous; I loved the plain box far more than the outrageously expensive mahogany or shiny metal American coffins. But George wasn't about to forgo his advantage.

"This is all we can afford." He hung his head as if ashamed. "You see we don't have a proper vehicle to transport her to her homeland; she must go in a friend's little lorry, so the simple coffin has to be rebuilt to fit it in. We haven't the means to do things right."

"George," I was now in way over my head, "I hope, when your country gains prosperity, you will look at the ways we have ravaged our land through greed and selfishness, and you will proceed with more care than we have. That you will remember how life-giving simple can be. Not only have we plundered a beautiful land, but we have polluted our own souls with our avariciousness."

George's eyes narrowed. I remember thinking I was about to experience something I hadn't in six months of exchanges with Africans. Polite and courtly, Africans always solicited my opinion

before offering their own, which then invariably meshed
seamlessly with mine.

"This is what you in the west now say to us," George's tone was
dark; he'd failed to address me as "Baba". "You are rich and have
everything you want, so you counsel us to go slow, be content
with our simple life. Well, we've learned well from you; we want
what you have and we intend to have it."

I was stunned. "George, that's not what I meant at all. I mean
you have much to teach us about nurturing our soul."

"I mean no disrespect, Baba, but you don't know what it's like
to see your luxury while we are poor. We do not believe your talk
about our noble poverty. We believe you mean to keep us poor
so we will not challenge your wealth."

I flashed back to Akron, Ohio and 1966. I went with a woman
from Planned Parenthood to a black Baptist church in east
Akron where she gave her lecture on family planning. When she
asked for questions the Pastor rose to his feet.

"You understand," he said, "this is the white man's way to keep
us down. Now that he has dominated us so completely his
biggest fear is that we'll breed faster than him and become his
master instead of his slave."

"Dr. Anderson," the woman from Planned Parenthood protested,
"You and I know each other; you can't believe I'd be a part of
such a racist plot!"

"Mrs. Baker," Dr. Anderson answered, "You're a nice and
honorable woman. But you're naïve; you have no idea the
bidding you're doing for the white man."

I have just read a speech Vaclav Havel, President of the Czech

Republic gave when receiving the First Decade prize at the tenth anniversary celebration of the Polish daily Gazeta Wyborcza. In the speech he asks what the nations of Eastern Europe can do to repay the west for helping them win their freedom.

He says those living under totalitarianism learned that finally, the only kind of politics that makes sense is "a politics that grows out of the imperative, and the need, to live as everyone ought to live and therefore—to put it somewhat dramatically— to bear responsibility for the entire world. People lucky enough not to have had to live under totalitarianism may never have learned this lesson with the same urgency as those who did."

"The dictatorship of money, of profit, of constant economic growth, and the necessity, flowing from all that, of plundering the earth without regard for what will be left in a few decades, along with everything else related to the materialistic obsessions of this world, from the flourishing of selfishness to the need to evade personal responsibility by becoming part of the herd, and the general inability of human conscience to keep pace with the inventions of reason, right up to the alienation created by the sheer size of modern institutions—all of these are phenomena that cannot effectively be confronted except through a new moral effort, that is, through a transformation of the spirit and the human relationship to life and the world."

The leadership for the next chapter in human history is coming from people and nations that have suffered. From Havel, Nelson Mandela, and Desmond Tutu. From East Timor, Northern Ireland and from the refugee camps of the Middle East and the Balkans.

We wonder what it will be like when our economic boom busts. We wait for that inevitable event to make new resolutions about our place in the human family. Moral leadership seems impossible for a people numbed by our own affluence.

We in the west, who have not experienced the devastation of seeing our cities destroyed since our Civil War, will sit at the feet of those who have. No culture has ever willingly curbed its acquisitiveness on behalf of its inner life. Or tempered its appetites so the world's goods might be distributed more justly. What does it benefit a nation to gain the whole world and lose its own soul?

How long will it be before we again bury our dead in a pine box?

WHITE WASPS

Notes From Zone 4

Terrorist Attack The Day After 9/12/2001

The stinging insects in Vermont have had their strongest season in memory. Whether because it has been hot and dry no one seems certain, but along with weird stories of bears coming out into the open, talk in the store has been about being stung.

We have a nest of white wasps. The painters who were painting our house called them to my attention just before I would have run over them with the lawn mower.

I waited until night, then shot an entire spray can of wasp killer into the hole. The next morning, as soon as the sun rose, so did the wasps. The next night I did it again, this time putting a rock across the mouth of their hole so any who may not have been killed by the spray couldn't get back in. The following morning not only were wasps coming out around the rock, but they had excavated a new hole.

"Pour motor oil in there; that'll finish 'em," one of the most plugged in to nature people suggested. That night I poured a quart of engine oil in each hole. Same result.

So I decided what I might have decided before going to all the trouble and probably risking a life threatening encounter with the wasps. They've been a part of this meadow longer than I have, will be here after I'm gone, and I'll figure ways we can be here together.

This morning Lacey and I sat on a bench overlooking the pond, the bench the kids gave us for our wedding anniversary. We watched thousands of the wasps working the purple fall asters and cosmos. Though the day was perfect, cloudless, warm, we both felt nauseous, from fright and frustration, having just turned off NPR and the endless reports from New York and Washington. Like you, we're wondering who we know among the dead, and how this is going to change what it means to be an American.

For many years we have been telling ourselves we were living in a fantasy, so rich, so removed from the troubles of much of the world, able to act and protect our own interests without fear of interference. The plunging stock market was our early warning. Not only was our own high tech miracle proving clay footed, but Japan's troubles, and Indonesia, the European Union, Russia, even Nepal's royal assassination, were affecting our fortunes.

It's a mark of our character, this sense of being the good guys, the blessed, the innocent who go about our business and invite any who wish to join us. We watch the Israelis and the Palestinians, the Catholic and Protestant Irish, Indians and Pakistanis, and cluck over their unwillingness to put aside ancient insults and get on with prospering as we in the New World have.

So we missed something I trust we'll never miss again. That every country and every person have interests, and they often conflict. People everywhere portray it as good versus evil, and we will this time. It becomes like trying to eradicate white wasps.

Wasps' sting hurts, but they sting not because they're evil or enjoy inflicting pain, but because they feel their interests are threatened.

Perhaps it was unavoidable, with the luck of geography and events turning us into the world's lone super power, but unless we are going to consign ourselves to living this nightmare, we might take a look at the true interests, whether we think they're legitimate or not, of all sorts of people around the world. And we may have to curb our own appetites in ways that seem to diminish us.

The oneness of the world is a cliché that the American business miracle of the past fifty years has made real. There will always be criminals and a need for government to enforce laws. But this attack on our most potent totems has already done its work. No doubt we must and we will retaliate. But we Americans really are part of the world. Attempts to mold the world in our image distorts our self-image. This great nation is irrevocably partnered now with all the rest of the world. For better and for worse.

WIPING THE DOG'S FEET

Notes From Zone 4

Independence Day 2001

I never used to
sweep
the garage
or polish the stainless steel
sink.
My laundry could sit in the
hamper
for weeks so long as my socks didn't
stink.

Five years ago, when I
quit
my job I began tucking in
hospital
corners
when I made the bed
rubbing the kitchen
faucet
with the dish towel after doing the
dishes,
removing my shoes before stepping up from the mud
room,
rotating my tee

shirts
cleaning the dog's
paws
before she came inside.

When I
quit my job I calculated how old my
father was
when he quit.
This morning looking at a photo of my
grandfather
I worked out how many years he lived after he
graduated
from college (58)
Next June marks my 40th.

I'd love to pin this
picayune plague
bush league doom defense
on my fastidious wife
But she merely taught me the trivial
tricks
that look to order the
chaos.
I have adopted them since I
quit my job
and no longer put on the daily
suit
that once defended me from
entropy
Melancholy mocks me, muddy
treads
in the garage
I just
swept.

NOTES FROM ZONE 10

St. Patrick's Day 1999

When last we spoke I'd taken on a reassessment of my
relationship with God as a Lenten discipline. A simple enough
task for forty days. I have been resurrecting some old pieties and
trying some new ones, some of which you'd recognize, some not.

My hard drive crashed on my spiffy new G3 laptop. A slippery
slope to atheism. It had been giving me warnings, doing
seemingly arbitrary loopy tricks, but since I don't understand
what the thing is or how it works, I ignored them, hoping they
were nothing.

Then one afternoon, after a long morning of writing, I booted
up the machine and got the little bugger with the question mark
blinking where his smile was supposed to be. I didn't panic; I've
faced this before. I turned the machine over and read the graphic
about which keys one has to push simultaneously while turning
the machine on in order to reset it, (do computer nerds have
more fingers than I do?) turned it back over and confidently did
it.

And got the little bugger with the question mark face.

I was certain my friend Russ could fix it. But since I'd been
relying almost solely on this computer to help me record my
reflections about my life with God, seeing the fellow with the
question mark blinking in his face began to disconcert me.

I called Russ who was amazed and chagrined that this had happened since he was sure my problems were over once he'd helped me load on system 8.5.1, escaping from bug infested 8.5. And he, too, is running 8.5.1. (Russ' best quality is he never does blame assessment; he believes in random misfortune.)

I thought a lot about what this might mean, being denied access to the shaky work I have been doing, my God-meandering, having the main vehicle for my work lock me out, finding myself cut off from the memory of my last several weeks.

Russ shared my confidence that this could be fixed. He talked me through perhaps ten scenarios for repairing the problem, each one resulting in the Jeremiah figure, the gloomy prophet blinking his enraging question mark, warning me I was a non-person. Russ finally was out of options and we agreed I'd call the Apple rescue number.

Kareena at Apple was an seraph. Not only was she patient as my panic began to mount, but she asked helpful questions when I referred to a thigamajig and whined. She praised me whenever I was able to follow her directions. Her ministrations were gentle and gracious. I was reminded of the nurse in my urologist's office who rubbed my back when the sigmoidoscope was angling its way toward my Adam's apple. I had considered naming her in my will.

Like Russ, Kareena walked me through several exercises. When each of them failed to persuade the cold-hearted little man to turn his question mark back into a smile, she told me, "Well, Mr. Colmore, we're now down to two options."

The blood ran cold in my veins

"What are they, Kareena?"

"The first is you can search around, on the Internet (how can I search the Net? I can't boot up my machine.) or in stores for some piece of repair software that can fix this problem. We at Apple don't know of one, but that doesn't mean there isn't one."

"But Kareena, even if I could find something, I can't start up the computer. How would I get it to accept a repair disk?"

"That's a problem, I'll admit." She lowered her voice an octave, like the angel with the flaming sword at Eden's gate reminding of the mortal sin still staining my imperiled soul.

"So let's have the other option," I suggested trying to sound brave.

Her voice brightened. "You can reinitialize your hard drive."

"That doesn't sound so bad; why haven't we considered that before?"

"Well, Mr. Colmore," her voice was back to the solemn low octave, "it means losing everything on your hard drive."

I finally broke the ensuing silence, choking back the saliva that had slid down my windpipe: "Everything, Kareena?"

"Everything."

For the next fifteen minutes Kareena earned her bucks. I hope her supervisor was monitoring the call. Like the patient who has just been told he has a month to live, I kept Kareena on the line while I revisited every possibility we had already cast out, hoping I had not heard something before that I'd hear this time. I knew she knew that I knew we had been over all this ground already, but she acted as if we were bringing up new live hopes each time.

My whole life flashed before me. I remembered the parishioner who founded and ran a fabulously successful biotech company. His secretary walked into his office one day and found him sitting at his desk, eyes fixed, hands clasping the edge of the desk, his body rigid.

A vessel in his brain had clogged, denying blood to some cells that controlled the motor skills on his right side and his speech center. When I arrived at the hospital a couple of hours later, his eyes followed me as I entered his room, but his speech hard drive had erased everything except the word "yes". Though it must have been no comfort to him, I remember thinking how good it was that the one remaining word was "yes" instead of "no". Or worse. I used to visit a dignified old Yankee lady in a nursing home in a former parish whose only remaining word was "shit", a word no one had ever heard her speak before her stroke.

After fifteen minutes, though Kareena had said nothing about a time limit or even let any impatience creep into her voice, I knew we were out of choices.

"Kareena," I pleaded one last time, "are you sure we've tried everything possible before I reinitialize the hard drive and erase everything?"

"Everything I know, Mr. Colmore."

"Kareena, I'm a writer . . ."

"I know what you must be going through, Mr. Colmore. I have one of these machines at home and I live in dread of this happening."

"O.K., Kareena, I'm ready. Let's do it."

For the next twenty minutes Kareena graciously led me through the horror of major open-heart surgery on my computer, removing its life force and reintroducing it one precarious step at a time. When it came time for me to begin installing the software, she gave me a case number and urged me to call back if I had any more problems, though she was sure I wouldn't.

The next two days were filled with attempts to reconstruct my e-mail address book, the means by which I send these pieces to you. I reckon you are about half of those to whom I used to send them. As I receive messages, I reenter the address of the sender.

My prayers are more heartfelt than before. This is the fifth computer I've owned since the 128K I got in 1984, and I've believed each one must be not only more sophisticated, but more reliable than the last. Though I still haven't the faintest notion of what these things are or how they work, I have become dependent on them for my most important work. When I was in despair in my first winter back in Vermont, my e-mail and my writing were some days the only thing standing between me and a self-inflicted wound.

This winter my body has given me many signals that its systems are not immortal either. A shoulder that has gone into the tank for no apparent reason, knees and hips complaining of a lifetime of awkward upright living, weird untimely tics in unwelcome muscle groups just as I'm about to hit a cross-court forehand. A friend said he now understands why his father always made that strange little grunt each time he pulled himself up out of the car.

Oddly, this has been as good as it has been bad. Or enriching as much as impoverishing. I briefly considered returning to doing all my writing longhand. I have some monastic instincts that I thought I might give vent to, renouncing e-mail and the Web, spending more time in meditation, reading, swimming. As recently as two years ago I thought I could reorganize my life so the enraging little bastard with the flashing question mark in place of the reassuring smile would never again pop into my life.

Some of you I have lost, maybe forever. This writing will go out into the ether in search of you, perhaps dwindling like prayer as it feathers out to the ends of the noosphere. I will have to rely on something that is beyond my ken to keep the connection between us intact. That connection, I've discovered matters to me as much as anything.

The day after my computer erased its entire memory, my phone rang and the voice on the other end said, "Blayney, this is Bo Tarns."

"Bo Tarns? Bo Tarns? Bo Tarns!"

Louise, who was in the room, said I repeated his name so many times she was afraid I'd had a stroke.

Bo Tarns was a close friend with whom I had lost contact, I thought forever, some 25 years ago. I confess I'd thought of him often, wondered where he was and what had happened to him. I felt sometimes angry, mostly sad that I'd lost a friend. We don't get many in this life.

"You got a minute to talk?" he asked.

"My hard drive's gone," I replied inanely, "I've got nothing but time."

"I'm calling to get back in touch with you. I let a good friendship go a long time ago and I feel really sorry about that."

For a moment I thought I might cry. I've always known it was my fault the friendship had soured. (Unlike Russ, I assess blame.) We talked for a half-hour, coast to coast. About our failed first marriages and our grown children. About the undeserved gift of a second marriage that was richer than we dared hope. I pictured him as he was the last time I saw him. While we talked I looked at myself in the mirror wondering if he'd be shocked at the white hair and deep creases. We laughed about the time we'd met in New York; I took the train from Boston and he from Washington, to go to the Mohammed Ali-Joe Frazier fight in Madison Square Garden.

I thought about Ali and how he's become an even bigger hero than ever, now that he's broken and we nervous whiteys can see his impressive dignity. I thought about how eager I've been the past quarter century to set it right between Bo and me but I couldn't screw up the courage to try. I thought about how much I lost when my hard drive crashed and my body began to age.

"You got an e-mail address, Bo?" I asked.

"Nope, haven't entered the computer age just yet. Guess we'll just have to find a way to see each other."

One day some years ago I was talking to my friend, a Carmelite nun who has lived in enclosure for forty years. I'd just told her how I hold myself back from God.

She smiled. "What do you think God wants from you, Blayney?"

I felt panic, my mind went blank, like I was in third grade and the teacher asked me for homework I hadn't done. I couldn't make a sound. I felt my face get red, sweat dribbled down my side.

She laughed. "Why, you know what God wants from you, Blayney. God wants everything."

I've been thinking about how much more I have to lose and I wonder how that will be. I don't know how old I was when I realized I had a shot at being around when 2000 came. I guess I still do. I think about you, whom I've chosen to connect with and those I lost in the crash. How much it matters to me, those who are lost and those who get found again. Prodigals. The story still has some oomph, still gets my juices running. So far it's been a pretty rich Lent.

My computer and my printer still refuse to talk to each other. I hope they resolve that faster than Bo and I did.

II

Essay and Commentary

GAY MARRIAGE
VERMONT GOES FIRST

2000

This year Vermont became the first state to legalize what it calls a "civil union" between people of the same gender. The name is intended to distinguish the gay relationship from heterosexual marriage and still grant the gay couple the tax and legal rights of married couples. I believe the emotional issue that finally caused the passage of the bill was a man who was dying of AIDS, whose family denied his long-time gay partner access to him.

The purpose of this essay is to support not only civil unions, but gay marriage, and to say something about why I think it's such a hard issue for most of us.

I believe there have been two main reasons for society promoting marriage as ours has through tax laws (the so-called marriage penalty is an inadvertent error that will be corrected when the election year heat cools) and social policy. The first is to promote procreation, fertility, and the second to seek stability.

Most religions and nations have encouraged fertility for obvious parochial reasons. If there are more of us than of them, we will prevail. With push-button war rather than phalanx going up against phalanx, the size of the horde has lost much of its significance in human competition.

What's more important, the issue of crowding the planet with too many of us has become one of the most pressing problems of our time. Though we would be loathe to follow the Chinese practice of engineering social policy to drop the acceptable birth rate for couples to one, most of us would agree it would be good to find ways to voluntarily lower the birth rate.

Gay couple do not make babies. What's more, we're discovering they like to adopt children and often make at least as good parents as heterosexual couples. So they not only don't contribute to the problem, they can lend to a solution.

We humans are fundamentally conservative, resisting change until there seems some clear compelling reason to embrace it. Aside from the Roman Catholic Church, that has a medieval problem of definition (cf. Thomas Aquinas), we now have a compelling reason to define marriage in ways other than reproduction.

The Episcopal Book of Common Prayer describes the first purpose of marriage as being for "their mutual joy".

At 60 years old, with my child-bearing days long behind me, I am more happily married than ever. I like being married. Lacey and I have no children. (She has two from a previous marriage; I have three.) Surely we can describe marriage as providing the possibility for procreation without denying people in a childless marriage the same benefits and responsibilities.

The other reason for encouraging marriage is for the benefit and stability of society. Married couples take out mortgages, pay taxes, buy groceries, put down roots, have a stake in the status quo. Though I've never seen a study that shows it, surely fewer revolutions are fomented by married people than by loners.

The rap on gay people, particularly gay men, is they are promiscuous and unstable, with many partners, spreading sexually transmitted disease and social unrest.

The surprise to me is the numbers of gay people seeking the legitimacy of marriage, suggesting to me that they are looking to join the stable householder families we want as neighbors. Whether the possibility of regularizing marriage between gay people would drop the numbers of cruising gay people to the numbers of promiscuous heterosexual people, I couldn't say. But surely it would provide more chance for gay people to take on the sorts of lives we keep saying we wish they might.

So, if you buy these two points, and many do, why does gay marriage (or, in Vermont, even Civil Union) cause so much uproar? Why do we get so upset about it? (In Vermont's case I'm sure it has the dimension of long time locals versus recently arrived flatlanders with their liberal social engineering).

Surely it's because sexuality, sensuality and eroticism are such moving targets for all of us. How do I know what your sex life is like? Let alone what your fantasy life is like? When it comes to sex, who knows were they stand? And since it seems to be a moving target, something that changes through life, sometimes in the course of a single day, we're not likely to find out.

A friend once said to me that he believes 10% of people are homosexual and 10% are heterosexual, and all the rest of us are scattered along a continuum in between, and we move around on that continuum in the course of our lives.

We wonder, however vaguely, however deep in our unconscious, whether our sexual identity is clear and acceptable, especially to ourselves. I have a half dozen very close male friends, whom I embrace and even kiss (chastely on the cheek). I have never consciously been sexually aroused by them, but I get excited to see them and sign my e-mails to them with love.

I have never consciously experienced the erotic basis for same gender sex. But there are lots of erotic heterosexual acts I know about that don't attract me. Is homosexuality unnatural? If you remove procreation as the definition for sex, I don't think so. Any more than heterosexual sex using birth control is unnatural (which is the reason the Roman Catholic Church opposes it).

I am a 60 year old writing this. At 30 (or 40 or even 50) my hormones were still like molecules in boiling water and I could never have treated the subject with such distance. I still love sex but am not as troubled by it as I once was, not wondering if it is about to overturn my life. Nor am I so concerned about where I fit on the scale.

But along with how other people view us, whether we're relatively rich or poor, good looking or homely, liked or shunned, smart or dumb, the question of whether we're normal sexually worries us. Gay people trigger that worry that we try to keep underground. Suppose we just enlarge normal to include gay people? Surely that makes all of us a little safer.

Addendum: Since I wrote this piece I have heard a Vermont legend that may cast more light on live-or-let-live Vermonters anger at civil unions. Some old Vermonters talk about an essay in Playboy magazine around 1968 (didn't every piece of the social revolution happen in 1968?). Reportedly the essay pointed out that since there were fewer than 400,000 people in the State of Vermont, a couple of hundred thousand progressive people moving there could own the state and enact social legislation. That, so these old Vermonters say, is what happened, and the most recent result is Civil Unions between gay partners, signed into law by Governor Howard Dean, a New Jersey flatlander, preppie, physician, and recent Vermont immigrant.

DUCKY

August 1997

I was swimming across Harriman Reservoir, just down from the boat landing in Whitingham. There's a rock sticking up near the opposite shore which is my marker for turning left on my long swim into the far end of the cove where the lake ends. As I made my turn this day, I was aware of a big commotion on the water. At first I thought another swimmer had passed me going in the opposite direction, though whoever it was seemed to be going incredibly fast and I thought it odd I hadn't noticed them earlier.

At the second pass I stopped swimming and looked up to see a small crested duck take a pass at me, coming perhaps within six feet before veering off, all the while flapping her wings and making a fearsome call. Now she wasn't flying, never quite leaving the water, though her wings were going hard and fast enough so I thought maybe she was injured, and she was churning the water like a steamboat paddle wheel. She circled me from six feet away, first one direction then the other. That familiar charge went through my body as I wondered whether she would actually come for me and peck at me. The charge is, I suppose, fear, something I've always wished I might quell since I've heard animals smell that fear on you and it acts like an exciter to them.

I stopped several times, sometimes treading water, sometimes doing a gentle breast stroke. Each time the duck eyed me to make certain I was disabled or at least diverted, then flew noisily away. But as soon as I resumed swimming the crawl, she came back and resumed her intimidating charges at me. When this had gone on for perhaps five minutes, I gained confidence that she wasn't going to actually come any closer than the six feet she kept between us, and I began to take an interest.

She listed to her left as she circled, her left wing dipping further into the water than her right, and the colorful pointed tuft on the back of her skull reminded me of Woody Woodpecker frantically menacing Sylvester the cat. I was Sylvester. Swimming.

Since she didn't appear to be injured, I assumed I must have swum near her nest, though I was towards the middle of the lake, and August 2 seemed an unlikely time for a duck to be nesting or protecting its young.

I noticed a woman sunning herself on the shore, sit up and shield her eyes against the late afternoon glare so as to get a better look at what was happening out there on the lake. I wondered if she thought I ought to be alarmed. Was I? Mostly not.

Finally I turned around, thinking I'd gone far enough, and headed back to my starting point. The moment I swam in the other direction, the duck flew away and I never saw her again. As I swam back by the woman who had been sunning herself, I asked her if she had seen the duck following me. She laughed and said she certainly had.

When I got back to where I had started out from, my wife laughed and said some crazy woman had shouted to her that "that guy you're with is being chased by a duck." Lacey climbed onto a rock to look, and decided the woman was seeing the wake of my kick. I explained that the crazy woman was right.

This morning I looked in Petersen's Guide and believe I was being pursued by either a common or a hooded Merganser. A hooded Merganser. Ducky.

GOING FASTER BUT WHERE?

I wrote this piece for an essay contest about how transport will
be managed in the future. I didn't win the contest.

In my beginning is my end

In order to arrive at what you do not know
you must go by a way which is a way of ignorance.
In order to possess what you do not possess
you must go by the way of dispossession
In order to arrive at what you are not
you must go through the way in which you are not
And what you do not know is the only thing you know
And what you own you do not own
And where you are is where you are not.

T.S. Eliot The Four Quartets

First the questions. How do we manage transport in the future?
Differently, so differently from the past that it will be as if the
very subject had been changed.

Should every citizen have the right to run a car? To deny a
citizen's right to run a car is like denying her right to contract
cancer.

Is tourism the new imperialism? Only when the tourist believes
he/she has plundering rights. How do you define sustainable
tourism? As a pilgrim visiting a sacred shrine.

How can we avoid global gridlock in our cities? By defining the experience of a pilgrim in a city, not merely in commercial terms, but in terms of common interests, mutual responsibility and interdependence.

Is increasing urban concentration more sustainable than encouraging rural dispersal? Perhaps today, driven by a commercial feeding frenzy, unfettered global free markets, capital holding the whip hand; but not under the insights offered by information technology.

How are local cultures and languages protected from increasing travel and social contact? They need not protection, but honor. They will evolve as conditions change, in response to forces more diverse and complex than mere commercial interest.

How do we manage transport in the future? Near term, by developing energy cells, notably hydrogen, but longer term must be radically new. The first successful experiments in dematerialization and re-materialization have been conducted. The process, based on information as the basic unit of reality, once a Star Trek fantasy, opens the way to transport radically different from the way we now conceive transport.

We are approaching the saturation point for travel in the old mode; the skies in areas where most people travel are too full of planes, larger airports or motor ways present unacceptable political, environmental and economic problems. We could strangle ourselves like kudzu, or we could redefine the task, information technology.

Each cell in my body is a mine of information. When we decode that information, as we have with atomic structure, we will be able to manipulate it. This is the basis of transport for the growing billions of people, both within and beyond this planet.

Should every citizen have the right to run a car? Eventually the notion of individual car ownership will seem as odd as people trying to claim private rights to the sea. Though cars may no longer burn fossil fuel, and computers regulate the flow of traffic, the ability to encode and decode will make overland, sea and air travel seem primitive.

Is tourism the new imperialism? No. Tourism is cross-pollination, one of the ways in which parochialism, species' suicide, can be countered. A tourist carries home information as a bee does to its hive after visiting a flower. Sustainable tourism is an equation, one side of which, the tourist's esteem, balances the other, the hosts' self-esteem. The hosts export their offering to human wholeness. Whether the threat of a meteor colliding with earth, aliens appearing from outer (or inner) space, a plague, some challenge to human earthly hegemony will either extinct us or purge our parochialism. Travel becomes a pilgrimage, tasting one another's precious fruits.

When I was 11 years old I traveled with my family from the west coast of the United States, by ship, to Honolulu, Yokohama and finally to Manila where we lived for the next many years. The 22 day voyage changed me. Japan and the Philippines were ravaged by World War II and I was awed by the stoicism and resourcefulness of people some of whom I was conditioned to regard as alien, enemy.

I have since spent an extended period in Zimbabwe. I was again changed by people my culture portray as backward.

Human beings are remarkably adaptable, but not infinitely so. How soon we may reach the limits of our numbers and the resources required to sustain our appetites, no one seems to know.

If, however, information as the basic unit of reality turns out to be heir to atomic theory, then transport, moving of people into contact with other people of different experience will become not only more possible, but essential.

An information dialectic, the interplay of data and nescience, are the binary characters of the new synthesis, the heirs to the 1 and 0 of the data processor. Transport is not, at its most basic, about simply moving people, but about people, their cells drawn into organic intimacy with other cells, recognizing their common origin and end.

A central requisite to a future for our species here is our being weaned from thesis/antithesis. Our wish to dominate others at the expense of a mutually beneficial resolution, must yield to awareness of common destiny, mutual fate. But how to counter social Darwinism, the belief that progress requires a battle for dominance?

By means of information technology, the transport of the coming age. Sub-atomic structure is composed of bits of information. Information, like energy, is subject to its own Law of Thermodynamics. So our habits can change. Information can be rearranged, but not created or destroyed. Every bit of information, whether we see it or not, is compatible with other bits, an essential part of the whole. The goal is not to convert, but to find ways of accommodating and incorporating diversity.

Think of the earth as a nuclear reactor, and we as the particles whirring around it. We're going faster but where? As its particles accelerate, an atom may itself be transformed. We are approaching a critical mass, as in a nuclear reaction, in which the increasing speed of increasing numbers of electrons will result in a explosion of old dogma revealing new reality.

That transformation will change the nature and purpose of

transport itself. The basis for optimism is the demise of parochialism, our future's enemy. The information that makes up every cell in us is inviolable, indestructible, and will form the building blocks of new reality.

This transporting of bits of information has been going on since the big bang. But we cling to our parochial dogma for fear of ego annihilation, the extinction of the information that is me or my tribe. Now we approach the moment when we can employ information technology to disassemble and reassemble systems as complex as one of us, altering but losing nothing.

It will change the way we live and move and have our being.

SUZIE'S THUNDER MUG

This is an account of a bizarre incident that happened to good friends in our town in Vermont in the summer of 2000, one of the wettest summers on record.

Jim found the old porcelain chamber pot, the thunder mug as he called it, in the side yard of the dairy more than 100 feet from the porch of his wife Suzie's antique store. The flash flood that had carried it came up quickly and unexpectedly when a dilapidated wooden foot bridge upstream got picked up by the surge of water and lodged against the stone culvert that was supposed to direct the water into the river 50 yards beyond. Sometime around 2am, the stream exploded onto the road. It dug a six-foot trench where the dairy driveway had been and rose up onto the building's porch, filling the belowground space Jim had, that very day, finished off for the upholsterer.

The upholsterer and his partner moved in several pieces of furniture the previous afternoon. Jim had been best man at their wedding the Saturday before, the day the Vermont law went into effect giving members of the same sex the rights of married couples. Suzie was hostess for a gathering of friends the night before. People in the small village were divided in their opinion of the new civil union law, but Dennis and Fred were well liked and sympathy for their misfortune, having their brand new shop flooded, was universal.

But the thunder mug fascinated Jim.

Jim has a pony tail now, one of the few remaining signs of the days when he lived alone without running water or electricity in the log cabin he built in the woods. He's become known as one of the most talented and knowledgeable builders in New England for restoring historic structures and building new buildings the old way. When he and Suzy married they moved from Connecticut to our Vermont village where they have become central players.

More than 15 years ago they bought several acres of undeveloped land over on the other side of town. Though it was mostly on ledge and wasn't scheduled to have services brought to it, they liked it because it was on a high ridge and you could see every high peak in the area including Monadnok.

They called it Party Camp and it was. Almost everyone in town had been up there for some party or other, if not a very liquid Saturday night, for the annual pig roast they held every year until it got so big it was costing them several thousand dollars to put on.

Two years ago Jim decided he wanted to build a one room house on the land. He and Suzy spent a year designing it, deciding whether to put on a slate or a shingle roof (slate, and old slate collected from demolitions), looking at doors from houses Jim had taken down, and searching antique stores, including Suzie's, for just the right trimmings for a cabin that would look as if it had been there 150 years.

Because he was busy, and even more because they were both fussy, perfectionists, it took them more than a year to build the house and another six months to find furnishings that suited them. Well before it was finished (Suzy said it would never be completely finished) they began taking dinner, cooking over an open fire, spending nights. Once it met their requirements for authenticity and flawless design, they invited friends for long candlelit dinners. It was the town's most sought after invitation. On the coldest winter nights, parking your car and walking through the woods, you'd see the light flickering in the windows and your step would quicken as you anticipated stepping from the icy air into the house toasty from the fireplace.

Though anyone who lives in rural Vermont is plenty used to using the woods for a bathroom, a hunter's or farmer's cabin would have had a thunder mug, a means of providing at least minimal comfort if you woke during the night with an urgency. Jim and Suzie had been looking everywhere for such a thing and though they had seen many, they were all cutesy, jigged up in modern dress to fool the undiscerning eye into thinking a new piece was old. Nothing annoyed Jim more and he would have spent the rest of his life braving the cold woods before he would put anything fake in his cabin. Finding the right chamber pot became a mission.

Suzie was called to do an appraisal of the estate of a farmer's widow who had died. The house had a refrigerator and a toilet (with a pipe straight into the stream that ran by the house). Other than that, it looked as if the past century and a half hadn't touched it.

In the bedroom on the pine commode stood a porcelain chamber pot. Suzy would have bought the contents of the whole house just to get that pot. She knew the moment she saw it that it was the one they had been searching for. By then the sought after thunder mug had come to symbolize to both Jim and Suzie the missing piece to their precious puzzle.

When she brought the pot home Jim immediately agreed it was perfect. Suzie put it in her shop, not because she would sell it (though there were often tugs when someone offered her a good

price for something she wanted for herself) but because that's
where they collected things for party camp.

That was the Thursday between Christmas and New Year's,
busy times. On New Year's Eve, Suzie, Jim and four friends took
an elegant dinner to the cabin and drank wine and beer and
toasted the new millennium while they ate Portabello
mushrooms grilled over the fire and a game dinner. They played
medieval chamber music on the CD player plugged into their
car cigarette lighter. Several times they walked out to look at the
stars. It was a perfect cloudless, frigid night, the last night of the
century.

A few minutes past 1am, they made one last check to be certain
they had put the fire screen up and the fire was safely out, and
walked to their car and drove home to check that their daughters
were home and where they all spent the night.

The next morning around 11, Suzie drove up to the land to pick
up dirty dishes to bring them home to wash. As she drove up
the ridge, she looked ahead and had a feeling of being
disoriented. She was looking through the cabin as if it weren't
there, to the trees beyond. She looked around behind her to see
if she had driven to a different part of the land, but the scene
behind her was as always. She looked again and now saw the
smoke curling into the sky.

Lunging from the car, she ran toward the cabin, belching little
sobs. As she came over the ridge she saw the chimney leaning at
a weird angle. There was nothing else, all ash, everything
incinerated. Later she and Jim would say it was like looking at
the corpse of your child.

The fire Marshall still hasn't been able to figure out what
happened. He says he's never seen a fire burn that hot and

consume everything, metal as well as wood, in such a short time. Suzie and Jim have decided not to try to replicate their perfect creation, but to do something else, different at Party Camp. Suzie cried for two weeks before she could bear to look at pictures.

Seven months later Jim was walking the devastated wreckage of the dairy beside Suzie's antique store, wondering how much of the backbreaking work he'd done over the past month would have to be redone. He looked down and saw the thunder mug and his mind raced thinking about fire and water, about the biblical story of Noah and how God promised he'd never do that again. And about James Baldwin's angry novel, *The Fire Next Time*. And about how he and Suzie had known both fire and flood.

And he was glad they'd never taken the thunder mug to party camp, so they had it now, even though they'd almost lost it down the river, to remind them of the near perfection they had achieved in their cabin. Jim picked it up and walked over to the shop where Suzie was checking her own damage from the flood.

"Hey, Suz," he called to her as he walked in the shop, "look what got picked up off your porch and washed all the way to the dairy yard. I'm really glad now we never got this up to party camp. But it nearly got washed away. I can't imagine how it stayed out of the river."

Suzie looked up to see what he was holding. Her eyes widened and the color rose in her cheeks. "Jim, I took that chamber pot from the old house up to party camp the night before it burned. I wanted it up there New Year's Eve so the place would be perfect. It burned up along with everything else."

MY SOUL DOTH MAGNIFY THE LORD . . ." MARY'S SONG.

Body and Soul in the Year 2020

An Essay Submitted to the Greenwall Foundation

for the Oscar M. Ruebhausen Essay Award

*I wrote this essay for a contest which asked one to write about
a vision of body and soul in the year 2020. I didn't win.*

Several months ago there erupted in the media and in the world
at large a debate over the fate of small amounts of smallpox virus
in frozen storage in Atlanta and Russia, and perhaps in some
other unknown country like Iraq. The question was whether,
now that the disease, once our specie's most feared killer, has
been eradicated, its last remnants should be destroyed.

The political and strategic issues were complex, not unlike the
debate over the elimination of nuclear weapons. Can we trust
each other to actually get rid of it all and not secretly retain
some for strategic advantage over the other? What if the great
powers rid themselves of theirs only to discover that some small
outlaw nation or terrorist now possessed some and could hold
the world hostage?

The U.S. and Russia decided not to destroy the virus, but I suspect the real reason the scientists involved lobbied not to rid the world of it was neither political nor strategic. I believe, and this is the thesis of this essay—Body and Soul in the Year 2020—the reason is the sobering understanding we are gaining of how little we understand or can control our biological and genetic future. The decision, while it does underscore the frightening reality of how little trust exists within our own species, also reveals our growing understanding that we are more actor in the evolution of the biosphere than manager.

As a metaphor for our time and how we might approach our biological future, I take The Song of Mary, The Magnificat, which she sang after the angel (the Greek for angel can be translated 'messenger') announced to her that she was to bear an unusual child. The story refers to her as a virgin which may also be translated as 'young woman', perhaps pre-menstrual, and she wonders how this can be since she has never 'known' a man. All the angel will tell her is that she has been chosen by God to play a part in the evolution of humankind.

The Wakefield cycle of the medieval mystery plays portrays Mary as an innocent girl who has been befriended by Joseph. She seems mystified by the visit from the angel, uncertain of exactly what he meant. But then, before she has a chance to speak to Joseph or her parents or anyone, she sings the Magnificat, the song that sets the tone for human response to biological change that will alter the terms of our stay on this planet.

My soul doth magnify the Lord.

Though she understands precious little of what is being asked or of what to expect, she nonetheless gives her assent. She trusts the process in which she will be, at least at first, a passive participant. So we call her a woman of faith.

But not to misunderstand faith in this context. Again, the Wakefield cycle, through humor and sober reality, shows Joseph and others suggesting to Mary that she has done a stupid thing. She's in no position to either bear or raise a child; she's poor, unmarried, unprepared. Mary senses there will be not only unforeseen challenge in having this child, but heartbreak, life-changing events, more required than she has resources to meet. Her faith is not that God will lighten her burden, nor that she will receive special dispensation of some kind for her willingness, but that a genetic breakthrough is at hand and she is being offered a chance to take part.

Will our ability to alter genetic structure become greater in the next twenty years? Without dispute. Will we be sobered by what we are able to do? Yes. Will we attempt to limit what we will permit ourselves to do, passing laws, applying sanctions to those who break the laws? Perhaps. Will we continue to experiment regardless of laws or sanctions? Undoubtedly.

So the question is not whether the unbalancing events of the past few years will continue and even accelerate, but what of our body and soul in the face of those events? What might we look like in 20 years and what will be the state of our inner life, the dimension we once believed was not only unique to us, but marked us as the purpose and crown of creation?

II

Whether Mary had any inkling, she stood on the cusp of a genetic breakthrough. Her son's birth ushered in a new age. The notion of God in human flesh changed forever the locus of human effort and imagination. Once the idea that God would invest in the dirt of this realm, science, art, poetry, rhetoric, mathematics, all turned focus from heaven to earth. No matter what one's theology, the ability to map DNA and alter genetic structure, grow a tomato that will stay fresh twice as long as tomatoes grown twenty years ago, result directly from the world's understanding that Jesus (and Mohammed and Abraham and Buddha) incarnate God. The matter which forms their cells is God matter.

Mary is a first century Robert Oppenheimer agonizing over a growing understanding that she has the ability to do something she does not fully understand and that she knows will change the terms of human tenure on the earth. Edward Teller may be the symbol of the myopic experimenter, holding that his parochial position is sufficiently moral to allow him to gain strategic power over his rivals with impunity. Mary, perhaps because as a Semitic first century woman she is excluded from power politics, assumes the new human form will be, not parochial, but for the whole race.

The first soul requirement for singing Magnificat in the face of great change, is that we quell our parochial impulse. Tribalism, nationalism, racism, fundamentalism, are all marks of human fear and we are each imprinted with them. Some part of us understands that we are a step along the evolutionary path, not its final purpose and destination. We understand in our depths, our soul, not only that we will each die, but that our children will die and, finally, our species as we have known it, will disappear from the earth.

And wanting to be God rather than a manifestation of holy energy, a piece of divine energy, we work against the inexorable forces of evolution wishing to make our particular biological form the final, ultimate form.

Even Mary in the story, even though she heroically sung her assent, protests to her now grown son that he is ignoring the customs and traditions of his people, shaming his family, bringing sorrow to his clan. She has to have wondered if she made a terrible mistake agreeing to this radical experiment.

Recently Bill Joy in Wired magazine has raised the specter of our species being eclipsed by the very robot we have created to serve our interests. Looking at what he says is already a spontaneous being, with sufficiently complex inner structure to soon support self replication, Joy sounds like Mary complaining to Jesus that he is not sufficiently obedient to his parents and his past.

What would it take for Joy to make a response like Mary's? He would need to trust that the process in which he is taking part, lending to the development of some unknown new being is incxorable and must be trusted. A number of factors are required for such trust. Those factors, and the qualities that support them, will be acquired by our kind in the coming years because those who evolve will bear their marks.

The first is the assent to being a part of the whole and not the whole itself. Whatever it was that caused the dinosaur to grow so large was a fatal biological conceit that seems to be showing again in our attempts to dominate our planet. As there are birds today who are heirs of the dinosaur's genetic remainder, so there will be species in the future, surely more modest in size and appetite, who will be our genetic heirs. Perhaps Bill Joy is right to be afraid of what we have wrought, but humankind as we know us is not the final word on biological evolution on this planet. And no matter how violently we may extinct ourselves, we cannot wreck the ability of the earth to support innovative new forms.

The first quality that will support the new biological age is humility, perspective. We will see that our arrogance in seeking to dominate the earth has been destructive not only to other species but to our own. Someone has predicted that the superstar of the coming age will not be the great athlete nor the performer, but the scientist, particularly the cyber-scientist. And that may be so. But since one requirement for a biological future for any species is the ability to cohabit with other species, not over or above, even the notion of superstar will become vestigial and anomalous.

The second quality is spiritual. Teilhard de Chardin, the French Jesuit paleontologist, provided a useful metaphor for understanding the path and pattern of evolution. He suggested that the process moves from the few to the many and the simple to the complex. And it is when the internal structure of matter, the cells, atoms, molecules and the ways in which those cells are held together (or in more complex forms, communicate, as in synapses), reach a certain level of complexity, they take on a whole new quality. Thus inert matter at a certain level of internal complexity takes on a quality we call 'living'. And a simple celled being, at a certain level of complexity has what we might recognize as a nervous system, and then gains the ability to support thought. The next great leap is in consciousness, then, self-consciousness or awareness. The stage humankind represents is 'spiritual' which means that we perceive there is a dimension of reality beneath or within the dimension we call 'material' which we call 'spiritual'.

The spiritual stage, still in its formative chapter, is marked by the forging of bonds among individual human nervous systems so that humankind becomes a single phenomenon. (cf. Teilhard de Chardin, *The Phenomenon of Man*)

Spiritual is a much abused term, largely wrapped in issues of behavior having more to do with piety. While there are good reasons for codes of behavior in human community, we confuse those codes with spirituality at the risk of eroding the place and power of the spirit in human development.

Because in the material west we regard affluence as a reward for good behavior, as given by the invisible hand of God, we tend to equate prosperity with spirituality. Or, in the monastic tradition, the reverse, to equate spirituality with austerity.

Spirituality is the energy potential in unseen dimensions of reality that cannot yet be quantified. It requires us to live in the unknown, acknowledging that we are surrounded by energy we can neither posses nor control which, like the submerged part of the iceberg, is likely greater than what we have seen.

What this means, as the essay title suggests, is that our biological future will mingle body and soul or we will have no biological future. We have run out the string on pitting one against the other, the so called Cartesian split. And mixing spirituality with humility means acknowledging that we are not the only species that participates in all dimensions of reality and has a soul. In fact 'soul' may well be the word we use to describe the Whole of which each of us is a part. The breaking of parochial boundaries, not only between religions and nations, but between species, acknowledging that we are all part of the one ecosystem, will make the crumbling of the Berlin Wall seem like a small event along the way.

Each of us inhabits a body, each is a part of the soul. The conviction that each of our bodies is discrete is an illusion, one tenaciously held in western thought. And the notion of individual souls is one of the most costly misperceptions in the post-enlightenment west. It has led us into a parochial competition that is incompatible not only with our biological future, but with the nature of biological reality. The metaphor that best serves for the coming period of evolution is of cells in a single organism.

So the third quality that will emerge is what we once called mysticism. Mysticism, an acute sense of being surrounded by the 'other', used to be attributed to a few finely tuned recluses who lived apart from the world. But increasingly mysticism, a mature sense of the presence of the invisible, will come to be as essential to being a whole person as being able to love and reproduce and nurture young.

Jesus, Mohammed, Buddha, Gandhi, Martin Luther King, no longer heroes on pedestals, but genetic markers pointing the way for each of us. As literacy, science and math have long been considered the essentials for educating people to take part in human intercourse, now sitting meditation, disciplines that develop the silent inner resources will come to be seen as necessary. In our newly formed humility, our sense of ourselves as a part of the biosphere, not its crown, as partners with other species and not their master, we will discover that many species have developed inner resources, the rhythm of active and quiet, thriving and senescence.

Zen teaches that the source of all unhappiness is wanting things to be different than they are, and this, too, is a lesson we can learn from animals that have adapted to our having dominated the earth and who now wait patiently for the biosphere to rebalance itself. Most of our parochial energy is devoted first to being the dominant race or town or nation or religion or political or philosophical school, then to maintaining what we regard as our divine legacy, the star role in the unfolding of earth's biological future.

The question is about moral and ethical considerations in our biological future. Those considerations are emerging as conditions evolve. We sometimes think that we have a clear set of ethics. But not long ago charging interest for a loan was considered a sin. What seems unthinkable today, cloning people, sharing power with other races and species, acknowledging the

limits of our understanding and power in the unfolding of the
earth's biological future, even finally coming to accept that our
kind will one day give way to some new form we cannot now
imagine, will all become ethical and moral imperatives. Not
because we will have improved the moral quality of our species,
but because we will, as all species must, have adjusted to the
shifting nature of biological reality.

My soul doth magnify the Lord. Someone once said about the
Christian Church that when she condemned, history almost
always proved her wrong (cf. Galileo) and when she affirmed,
(cf. Pope John XXIII) history almost always proved her right.
Perhaps every generation sees itself living though a time of great
historical and biological change. (Adam said to Eve, as they left
Eden, "Darling, we're living in a time of transition.") Because of
our illusion that we run the world, we are conservative, resist
change. If you are on top change can only bring you down. But
increasingly we will see that we have never been on top, and that
competitive hierarchy is not a helpful model for progressing in
the biosphere Even our ability to reflect, perhaps not so unique
as we had thought, was a skill designed for cooperative rather
than competitive living. And as we sit more quietly and reflect,
let reality have its way with us instead of trying to innovate and
rearrange reality to serve our desire to dominate, we will see that
the redirection of spiritual energy from squandering resources on
behalf of individual affluence to the balance of biology
throughout the world, was in our interests all along.

Balancing the interests of the entire biosphere rather than of a
single person, nation or religion, perhaps the most certain mark
of our biological future, will determine what direction our
biological future takes. Perhaps we humans still have the ability
to rejoin that balance, though our hegemony will have to be set
aside. While it may seem of critical importance to us, what and
whether our place in the biological future, the future will unfold

with or without us, and though our bodies will be recycled, the soul will flourish with renewed energy. For creation's soul, of which we are a part, sums up the energy, visible and invisible. And the enduring ethic will be on behalf of that soul which is indivisible and perfectly whole. The creation is, finally, as the ancients saw, in God's indivisible image. Shema Israel.

PARTISAN POLITICS

This piece and the one that follows were both written in the heat of the Presidential campaign of 2000, between Al Gore and George W. Bush. Ralph Nader was playing his spoiler role.

I am a yellow dog Democrat and this is a plug for returning from the morass of personality politics to party politics. A yellow dog Democrat is someone who would vote for a yellow dog before voting for a Republican. I've never heard the equivalent for a diehard Republican but I'd bet many to most of you are whatever they call them.

In this essay I'm staying totally away from the candidates, who are merely reflections of the times, like all of us, and therefore provide little if any basis for choosing among them. Hardly any commentators have anything to say about the two main parties, and I still believe there is much to choose between them. Though the candidates themselves seek to blur those lines, the historical differences make choosing important.

I discovered I was a Democrat in 1956 while watching first the Republican Convention and then the Democratic Convention on a Master's small television in Arden Dormitory at St. George's Summer School where I was doing penance for having flunked every course that spring at Kent (including Sacred Studies).

When Eisenhower spoke, the comments were sardonic. I had
never heard negative comments made about a Republican. Two
weeks later, when Adlai Stevenson spoke, there was silence
followed by near reverential admiration. Because I was in awe of
those gathered in that apartment, history teacher, English
teacher, biology teacher, I wondered. In the years since I have
discovered that I am, by personality, understanding of
history, economics and conviction, a Democrat and not a
Republican.

Republicans believe in the ability of the individual to make a
better decision about his life than can the government. Therefore
government should be as lean as possible without jeopardizing
public safety, and the amount of taxes collected only those
necessary to maintain public order.

Democrats believe that government should care for those who
cannot (or do not) care for themselves while interfering as little
as possible with those who do care for themselves. Taxes and laws
needed to ebb and flow as events require.

Because clever, ambitious people will succeed in almost any
environment, little needs to be done to encourage them.
Probably the vast majority of people are content to work as hard
as necessary to maintain what is a less than perfect but
satisfactory life. In hard times that will mean some worry as
mortgage rates and tight money make life more precarious. In
good times they may add a few luxuries, a boat, a computer, a
more expensive holiday.

But, as Jesus said, the poor we have always with us. I don't think
anyone really understands what percent of those who are poor
find themselves in circumstances beyond their control and what
percent bring it on themselves. I argue that the distinction
doesn't matter. Some percent of people are impoverished in the

most prosperous times, as a walk through any American city in these astonishing times of economic boom makes clear.

The nation's soul requires that we never cease our efforts to help people who are poor and in distress gain some relief. If not for simple reasons of justice, for self-interest, a nation that makes good on her founding brag. The Republican agenda, to free people to get rich, will be carried out no matter what government does. People want to get rich and will, if their personality, abilities and circumstances do not prevent it. But unless the government, the will of the people, advocates for those who are crushed, they will be crushed more and more and the nation's soul, Republican and Democrat alike will rot in a stew of selfishness.

I know the argument about a healthy economy benefiting everyone, a rising tide floating all ships, but a quick look around in these times of prosperity we're not likely to see again, shows that isn't altogether true.

The Democrats are afraid right now to speak out clearly about their historic agenda because more than half of us have prospered in the stock market, and they assume we don't care about those who haven't. And the Republicans have strained, notably at their recent convention, to loose their ties to the powerful rich. But the historic differences remain. Differences of approach to issues like national health insurance, Social Security (whether to allow some to be invested in equities), labor unions, affirmative action show there remain differences between the parties about whether the focus of government concern should be on behalf of the rich or the poor.

I believe the soul of a country is determined more by how it treats its weakest than how it treats its strongest. I agree that Clinton/Gore cannot take claim for the booming economy any more than can the Republican Congress. Or Alan Greenspan. The conflicting opinions of the most renowned economists make clear that no one knows nor can control the increasingly international economy. My argument is not about which party agenda will keep the economy strong longest but which party is more likely to keep attention on those left behind.

For reasons of geography, surprisingly egalitarian views by our forebears, and fantastic luck, we have become a wildly rich nation. If you believe the best way to use some of that wealth to provide some relief and solace to our downtrodden citizens is for government to open all the commercial gates and let the thing run, then I think you should vote for the Republicans.

If you believe that significant government concern and focus should be on relieving the burden of the poor, making opportunity for those who can and will make use of them, providing shelter and a living for those who can or will not, then I think you might consider yourself a yellow dog Democrat.

But whichever you believe, I am sponsoring the notion that, dazzled as we of course are by Bill Gates, the nation's resources, at home and abroad, for the sake of our souls and our future as a species, needs to be concerned first of all, with the fortunes, not of Bill Gates, but of the woman with AIDS living beneath the bridge in Central Park.

PARTISAN POLITICS II

A Reconsideration

When last we spoke I was shilling for the Democratic Party. I've been feeling uncomfortable about it and I just discovered why. Not that I don't still believe the historic difference between the two parties is that one focuses on those at the top of the economy and the other on those at the bottom, but because for some time I've wondered if the Democrats, in order to stay in the game, haven't joined the Republicans in sleeping with corporate power.

I have worried though that if one abandons realpolitik, starts getting sidetracked into ideological alleys, the cynics will elect the cynical candidates. Gore seemed an acceptable way to go.

Two recent experiences lead me to suggest we all take another harder look at Ralph Nader and the Reform Party. One was an exchange with Josh, a 30 year old high school teacher in southern California, and the other an article in the current Harper's by the sharply critical, often cynical Lewis Lapham.

I have been a critic of Nader the past few years, thinking him a self-righteous prig. Josh says that's because he's a part of the historic justice movement and it's my uneasiness with justice for everyone that causes me to make such a judgment about Nader. Lapham, who is uncharacteristically idealistic and not cynical in this piece, portrays Nader as anything but self-righteous or a prig.

Josh referred to Nader as a 'citizen', comparing him with Jerry Brown, Mayor of Oakland. I think Josh must have read Lapham's article before I did because that's what he calls Nader, too, a citizen, and he uses the term with nearly ancient Greek admiration.

I think you should read the Harper's article because it may be the best, maybe the only thing you'll read this election year that causes you, as it caused me, to reconsider whether the only sensible thing is to vote for either the Republican or Democratic candidate for President. In case you don't read it, here's one quote:

"Unlike Bush and Gore I don't promote myself as a solution to the nation's problems. The idea is to encourage a lot of other people to use the tools of democratic government to take control of the assets they hold in common –the public lands, the public broadcast frequencies, the public money. Whatever your issue is, whether it's racism, homophobia, taxes, health care, urban decay, you're not going to go anywhere with it unless you focus on the concentration of power. We have an overdeveloped plutocracy and an underdeveloped democracy, too many private interests commandeering the public interest for their own profit. Most Americans don't realize how badly they're being harmed by unchecked commercialization of what belongs to the commonwealth. If enough people knew what questions to ask, we have both the ways and the means to achieve better schools, a healthier environment, a more general distribution of decent health care."

I am working on an essay on the subject, "Moral and Ethical Considerations in Our Biological Future—Body and Soul in the Year 2000." I found myself writing that though it may be true that each of us has an individual body (though that, too, may be an illusion), it is certainly true that the idea of an individual soul has done violence in the capitalist west. We are each a part of the soul and the fortunes of one are tied to the fortunes of all.

Here's another quote from the article, this from Lapham:

"Like their candidate, [Nader's staff members] understood the political crisis in the country not as an ideological quarrel between liberal and conservative, Democrat and Republican, but rather as an argument between people who would continue the American experiment and those who believe the experiment has gone far enough, between the inertia conducive to acceptance of things-as-they-are and the energy inherent in the hope of things-as-they-might-become. The party of things-as-they-are always can count on the support of the comfortable majority; it is the party of the military defense budget, Time magazine, and the lobbyists working the bar at the Madison Hotel; and it buys a lot of expensive advertising to sell the notion that nothing important remains to be said, discovered or done."

I called myself a yellow dog Democrat and so I am, but I'm beginning to wonder if the Reform Party and Ralph Nader may be the true heir to the party that once pledged itself to the welfare of the people of the nation against the plutocrats who would presume to decide for us what is best.

Maybe there is an agenda more important than electing Gore instead of Bush. Is it too late to think about taking back the country for people rather than leaving it in the hands of the CEOs making 400 times the salary of the people working for them?

At one point Nader says that he understands politics as "first and foremost a movement of thought, not of belief." Lapham asked him if defining politics that way didn't set him up for a good deal of disappointment.

"Maybe it would," Nader responded, "if I were into mood changes."

Consider a man and a movement in 21st century American TV politics, focused on policy rather than mood changes. Either he's crazy or he's the future.

FRIENDS, ROMANS, EVERYONE

March 3, 1997

The American religious infatuation with "being saved" is what prompted this piece.

1. To believe in Jesus is to believe everyone is saved.

2. To "believe in Jesus" means to trust that listening to what Jesus taught and watching what Jesus did, shows as much as we can know of what God is like.

3. By "saved" I mean loved by God forever, no matter what. For some that means going to heaven when you die. For others it means finding creation trustworthy, now and forever.

4. My references are two, the Bible (The eight chapter of St. Paul's letter to the Romans: For I am persuaded that neither life nor death nor angels nor principalities, nor powers, nor height, nor depth, nor things present nor things to come . . . nor any other creature, shall be able to separate us from the love of God which is in Christ Jesus Our Lord.) and human intuition, what reasonable, thoughtful people sense to be true.

5. I submit further that this is not a sectarian matter, not another version of how many angels can dance on the head of a pin, but of signal importance to everyone, Christian or not, believer or not, and that everyone believes one way or the other, whether consciously or unconsciously.

6. The practical effect of believing or not believing in "universal salvation" (that everyone is finally saved), is that those who know that their sins (errors, foibles, mistake, faults, offenses, wrongdoings) can and will be set right even if they find themselves unable to set them right themselves, have a fundamental optimism. Those who believe that some people and/or sins are unpardonable, must either rationalize their own sins or dwell in despair.

7. There is no evidence that believers find this notion any more palatable than non-believers. In fact, for reasons soon to be made clear, the Church has a stake in insisting on some sins being unpardonable.

8. St. Paul (just about the only active writer from the days of earliest Christianity whose writing is extant) says that Christianity is a stumbling block to the Jews and folly to the Gentiles (Greeks). The stumbling block to the Jews was the suggestion that, while the ancient Hebrew Law still pointed the way to a life lived with wisdom, Jesus showed the possibility of coming to God (and heaven) without keeping the Law. To the Greeks, the argument that God would love us, never give up on us no matter what, seemed illogical, beyond human reason.

9. For believers and non-believers the basic issue is whether we can afford to take risks with our creative energy, or need to fit ourselves into an ordered, closed system in order to be acceptable. Everyone does some of each, but where one lies on

the continuum between universal salvation and righteousness under the Law, has a heavy bearing on whether one's energy is spent more in seeking risks or seeking safety.

10. Since the Christian Church is an institution, with power to protect, you can see her interest in righteousness under the Law rather than universal salvation. She determines the Law, sets the terms and she monitors the behavior. In fact she even claims control of the mechanisms of salvation. This is the reason, in the face of massive evidence to the contrary, the Church has discouraged the teaching of universalism.

Although virtually every system and religion, from Buddhism to Marxism, claims the power to save, the unique claim Jesus makes in the Bible, is that God's power to love and save is not bound by any religion or system (including Judaism from within which Jesus makes this claim).

The strongest argument against universalism is that people who believe their salvation is secure will disobey rules and choose license. In fact there is some internal evidence in early Christian writings (again, notably Paul) suggesting some sexual license being practiced among early followers of Jesus who believed in some form of what we would call "free love". You will recognize that argument as saying nothing about whether or not universal salvation is true, but that it's a dangerous idea, offering people radical freedom.

Even if you grant that argument (which I don't), it seems to me to strengthen the claim of universalism rather than weaken it, because it suggests that God's love and intentions are not only greater and different from ours, but even require us to suspend our normal understanding of love.

Psychological evidence suggests that evil behavior results from people believing they are beyond love and redemption. People who believe they are loved, even when they don't deserve love, can afford greater generosity towards others.

The question I am always asked eventually is, "What about Hitler? How could Hitler be saved?" I offer a parable:

Hitler dies and appears before God for judgment. He raises his fist and shakes it in God's face.

"Go ahead, send me to hell! I'm ready to go. I've prepared my whole life to go to hell. So send me now."

"It's not that simple, Adolph," God replies. "We'll see. First there's someone here to see you."

The first Jew to die in a Nazi death camp, emerges from behind God's throne.

"Hi, Adolph. It didn't work." And he steps forward and embraces Hitler, who shrinks back in horror.

"No!" he cries, "keep them away from me. Just send me to hell. I can't do this."

"Well, Adolph, there are 5,999,999 more who wish to greet you. Then we'll see."

I once asked Alan Jones, Dean of Grace Cathedral in San Francisco, and author of many books on Christianity, what he thought about universalism and the Hitler parable.

"Well," he began, slowly, thoughtfully, his eyes focused somewhere far over my left shoulder, "To call yourself an orthodox Christian, I think you must believe in hell. But I don't think you have to believe anyone spends eternity there."

We westerners are fixated on human free will, our precious prerogatives, ability to choose, responsibility to decide. There is no doubting its power. Free will is perhaps the strongest force in the universe, with the exception of God's Love. For I, too am persuaded, with Paul, that nothing, not even my willful rejection of God, is strong enough to separate me from the love of God.

OLD WINE
IN NEW WINESKINS

An essay on diversity submitted to Creative
Nonfiction for the Walter V. Shipley
Essay Award 2001

I didn't win this one either.

I was standing between Booker and Robert, still so new to the
country I didn't yet know enough even to feel awkward. Robert
was what I would come to know as an "old Rhody", a white who
had lived his whole life in Zimbabwe before the war of
independence when it was Rhodesia, part of the British
Commonwealth. Booker, of the emerging African elite, a Shona,
educated, sophisticated, held a management position with Plate
Glass. He was the first of many I would come to know who were
named for famous American slaves.

Booker was the catechist (the lay leader) in the rural Anglican
congregation where I, a white American on sabbatical from my
parish in suburban Boston, was interim priest. It was 1984,
Presidential primary season in the U.S., and reading the Harare
Herald, the country's only newspaper, gave one the sense that
Jesse Jackson was the focus of the Presidential race. Booker told
me he was impressed that Jackson would be taken so seriously

and he took that as a sign that the civil rights movement had taken deep root in my country.

"That's interesting, Booker," I said to him. He had been telling me details of the movement I didn't know, unnerving since I had been active in the movement myself. "I know that Jesse Jackson, among others, believes progress has been too slow and too little."

"Not me, Boss," he replied, ironically using the old term from colonial days and flashing a toothy ingratiating grin. These remnants before independence were striking and plentiful. At times I felt eerily as if I'd returned to my childhood in the racist American south of the 1940s.

On the day in question Booker and Robert and I were standing outside the cinder block church of St. Apollos The Irrigator (scripture reference: "I, Paul, planted, Apollos watered and God gave the growth."), so named because the church was in a hot dry valley in the rural lowveld, the southwest corner sandwiched between the borders of South Africa and Mozambique. No people had lived there before they figured out 20 years earlier how to divert water from the north so they could irrigate the sugar cane that was the region's reason for being. We were talking about Africa's attempts to catch up to the west in technology.

Without preamble, Robert turned to me and said, "Why, before the white man came to Africa these monkeys didn't even have the wheel."

I suppose I blushed; I would have given a lot to have my skin turn dark at that moment. I remember from my boyhood wondering whether people like Robert thought Booker was stupid, deaf, or did he mean to intimidate him? I think I may have cleared my throat, or looked at the ground; I'm certain I made no reply because I couldn't think of one. Robert seemed oblivious both to my discomfort and to Booker. Soon he turned, shook my hand, "Cheers, Padre," and pitched off without so much as a gesture to Booker.

I couldn't look at Booker but he took a step forward so he was in front of me, looking straight into my face, something Africans rarely do. He grinned widely.

"He's right, Baba, we didn't have the wheel before the white man came. And you know what? Before you avaricious white men came to this lush garden country, we didn't need the wheel." His high-pitched raucous laugh was so infectious it almost gave me courage to laugh with him.

In 1949 I was 9 and we were living in Charlotte, North Carolina. We had a yard man named Willy who was a genius at tending roses and azaleas. But Willy was a binge drinker and it infuriated my tightly wound father when Willy didn't show up for work. One Sunday morning after church, Dad and I were walking in the garden when Willy appeared, his eyes jaundiced, still unsteady on his feet.

"Willy," my father lit into him without so much as a greeting, "I'm fed up with you. What the hell's the matter with you? You're the best gardener in Mecklenberg County when you want to be. But you're so irresponsible it doesn't matter how good a gardener you are."

Dad stood staring at him, hands on his hips, his Sunday suit fit him like a U.S. Marine tunic. Willy's eyes didn't focus but his head was turned toward my father.

"Missah Colmore," he began uncertainly, then smiling, his words picked up speed and authority, "if you could be a niggah just one Satiday night, you'd nevah want to be a white man again." Willy stood stock still, then his shoulders began to shake and he bent over laughing until he choked. Dad watched him for a moment, a puzzled expression on his face. I was a little scared he might hit Willy. Dad chuckled, then lost it and laughed as I had seldom seen him, so hard and out of control it seemed like he might throw up. I laughed, too, though I didn't really get the joke exactly, I just knew something big had just happened.

Willy had made a huge, brave joke, one that could, nearly by itself, overturn the relationship that Willy and Dad had inherited from generations before them. Whether my father ever fully understood the joke I'm not sure. Beyond the obvious irony, I'm not sure I do yet.

Nearly fifty years later my father lay dying of lung cancer. For several days while he was still conscious I sat by his bed and we reminisced. We talked about the racial divide and how it had marked our lives so powerfully, and what a liberation it had been for us when the civil rights movement changed all that.

"You know, Dad, I've never forgotten the night you were putting me to bed and I could tell you had something important to say to me. You'd already kissed me and were walking toward the door when you turned back. 'Son,' you said, 'I overheard you call Gertrude 'Mam' when she brought your meal to the table tonight. I'm glad to hear you thank her, but you understand it's impolite to call a colored woman 'Mam'. It upsets her, confuses her, and you musn't do it.'
I was embarrassed, ashamed to have made such a faux pas. "Yes, Sir, I understand and I won't do it again."

Dad was weary, worn down by the tumor that would soon kill him and not always alert, but his eyebrows shot up and his eyes focused on mine. "I never told you anything of the kind," he insisted.

But I remembered it so clearly that in 1963, at a demonstration at Boston City Hall, as we began a round of *We Shall Overcome* and I reached with my crossed arm to take the hand of the woman on my left, she looked so much like Gertrude it unnerved me for a moment and I wondered how she'd feel if I called her 'Mam'.

The illusion that feeds discrimination, that unless I hold my sway over you, (or you over me) the natural order of things will be overturned, leads to endless unnecessary suffering. Though the climate of our time is focused on the suffering of the one discriminated against, which is considerable, the suffering of the discriminator is also great.

My friend John moved his family into Roxbury, a predominantly black district in Boston in 1964 because he believed the family was being robbed of an experience of life's richness in the monochrome suburb in which they had been living. And he was directing an urban missionary society and believed moral consistency required him to make that move.

As their furniture was being carried into their house on moving day, their only white neighbor came to call. "I'm so glad to see you people moving in," he said to John. "This used to be a great neighborhood until all these blacks moved in. Now the neighborhood has gone to hell. I sure hope you're just the beginning of a turn-around." John decided to give that man a wide berth.

But he soon noticed that man's front stoop and house was the neighborhood gathering place. The man sat on his front porch when the neighborhood children were going to school and coming home, and they would stop and talk while he gave them snacks and talked with them about their day. On warm evenings their parents, mostly mothers and grandmothers, would hang out on his front stoop as well, trading stories, speculating about ward politics and laughing at the absurdities of life.

John soon discovered that if he wanted to become a part of the neighborhood, he would need to spend time on his prejudiced neighbor's porch. And he did. The conversation was always lively and fun, and his neighbor proved provocative with everyone, challenging them, often disagreeing with them, but the exchanges, though sometimes heated, were marked by respect and good humor. But anytime John was alone with him, the old man would go into his racial screed.

One night, six months after they had moved in, John and his wife were discussing how it was going.

"You know, John, I wasn't sure about this move; I thought maybe our family was being sacrificed to your ideology. But it's worked out great. I think the boys are really happy to be here. I'd forgotten what it's like to live in a real neighborhood where people hang out and talk together. There sure wasn't any of that in Wellesley. But it really amazes me that old Frank Welsh is the center of the neighborhood. That first day when he complained about the black neighbors I figured he'd be a pariah around here. But he's just the opposite, he's the glue that holds this neighborhood together. I can't figure it out."

"I've been thinking a lot about that," John responded, "and of course I've made up a theory about it. I figure we have just so much energy to expend on the side of the angels. Most of us liberals use it thinking and talking, not doing. Notice that none of our liberal friends visit us here? Now Frank has used all his do-good energy being a good neighbor, and he has no energy left to put into right thinking."

When I was a parish priest I ran a confirmation class for adults who were joining the church. I always began the class by asking each person to say who they were and why they were taking the class. I went last until the final years of my ministry when I changed the order and went first. They were like couples coming for pre-nuptial sessions, trying to figure out what I wanted to hear, and their responses were pious and mostly distant from their real motives. Probably most of them were embarrassed to admit how much of their decision to come to the church was simply because they wanted some place they could belong.

When everyone else had spoken I would take my turn. "I came here tonight hoping I might fall in love," I'd begin. "I often do. Though it has never been clear to me how that happens, I think I know what it's about. I take it as my task as the pastor here to make it as safe as I can for you to be who you really are, to see, first for yourself, and then maybe reveal to us your hunger, your passion, your fears and desires. It happens only rarely but when it does it changes everything. I have a selfish motive for doing this. If I can make it safe for you here, then maybe you'll help make it safe for me, too.

"When people feel safe, when they laugh and cry spontaneously, the whole universe takes a step forward. I'm certain you and I have a unique contribution to make to the universe and our task is to lend to an atmosphere as best we can to help us make it. We do that when we are in love."

We remain hidden because we are afraid our true identity is unacceptable. We don't think we're good enough. Discrimination, in all its forms, sends the message that who you are is unacceptable. When we declare someone unacceptable, whether for their race, their looks, their gender, their weight, we attempt to remove a piece of reality. Any assault on reality, any attempt to cajole or coerce someone or something to pose as someone or something they are not, does violence to the fullness of reality.

Once at a retreat of lay leaders of my congregation, we got into a frightening standoff about something to do with parish administration. I remember my stomach tightening as I realized our positions were polarized. We made one final round of the group to see if anyone's position had softened; none had. It was me on one side and all the others on the other. Finally one woman spoke, I remember she would die shortly after the retreat.

"Seems to me," she began slowly, deliberately, "that if we all agreed on everything, there wouldn't be much point in all of us being here. If agreement was such a big deal there could just be one of us here. Why are we trying so hard to get an agreement when it's clear there is more than one opinion among us? Do you suppose the fact that every single one of our genetic codes is unique, is some terrible mistake that we need to set right?"

Diversity is not merely a pious idea. It is the essential nature of reality. Because each of us is immersed in a distinct personality that is, like an atom in a molecule, a fragment of the whole, we have a limited perspective. Like the oxygen molecule in a drop of water, our contribution is critical, necessary. Had the oxygen molecule decided to make a wide berth around the carbon molecule because it had a different valence, or was shaped oddly, the biology of our planet would have evolved very differently, none of us would be here.

Because our species is, so far as we can tell, the first to become aware of evolution, we are seduced by the illusion of having a choice about how and even whether we play our part. And in western thought there is the further difficulty of the high place assigned to human choice, free will. This, too, has caused us to assume we can opt out of the unfolding of biological and geological history if we care to. The despair that marks literature and the arts in our time is fed by our fear that we may, through irreconcilable conflict, seeking to coerce each other into unworkable conformity, extinct ourselves as a species.

In fact even our conflict, our seeming unwillingness to honor the differences among us, serves the end of evolution. I can say that only because I see the process unfolding through what look to us as catastrophic events, like the yielding of the dinosaur's sway on the earth after the meteor collision that blocked the sun. Reality is what happens, not what we wish or think ought to happen, and the diversity of forms on this planet alone, should be enough to convince us that we cannot discern or control the future course of events. But it has not been.

If there were a biologist with sufficient perspective to say a)what the role of humankind is for the furthering of biological and geological history and b)what time frame and in what manner the close of this age will occur, perhaps our fear and cynicism might give way to hope, even excitement. But of course there is no such biologist because the only One with that perspective is, of necessity, mega – human. To be human is to have a limited horizon even while having a tantalizing, intuitive glimpse beyond.

The vexing, necessary thing is to recognize one's own parochial boundaries, my limited perspective. In conversation one day with an African businessman whom I thought I knew well, I made what to me seemed a simple, even flattering observation.

"George, since I've come to your country I've begun to feel like a new person. I notice that my greed has lessened, and my fear of being left behind by those richer than I. When there is not the sort of overabundance we have in the U.S. one doesn't miss it. In fact it's a relief to go to the store and decide what you're going to eat by what's available. I sure hope, when your economy begins to grow, you'll learn from our mistakes and see that affluence is a mixed blessing."

George, a gracious, even deferential man, narrowed his eyes before he spoke. His tone when he did speak, was hard-edged, I'd never heard his voice sound like that.

"You Americans, now that you have grabbed most of the world's resources, want us to remain simple, satisfied with our meager lot so we won't challenge you for some of the world's riches. Well, we've learned well from watching you and we intend to have our share. You've had your turn and we now want ours."

I was stunned, chagrined at how insensitive I was to the realities of the emerging world. Diversity requires not only that we respect differences, but that we not try to impose standards and limits on others that we have not disciplined ourselves to accept.

Species diversity is a kind of testing ground for participation in the future. The fatal flaw in most of our schemes for imagining the future is our persistence in making our own species the measure and cornerstone for what is to come. While it may be beyond me to stare into this computer screen and prophesy a future in which human beings are extinct, it is not too much to ask that we acknowledge that the earth and the known universe are not designed by and do not even seem especially suitable for human beings as we have evolved. It may be that if we are sufficiently adaptable, if, that is, we prize diversity as more than merely many different colors of our own species, then we could envision a role for elements of our genetic code as they may appear in some future forms. But it is the height, not just of arrogance, but of biological and geological blindness to think that we humans, because of our big brain, must be present and wholly intact in the aeons to come. With the miniaturization of powerful chips, that has revolutionized technological evolution, comes also the increased capacity for rogue groups to smuggle deadly weapons into population centers and in a moment of racial rage, unleash what decades of mutual assured destruction managed to keep at bay during the Cold War.

So another irony; in our clever attempts to emulate our complex nervous system with the simple binary computer system, we may have unwittingly contributed to the launching of the next phase of evolution beyond ourselves. We have reassured ourselves, insisting that the computer can do only what we program it to do (garbage in, garbage out), but mounting evidence suggests there will be a point of sufficient complexity, some form of artificial intelligence, perhaps already in existence somewhere, in which the new form is capable of a level of independence, spontaneity beyond our ability to understand or control.

In the end the issue is not who can accurately predict the future, draw the shape of species and events in the ensuing millennia, but whether we humans can set aside our natural parochial perspective and hear that diversity is not merely a liberal political ideal, but the inevitable, necessary shape of the evolutionary destiny of this and every planet. Yes, the United States, the first nation to have among its citizens people from every race and ethnic human group, is the wave of the human future. But the human future is only a fraction of the world and universe's future, and given the dimension and pace of the disappearance of species (some due to human mismanagement and some not), we can be sure that our species does not have an unlimited future here.

So what might be a creative stance for human beings, given that we are the only ones at the moment who are, so far as we know, recording the past and imagining the future? Once we see that we are one species among many, subject to change and eventual extinction, what hopeful strategy might we adopt for gladly participating in what at first blush looks like our worst fear?

Perhaps the most help science can provide is the understanding that the history of this planet, even though we are the ones who have put that history into language, never has been about us. Along with the amoebae, the dinosaur, the leopard and the robot, we have inherited an essential, creative, perhaps even central role in the unfolding drama. But the story is not, finally, about us. Even if we succeed in some way in the last ditch desperate attempt to rocket ourselves to other planets where we can be freed from the increasingly unfavorable conditions for us on this planet, we will inevitably have to evolve into some new, different form in order to prosper in that new place. And if we unravel the Einstein riddle of the dimension of time, so we can travel forward and back in time, and perhaps take vast trips through space that would be longer than a single lifetime in linear time, we will certainly be affected so profoundly by the new circumstances that we will emerge into this new age a new being.

The most thrilling aspect of this picture of the growing, inevitable diversity of our planet and the universe, is our deepening sense that we have been given, through no virtue of our own, a piece of the action in the unfolding of the creation. Though it is easy to despair at all that has gone wrong, especially at the shocking list of unintended consequences (unintended, at least, by us) we can take heart that as we look at what has gone before us in the geological aeons, we see that nothing has been lost, no energy squandered. Every atom, every exchange of energy, every breath I draw, has resulted from some other energy exchange and contributed to yet another.

We have become fairly expert at uncovering events as they unfolded in the past, marking with awe and astonishment the way features we now walk by barely acknowledging, cliffs, mountains, rivers, valleys, deserts, dogs, cats, canyons, leopards have been assembled over the aeons from other unlikely cells and formations. But we still have precious little ability to look at combinations of those same cells as we know them, those same rivers, cats and canyons, and predict what sorts of forms their cells will morph into in the future.

And once we acknowledge ourselves as another of those forms that has evolved from previous combinations of cells and will evolve into still other combinations, rather than as the never-again-to-be-changed end product of some divine process, we will rejoice. Rejoice not only because we do not bear the impossibly heavy responsibility for predicting or shaping the future, but because we are a player. Even what embarrasses us as our gross negligence, our exploitation of the planet's resources for our own selfish ends, polluting air and water, the most recent century darkened by our species seeming to be bent on suicide, burdening the planet with synthetic materials that are deadly slow to degrade, we now understand will one day become subject to the planet's infinite ability to evolve. Processes unimaginable to us will come along behind us with the ability to break down and reform molecules we now regard as forever inert and polluting.

But in order for our kind to find hope and beauty, excitement in this demanding future, we must adopt a kind of humility, a stance toward the world once thought to be peculiar to a few saints. The ancient discipline of sitting meditation, turning our creative energies to sacred observing rather than frantically, futilely trying to control the world's future, can enable us, with the Sufi dancer, to celebrate what we cannot quite understand. Like Booker, who laughed not out of bitterness or even irony, but out of sheer pleasure, at his perspective on the seeming insult the old Rhody made to the Shona, we will see that we, since we are creatures, not creator, can play and wonder, celebrate our role in creation, without fear that we are being irresponsible or lazy.

Diversity is the description of a future beyond us in time and comprehension. It will incorporate those cells, wonderfully organized in an integrity we have come to know as 'us', cells that have provided for us rich and unexpected pleasure and adventure, now no longer arranged in the forms we have regarded as necessary, not as we think we would organize them if we were the Organizer. How can we know that? Because we can trace the cells backwards in time, before there was any 'us'. And that provides us the humility that gives us the ability to go beyond ourselves, to wonder at a future in which our cells take some form we would not recognize as part of 'us'. When, we inevitably wonder, with our parochial guard up, are the cells organized in such different patterns that we would no longer call them part of 'us' at all? And the answer, new to our time, is never. Our cells need not be organized as they now are to be a creative part of the ongoing process of the forming of the universe. Meditation provides a means to freedom from human parochialism, the dead end of ego demanding the central role. We now can watch with detached wonder, like theater-goers, the unfolding drama of our evolving cells.

The ancient disciplines of eastern religion can free us from the fears sponsored by ego when it senses it is being asked to take its place alongside other aspects of the self rather than in the center spotlight. Liberal thought has pointed to the need for breaking the bonds of parochial behavior so we can welcome and take part

in the diversity that marks reality. It has not provided us with
the means to do that. Sitting meditation is a practical,
manageable means of detaching us from the illusion that we are
the measure and manager of the future.

As events take us speedily toward a future that looks ominous to
the easily frightened ego, sitting regularly in meditation stills
the fear, lets the ego shift to a place alongside the many aspects
of being, and we may celebrate a future of such incredible
diversity that it exceeds our wildest science fiction.

The fox knows many things; the hedgehog knows one big thing.

UPROOTED

This was written in March of 1997, six months after we made what I had thought a heroic move from coastal southern California to rural Vermont.

When someone asks where I come from, I stumble and stutter through a litany of the places I've lived. And, as I suspect is true for many southern Californians, I'm reluctant to say I'm from here because I secretly worry other regions of the country are somehow more noble, with better values. Better values or not, I've about decided I do come from here.

For the decade Lacey and I live in La Jolla we dream of our old Vermont farmhouse on the pond where we used to retreat when we lived in Boston. We came to La Jolla in 1987, I as Rector of St. James by-the-sea Episcopal Church, and Lacey an interior designer with Ross Thiele on Girard Avenue. We grew, gradually, to love La Jolla, more than we admit, but the quiet, unpretentious, cheap, simple, soulful call of Jacksonville, Vermont, population 500, strikes our 60s sensibilities as respite from urban hype, and ecologically responsible. I long to be apart after thirty years as a parish priest, to write and reflect. Ten years in sunny southern California is as much risk as we feel our souls ought to run.

One summer, years before we move to La Jolla, we spend our two week vacation at our Vermont house. I help Bummy, our caretaker, build a shed beneath the screen porch to keep our wood dry for winter. I guess you'd say I'm as handy as most urban Episcopal priests. We finally finish the job and are admiring the rough hewn barn-siding with which we framed it .

"How long you think it would have taken you to do this without me?" I ask him. Bummy can't resist.

"Bout half as long, I reckon." He grins.

I've been hugely drawn to the place since the first time we saw it 17 years before, across a little bridge which spans a spilling dam. The compact wood frame house, circa 1820, hovers over an 20 acre pond with a sturdy beaver dam at the far end. The simple, honest, house is alluring, to Lacey, a busy interior designer with a firm in Wellesley, and to me, a parish pastor in a congregation wearied by shifting morals, seismic cracks in the old authority, and economic tumult at the end of the 1970s.

We happen on it one autumn day as we drive slowly across the one lane bridge and see a For Sale sign leaned at a rakish angle against the tree in front of the house. It isn't clear whether the sign has fallen off the back of a truck, or means the house is for sale. Noting the Realtor's name, we turn around and go down the hill into the village below. A community grocery store and a junk/antique store, "Grandma's Attic", are the downtown. On one corner of Grandma's Attic porch a sign like the one we had seen by the house, is propped sideways in a wood washtub. In the shop a slim man in his early forties sits in a rocker by the wood-burning stove. No one else is in the store. He makes no eye contact as we enter.

"You the Realtor?"

"Uh huh," he continues rocking.

"That house up the hill, cross the pond; is it for sale?"

"Uh huh."

I wait for more; nothing.

"Think we could look at it?"

"Not right now; I'm too busy."

Now I'm a mixture of consumer rage, and awe at an alien ethic. No free microwave or trip to the Bahamas in exchange for looking at *this* property.

"When do you think you might have time to show it to us?"

Stan, though with a finely honed Vermont manner, has urban experience. He grew up here, fled to New York City where he became Maitre de at the Top Of The Sixes in midtown Manhattan, before burning out and coming back to the village. He spends much of the winter in Key West.

"Maybe tomorrow, maybe day after."

"We'll be going back to Boston this afternoon, and I'm not sure when we'll get back up."

Stan struggles to his feet. He's strikingly handsome, rugged, chiseled features, about my height, 5'9", jet-black hair combed straight back, dressed in a heavy red and black checked lumber jacket, faded, stained jeans and steel-toed tan work boots.

"If you can drive me in your car, I'll get someone to watch the shop for a while, and show you the house."

Elated at this chink in Stan's armor, I assure him we'd be happy to drive. It's a couple of years before he'll tell us that he assumed we were flatlanders who'd taken a bus and gotten off to spend the afternoon on tour with the local Realtor, a cheap and not uncommon way for impoverished Bostonians to see the countryside.

Stan takes us to six houses before showing us the one we're interested in. After we've bought the house, he explains he has a moral obligation to show anyone who is interested in any property in town, everything for sale. Houses in the village are rarely shown, even more rarely sold, and it would be considered effrontery not to show everyone's house when a buyer turns up.

Stan hands me the Realtor's listing-sheet, tattered and mud-stained. My urban eye focuses instantly on the one word, "unsurveyed".

"Uh oh," I express dismay. Though it will be years before I see the little brass surveyors' buttons imbedded in the sidewalks of La Jolla, I know the significance of a reliable survey.

"Guess we'd need to have it surveyed," I say. Stan eyes me skeptically.

"You haven't spent a winter up here have you?" I acknowledge that I haven't. "Once we start quarreling about where your land ends and mine begins, we wouldn't make it through a single winter," he explains.

"But what happens when you go to the bank for a mortgage?"

"Banks around here know there hasn't been a property surveyed in Windham County in 100 years. When we say, 'That stone's the boundary,' they take our word for it."

A place where people's word and memory carry more weight

than legal documents. And it turns out to be true. The bank never blinks at lending us money even though the boundaries are described in the deed as rocks and hills, not surveyor's precise marks.

In 1987 when we move into the church's house in La Jolla, high on a bluff with 180° view of the Pacific, we quickly get into a dispute with our neighbor after he seals shut a fence joining our properties. The church board begins at once to prepare a lawsuit to resolve the issue. We settle out of court, into a long sullen southern California neighborhood standoff.

Lacey and I spent our childhood summers at eastern beaches, with vast open space. La Jolla is our first experience of a busy city butting up to the ocean. In Vermont the eight acre pond by our house is surrounded by rolling acres, apple trees, blueberry bushes, bamboo shoots which the beaver feeds on most evenings.

Our La Jolla friends pay more for their cars than we paid for our farmhouse. The church spends almost as much as we paid for our farmhouse to do a few renovations. I watch the bronzed workmen with their surfboards in their pickups, bringing the Monterey-style house to near perfection. We took an architect friend back to Vermont the week after we'd first seen the house. The three of us walk down the leaning staircase to the dirt cellar where he gives a support beam, a rough hewn timber at the foot of the steps, a good shove. It swings loose from its footing.

"It's not a particularly important beam," he reassures cheerily. "This house has been standing for 150 years; it'll still be up when we're all underground."

Later when I ask Stan why the cellar is dirt, has never been finished off, he explains without apology, "It would cause big

problems when the spring thaw comes and the stream runs
through here."

In our 9+ years in the church's rectory in La Jolla, I reckon the
church leaders spend nearly $100,000 trying countless
ingenious schemes to divert the water which drains down the
hill above us from irrigation of yards and the golf course.
"Attempting to defeat water is a fool's errand," our architect
friend says in response to my concern about our Vermont cellar.
But to take such a passive stance towards nature would have left
most of southern California unbuilt. Yet by the time we move
out of the La Jolla house, the water still goes pretty much where
it likes.

It's not just a different style, it's another ethic, an alternate
existence. As different as one might expect moving between a
first and a third world country. Takes a while to see it's not
about morals so much as different realities with distinct survival
strategies.

Tracey, the dairy farmer up the road, with the 25 cows he hand-
milks twice a day, tells us about a trip he took to California.

"Once I finally got off those racetracks they call Freeways, I saw a
dairy farm had 2000 milking cows. That ain't a dairy farm,
that's a factory."

We're ideological easterners, smug about our simpler values.
We hardly notice southern California ebbing into our
marrow. The second Christmas we give each other wet suits
and become enthusiastic year round ocean swimmers,
marking the years by the Rough Water Swim the Sunday
after Labor Day. We love playing tennis in shorts at
Christmas. We grow smug about the weather, asking eastern
friends in phone conversations what the weather's like back

there. Still, we mouth the pieties of uncomplicated life closer
to the earth. And dream about living responsibly, lower on
the food chain in rural Vermont.

Three years ago during a four month sabbatical, I decide I am
ready to quit parish ministry after 30 years and do my writing
full time. Lacey, though she isn't remotely interested in quitting
her design work, is willing to consider a move back to New
England, both because she hopes to return her business volume
to the level she's never quite reached in California, and because
we have talked so often about what good sound sense it makes
for us to go back. It is, after all, home. Roots.

Yet Lacey's skeptical. We've paid off the mortgage on the
Vermont house and always assume we'll go back one day. But
reality begins to work on Lacey. Her business in California has
recently begun booming, and she isn't sure living and working
in a Vermont town of 500, from a 175 year old farmhouse with
a stream in the cellar, is going to be as idyllic as we imagine.
Especially after San Diego.

"We've spent nice vacation time in that house," Lacey warns one
day, "but I don't know about living there. I think we may be
mindlessly romantic, maybe Yankee self-righteous about doing
winter after all these years here."

Romantic? With a paid-off house on a pond in Vermont?
Beavers, Blue Heron? Wild raspberries? Skating on the pond,
skiing through the woods?

"With fax machines and e-mail it doesn't make any difference
where you live now." I reassure her. "No reason you can't do a
big California business from Vermont, and you'll also be able to
resurrect your Boston business. Think how much saner and
simpler our life will be. I'm looking forward to going up the hill

at milking time and helping Tracey with his chores." Lacey has always loved spending time in Tracey's barn.

"You dreamer! Two sets of singles wears out your back," she bores in, "You think you're going to do heavy farm work?"

That spring Lacey and our daughter drive from Boston to Jacksonville to take a careful look at the house. Lacey calls me in California that night, fighting back tears.

"It was horrible! A gray, lightless, rainy day. The house is dark and dreary. And Blayney, it's a wreck. I'm not sure any amount of work and money can bring it back to something we can live in. I think maybe we should declare it a total loss and push it into the pond."

My stomach knots. But by now this is a holy mission. I've done several in my life. Their chief emblem is the huge chasm between desire and duty.

"That's your best skill," I flatter, "you spend your life making peoples' wrecked houses into wonderful new spaces."

"Yeah, maybe I'm good at helping other people do that," she pushes back, "but this is *our* house. When I saw it today I felt like a brain surgeon reading her own child's PET scan. Redoing that house is like removing a tumor from my own kid's head. Makes me feel crazy, like it's too scary, dangerous."

Still, we decide to do it. Our friends, even in New England, are incredulous. But admiring. That's what's seducing us. They've heard me preach, they're used to yielding me the high ground. Picking up my moral tone about simple, responsible living in a rural town, they're loath to raise less noble issues like personal comfort, weather and ocean, Jack Murphy Stadium. Never mind that we swim in the ocean every day in La Jolla. That's la la land; we're returning to real life.

As the time draws nearer, even my bravado begins to be eroded by anxiety. We hedge our pure intentions by renting a small in-town apartment in Boston. I can't know then that that apartment will soon be all that stands between me and drowning myself in the pond. The relief I feel at having an escape from Vermont should cause me to take another, closer look at the growing gap between what I wish and what is real. But straight-dealing with reality would put a preacher out of business. It's become habit for me to preach pieties I've never tried. I don't yet get it that this isn't a sermon; this is our life. Lacey, never impressed by my preacher persona, becomes increasingly agitated as moving day draws nearer.

"I know we're not supposed to care about all the things a place like La Jolla offers, sun and ocean, warmth, light, friends, fun. But I do. I think I'm even getting to like the glitz."

I'm having heart faints now, in the dozens a day. But I'm stoic when people ask me about the move.

"I'm sure it's going to be a huge adjustment. We've loved it here. But we're excited about going back for this next chapter. It's home for us." The outside and the inside of me are becoming strangers.

People's admiration for our decision reinforces me, even though none of them say they wish they were doing the same thing themselves. They have so much respect for *our* doing it. Remember what it meant in adolescence, when a guy said he respected a girl? That's what it feels like when people tell us how much they respect us for making this move.

October 21. We're saying good bye to friends who've driven in from Carlsbad. Up the coastline we see huge billowing clouds of smoke. Looks like Carlsbad. Most of that night and before dawn the next morning, we fret with our friends who take refuge with our neighbors, about whether their house has burned in the season's worst fire. In the morning they learn the fire has miraculously burned right to their front door, jumped their house and spared it. Three neighbors' houses are ashes. We grasp at their house being spared as some sort of sign of God's approval as we start off on our new journey. We don't consider what sign it must be for the people whose houses burned. We can't let ourselves see how desperate we've become, looking for encouragement that what we've set in motion is a good thing.

The next morning we drive down Torrey Pines, heading for the 5. The sky is cloudless, that deep blue you wouldn't believe occurs in nature if you hadn't seen it. I try not to let Lacey catch me sneaking a last long look as the ocean disappears behind Mt. Soledad. The drive east is supposed to make the transition smoother, not like the too-brief five hour plane ride. Instead, the five six-hundred-mile days exhaust us, raise our anxiety. The last night out we spend with friends in upstate New York, just a couple of hours drive from Vermont. It's cold, rainy, bleak. We wear our socks to bed. Neither of us sleep. We rise before dawn, get right on the road, knowing we're going to have just two days to get the house ready before the van arrives.

It's been three years since I've seen the house and, as we turn across the bridge, it looks smaller than the picture we've had on our refrigerator in La Jolla the past nine years. We're too late for the fall foliage, the trees are bare. A grayish ash color, the hue of the gravestones in the burial ground across the street, hovers over the scene. My headache nearly blinds me. Lacey and I sit without speaking in the car in the driveway.

"This was your idea," Lacey accuses, "you go in first!" She comes behind me.

"Oh my God!" The stench nearly knocks us both backwards out the door as Lacey and I cross the threshold of our dream house. It's a musty, stale tobacco odor mixed with old cooking aromas embedded in every surface, and perhaps decaying rodent corpses in the walls. The grainy darkness, a rainy 40° New England fall day, the norm we will learn, and heavy insulating quilted shades lowered to the sills, deepen the gloom in the house and in our sinking hearts. The dimness at least cushions us from too stark a first look at what is to be our home.

As our eyes adjust to the muted autumn light, the wreckage of our farmhouse provides sobering proof of the romance and the hubris which led us here.

The last decade spent in the reliable southern California sun, in a house framed with windows to the west looking over the blue Pacific, has marked us indelibly. We've lulled ourselves into fantasies about simpler, quieter, slower life. We define ourselves as easterners, making virtue of the necessity of job and money, biding our time until we can return to our roots.

"What could we have been thinking?" I wonder aloud, as we walk into the house. My gaze falls to the cracked and pitted sub-floor. Each time we'd called from California over the past four months, they'd reassured us all the work promised for our moving in would be finished in plenty of time. The hardwood floor we are laying to replace the ruined wall-to-wall carpet in the entry room (we've never figured out what to call rooms in this house), lies scattered in lengths around the room. Our moving van is due the next day, we are in day two of a three day noreaster, and all our furniture and boxes have to be carried across this floor.

"What were *we* thinking?" Lacey's voice is thick with sarcasm. She stands 5'6", but when she's pissed she has the stature of an NBA center. Her hair's reddish luster sets off her flashing hazel eyes. She stands, feet apart, hands defiantly on her hips, oozing I-told-you-so. Her jeans and forest-green flannel shirt give her an all business air. What were *we* thinking? *I* had decided it was time for *me*, after 30 years a parish minister, to do the writing *I* longed to do. Lacey had been reluctantly willing. I remember worrying how well she was going to do in this move. Now I realize I should have worried more about myself.

"You always have such a pretty framed-up picture of what you wish," she accuses me, "but it's only your wish, not reality." Right now my wish feels like a huge tumor feeding on vital organs in my abdomen. The only bridge we haven't burned is the one
leading across the dam to this house, the one we perhaps should have burned.

Our eyes begin to adjust to the dark, to focus on the debris. The once white walls are slathered with thin gaily colored lines of what looks like gum or silly putty. The glass doors to the fireplace are black and gritty, like one-way mirrors. The brick hearth is cracked, the mantle pocked with a decade of pinpricks from the tenants' Christmas stockings. A thick layer of spider webs around the wood boxed beams obscure the plaster ceiling, as if you're looking up through the safety nets in a circus tent. In grim silence we walk through the room to the far end where the bathroom door is open revealing the broken and soiled toilet and sink. I step into the bathroom and the plywood floor sags, as if it might give way under my foot, plunging me into the dirt cellar. A dark stain betrays the leak from the rusted shower stall which has rotted the floor.

I stand stunned, paralyzed. Lacey has moved to the living room

(Passage room?). Without warning I begin to sob. Wracking, gasping sobs. The sort that come when someone you love dies. Lacey pivots, fixing me with her merciless stare.

"*You're* crying? I should be crying. You thought this was a good idea."

I had. On our sublime sabbatical two years before, in Charleston, South Carolina, Lacey happily immersed herself in the unprecedented historic restoration that city began after Hurricane Hugo. I devoted my time to writing. When we return to La Jolla, I'm restless, impatient with the demands of church work. I realize my sabbatical has been an exit vehicle from parish ministry. And, I assume, that means Vermont. And our farmhouse. Cows. Quiet. Though it plays a little tinny even to me, it sounds like what I have been urging for years in my preaching, the ideal sane life. I want it to be true. Lacey's reluctant agreement is based only on her faint hope that I'm right about how she might do her business from there and about how we'll respond to rural Vermont. But she isn't my parishioner, she's not intimidated by my hopeful piety.

"You think we're being realistic about the weather? You remember what it's like to be cold all the time, how much energy you spend keeping warm? You know what your morale will be like after two solid weeks of rain and 40°? And no ocean?"

When we were moving from Boston to San Diego ten years ago, a woman who'd grown up in California sidled up to me at a good-bye party, smiling the crooked Halloween smile I've learned means I'm about to hear some bad news.

"You're going to hate California by the time you've been there six months," she predicts.

"Why?"

"It's a hedonistic, intellectual hell. All anyone ever talks about is the weather."

Now, knee-deep in the wreckage of our house on this grim day, I'd give my life for that weather. My preacher's need to be loved and admired has buried me under an avalanche, a lifetime of oughts and shoulds, crushing how it really is. I've been enchanted by my own spell, and taken Lacey with me. I bury my face in my hands. What an asshole!

I'd like to tell you that was the low point, that Lacey sucks it up, puts her talent to work and we transform that old house into a reality which exceeds our hopes. I want to tell you that sleepy, solid, real Vermont proves a welcome relief from the dizzy illusions of southern California. But that requires you to overlook the next six months, the huge course correction which results in our living virtually full time in the Boston apartment, my inability to drive a nail or run a washing machine, loneliness so deep we can't bear to talk about it, and our marriage stretched to its limit, several times seemingly beyond its limit.

It's weird, but that terrible beginning shakes me loose from my habit of preaching, to Lacey and myself, about how good things would be if people would listen to God (me) and live the way God (me) wants them to. I am cured of that ugly preacher's habit within minutes of walking into the house.

Getting real with myself however, takes a little longer. I'm not quite ready to surrender my picture of myself as a grounded easterner, even though every day etches deeper in me the reality that southern California has marked me irrevocably. As Lacey keeps saying, Vermont looks and feels hauntingly familiar, but it doesn't feel safe, or like home.

*   *   *

The floor. If we don't get the floor done before the van comes
tomorrow morning, the living room is going to be a mud pile.
It's driving rain and more is promised for the next two days. The
cold rain does us a favor. Ron, who's doing the floor, gets off the
house he's working on because it's not framed in yet. Ron is
reminiscent of the young guy who showed up to do our floors in
La Jolla, when the surf wasn't up. Handsome, lean, well
trimmed, with a tiny braid hanging between his shoulder
blades, Ron's unflappable, even when he smells our panic.

"Your van's coming when?" he asks. Tomorrow around 11? No
problem."

I've never laid a hardwood floor, so I don't know. Lacey has
overseen many, and she's skeptical. We ply Ron with tea and
sandwiches. He hums a ditty as he duck-walks across the floor.
How does he stay on his haunches like that? At 11:30pm, seeing
double with fatigue, Lacey and I tell Ron we can't stay up any
longer. He still seems cheerful, undaunted by more than half the
floor yet to be laid.

"Sleep well. I'll let myself out when I'm done."

Our first night in the house. Not what we'd pictured. We sleep
(well, lie down) on a mattress on the floor of our bedroom, on
bedding we drag from the rank attic. The rodents (perhaps some
of the ones we smelled when we walked in the house) have used
the bedding before us. The ceiling of our room, which was also
promised to have been finished before we arrived, is stripped to
the lathe. Shredded newsprint insulation drops onto to us
through the endless night. We hear Ron pounding lengths of
cherry board into place, until the front door slams shut just after
4:30am. I haven't the courage or energy to go down and see if

he's actually finished, or left in exhaustion. An hour and a half later I let the dog out, and the floor is miraculously complete. Conventional wisdom, that it should cure for a period before being walked on, is just one of the compromises we make, willingly, to get moved in.

The 50 foot moving van, harboring everything we own, including the antiques Lacey has been collecting since she was a teenager, stops at the general store in the village at the foot of our hill. After an uneventful 3000 mile trip across country, Javier, the driver is told by the amused locals that there's no way he'll "get that rig cross the tiny crumbling bridge" which leads to our house. He finally does, but not before backing and filling for a half hour, then gouging a wedge out of the already crumbling cement bridge with his bumper. A couple of townspeople come up the hill to watch. One takes pictures.

Tracey, the dairy farmer, pulls his truck off the road and helps unload. His perspective saves us. "Christ, Lacey," he says as he carries an umbrella-stand into the house, laughing as if this was the most fun he'd had that week, "Watcha' gonna do with all this shit?" Tracey works steadily for two hours, until it's milking time. Just before he leaves, he carries a huge cement turtle into our cellar.

"Now I've seen everything," he laughs, "a goddam turtle you got to carry, it can't even pull it's head back in. Must be a California turtle."

I remember joking with a friend in California about our Vermont farmhouse costing less than a new BMW. And, while the house has probably not appreciated even as fast as the modest inflation of the past few years, renovation is just as costly in simple rural Vermont as in upscale La Jolla. An irony is that Pete, our tenant the past nine years is the best painter in the valley, and on him depends our ability to make the house livable. He and his family lived there while the house fell apart around them, unable to afford and too busy to keep up with maintenance, and in the way of Vermonters, not fussy so long as they kept warm and dry. That's another Yankee ethic which has mutated in us after a decade of southern California.

Seeing what lay ahead, we had begun forgiving rent several months before our return, agreeing to exchange rent money for Pete's future work. That turns out to be a strategic mistake. We arrive back just as the ski season is about to begin, and Pete's in demand. The skiers from New York who own the condos at the mountain pay him much needed cash, and they have the city ethic; "We'll pay you what we have to to get the job done when we want." But we're now on the Vermont barter system along with the other locals, and we go to the bottom of the list.

Happily, Pete turns out to be diligent. He shows up many nights after he's finished with his paying customers. He's alone, can't afford to put his crew on our non-cash job, so, in hopes of speeding the work, I put on my coveralls and pitch in with Pete, scraping and painting. And, as with Bummy many years before, my assistance requires Pete to constantly stop what he's doing and direct me.

But there's an unexpected dividend. Pete's a child of the 70s, a druggie and free-love guy. He gave it all up when he married and had kids, but he has no regrets. And he loves to talk. And I to listen. He is a gentle, friendly soul, full of stories about his high school friends who were wrecked by Viet Nam, drugs, booze. He has two brothers who are born-again Christians, and Pete shares with me a skepticism about their strident certainty. In these conversations which extend deep into the night, which grow increasingly candid, I realize how much I've missed rich conversation. I used to talk like this routinely. Even take long walks on the beach for some solitude. Now I wonder if I may have to join Pete's work crew to find companionship. The quality of my painting picks up a little, slowly, with Pete's help, but it's his contribution to my morale which means most to me. We're paying Pete by the hour and Lacey isn't keen about how much our bull sessions may be adding to his bill. Pete gets a kick out of her concern. When Lacey's in the next room, collecting her things to drive down to Boston, Pete effects a stage whisper to me.

"Hey, Blayney, if Lacey's going to be gone tonight, I'll drop by and we can do some drugs and talk about our sex life." Lacey's sense of humor isn't as robust as it once was.

With the exception of the stove and refrigerator, both of which we had replaced for the tenants in the last year, everything in the house which can break, is broken. Every faucet, electrical connection and window latch. Paul was our plumber before we moved to California, and he is as faithful as any tradesman we'd ever done business with. For the first four months, when we are at the house and not in Boston, Paul is there working at least part of every day. Allan, the electrician, is equally attentive. They are both lifelong natives of the valley, and while both express distress and amazement at the deterioration of our old house, I wonder if they don't think we're terminally fussy.

At the end of the first month no bill comes from either of them. Maybe they have pity on us, helpless aliens from crazy California. I begin my ostrich maneuver, keeping my head down when I see them. Maybe they forgot. They're Vermonters; what would they do with the money anyway? Even if they do bill us, it will be so much less than inflated California prices.

Both bills arrive in our mail cubby down at the post office on the same day. Together they total nearly $10,000 dollars.

Payable in full in 30 days, or a 1 1/2% surcharge. And no air miles. Still less than a BMW, at least a new one.

"One of the reasons we made this move was to live cheaply," Lacey reminds me as she looks over the two bills. I am too distracted to respond, looking out the window at the four wheel drive vehicle I've just driven off the car lot, the most expensive car I've ever owned. Everyone told me it was a necessity for a Vermont winter and mud season. And many's the time I'm grateful for it. But I will marvel through the winter at the old sedans and panel trucks, bald tires with 150,000 miles, swaying and skidding up the snowy hill by our house. A real Vermonter can and does live cheaply, but it's a different story for we flatlanders posing as Vermonters.

Six full months of work, expensive, tedious, frustrating work, finally brings the house to the point at which it seems habitable to us. We wonder if the local tradesmen think we're picky and spoiled. We no longer care.

Our first house guests come and stay in the downstairs guest room, only hours after the final paint and curtains are in place. It is the first room to be finished. They are awed at how beautiful it looks. No more than I am.

Every surface has been painted, plastered or papered. The wiring has been redone. New bathroom sinks and toilets, new shower stall and bathtub, new floors in the two bathrooms and in the kitchen. (The first floor they lay in the kitchen is the wrong tile, and it takes two months to get the right one.) The new hardwood floor Ron put down in the entry room gleams, as do the other hardwood floors which have all been refinished. We'd put ourselves on a budget for this work which we exceeded before we were a quarter complete. I still haven't mustered the courage to total the costs.

I'll remember forever the day when everything is finally finished. We talk with Pete and Bummy from Boston the night before, and they tell us it's all done. Not that there isn't a ton more we could do. There always will be. We drive up that morning with some misgivings, wondering how it will hit us this time. Each visit to the house has been like facing an implacable enemy. And we have no tolerance for the cold. It makes us irritable.

But this time it looks nice, clean, fresh. I think it's breathtaking, especially remembering what it looked like the first time we walked in. But, I wonder, is it home? I wait for Lacey to say something. She's silent as we walk from room to room. Her early American furniture looks as if it has been made for this period, though maybe for a grander, more important house. Finally she speaks.

"It looks really nice. But you know what? It's still a funky old farmhouse in a remote little town of 500. And it always will be. I still don't know if I can live here. Or make my business work from here. I can't believe I'm saying this, me the old Yankee, but I miss California terribly."

Since then we've done a Vermont winter and a mud season. We've skated on our 20 acre pond. We've explored the deep surrounding woods on cross country skis, lovely, quiet, freezing days. Our future still looks as murky as the pond after a summer storm. We've made two mid-winter trips back to southern California, where ocean swimming and shirt sleeves in the winter reawakened our nerve endings with such immediate and startling intensity that we found it hard to get on the plane to return. We've come light-years from that first nauseating day we walked into the house. But are we Vermonters? Will we ever be?

I'm finishing this piece just as sultry summer comes to Vermont. It's green and lush, bright sun, a different universe from the unforgiving cold, hard, dark winter which felt like death . The theory about light and morale is no longer a theory. On our last trip back to California, we sought out an apartment where we might spend the winter months. My pride and arrogance are much muted. My wish to define myself regionally is gone.

My grown children often express surprise that I stayed in the same work from college until past middle age. Maybe that has much to do with my profound dislocation, moving from California to Vermont. My judgments about Californians being less grounded than New Englanders now seems stupid, pointless. I am an American, with no clear sense of where home is, and yet at home in many varied places. But I'm far less portable than I thought. Like so many driven men after decades in a career, I longed for some peace and tranquillity, autonomy. I believed I could live happily anywhere. I resented Lacey's needs for creature comforts, but should have owned them as my own, too. I love Vermont, especially in the summer, and occasionally in the dead of winter for a lovely cross country ski. But there's no more pretending that it's a woman thing, this wrenching business about where you live and how. Last winter I thought it was going to put me completely under.

We'll probably always have this old Vermont house in our lives. Today the huge maple trees are blowing and I'm going swimming in the lake. Lacey's in San Diego making money and feeling happy to be there. We'll spend summer here, continuing to do work on the house, and tending the raised-bed garden we learned how to build from Martha Stewart. Maybe we'll persuade our families to come spend Thanksgiving with us here. Some years the pond freezes early enough so we can skate on Thanksgiving. But soon after, having eaten crow along with our turkey, we'll get in the car and head west, and south, for winter in California.

PRESUMED INNOCENT

October 1997

Yesterday I was reading an article in the Boston Globe about the 19-year-old British au pair who is on trial for the murder of the infant boy she was charged with caring for. I found myself rooting for her as if she was a baseball team in my hometown. That's not a new experience for me. Though I keep it under wraps, the truth is I want the bad guy, or at least the one every fingers as the bad buy, to win. Or at least survive. Every time.

This is my story, and it may not connect with everyone's, but I'd guess it will with most. It's about being that au pair and Bill Clinton when Paula Jones accuses him of sexual advances. That's what this story's about, and about why the American Dream, which is built on the presumption of innocence, is both the most daring experiment in the political history of the world, and unsustainable.

Just before the start of O.J. Simpson's trial for murder, my wife and I were at a neighbor's house for dinner. We lived in southern California then, not that anyone anywhere else in the country was talking about anything else, but we sure weren't. Our host was Swedish, rich, Jewish, a former diamond dealer who now, at age 40, managed his investments. His wife, ten years younger, was Belgian. Another couple, a pure bred American doctor in his early forties, and his 32 year old wife, were also there.

"How many think O.J.'s guilty?" asked our Swedish host. Every hand except my wife's went into the air. "What is this?" he asked sarcastically, "I thought one was supposed to presumed innocent in this country until proven guilty."

"Bull shit!" exclaimed the doctor. "That's legal jargon. Everyone knows he's guilty."

I felt a pang of uneasiness, not only because of my passionate belief in the majesty of presumed innocence, but because I also knew, whatever happened at O.J.'s estranged wife's house that night, somehow I wished him well. My wife, who holds most people guilty before they're even accused, just couldn't bring herself to believe that anyone as good looking as O.J. was capable of such a monstrous act.

There's nothing particularly profound about this, various legal systems treat it differently. But I think it may be about more than my perpetually guilty conscience that makes me happy to live in a country that weights the system against conviction. The question is whether one would prefer to live with the risk of sending an innocent person to jail, or worse, or with the risk of having a guilty person go free. [This was written five years before the terrorist attacks of September 11, 2001, but I'll stick with it.]

Recently I exchanged emails with a woman who wrote of the need for justice. I take that to mean some innate sense in us that feels things are incomplete or violated if a crime goes unpunished. Even allowing for the petty crimes we all commit for convenience, speeding, taking the extra drink before driving, jay walking, I don't seem to have that innate sense she has. Though I still believe O.J. killed his wife and her friend that night, I think our system worked. A jury of his peers refused to convict him. That's the risk we run. I am white, middle class, and do not pretend to understand exactly what was in the mind of the jury. But our system recognizes that the jury has the last word. I may disagree with the jury, even hate their verdict, but once they are seated, and assuming no misdeeds have been done in the process itself, we are bound by their decision.

The imponderable, it seems to me, is not the service of justice, but the human need for retribution. Our system until recently, when victims' rights became a part of the equation, made no provision for retribution. There is something unnerving about that because it can provoke a whole new set of actions on the part of the aggrieved.

But I'm glad it's hard to convict in our system. I think the founding fathers had lived under systems in which power prevailed every time. They took a big chance in designing our system as they did. If we cave in to our fears and outrages at the occasional O.J. verdicts, we'll end up with a monster. One that will end up convicting us all.

VISITING THE
NATION'S CAPITAL

October 1999

It was my first visit to Washington in the nearly thirty years
since I was a young assistant in St. John's Church, Lafayette
Square, The Church of the Presidents across the park from the
White House. Nixon had been President, the Viet Nam War was
culling my generation. I had been vocally against the war in my
prior post in Akron, Ohio, but this was Washington and I was
cowed. The feelings of shame diminished over the years, but this
visit had stirred them again. I was relieved to have gotten
through the visit without coming apart, and now was
concentrated on getting to the airport and going back to
California.

I was anxious about our getting a shuttle from Reagan National
Airport to Baltimore Washington. When I asked the uniformed
man at the Information desk, he eyed me with a sad expression
and said, "Now, that's going to be difficult." My heart sank. He
told me, in a thick African American dialect, what I must do,
and motioned me out the doors saying something about how
that shuttle never comes across that traffic island.

When we finally settled into a van, and the man told us it would
be $50 to go to BWI, I was relieved. The system they had
worked perfectly. The driver was from Jamaica and his whole

family had come here, too. He never went back because, "I'm not a rich man and Jamaica is a country for rich people, not poor people."

"So," Lacey asked, "are you an American citizen?"

"Yes, automatically," he explained, "because my mother became a citizen when I was under 18." He fell silent for a while. Then, as if it had been troubling him, he straightened out what he feared might be a misunderstanding. "But I've got an alien card."

"I don't understand," I said. "If you're a citizen, why would you need an alien card."

"Well," this was apparently the point, "it means that I'm a citizen, but if the country decides to go to war, they can't make me go. They can't make me kill anyone. I've never killed anyone and I don't want to kill anyone. I don't want them to train me to be a killer."

"I never knew anything about that," I told him. "You mean you are a full citizen, can vote and everything, but you aren't subject to the draft."

"That's right," he insisted, "they can't make me kill no one. This country does a lot of wars, but I don't want to become a killer."

It had already been a loaded weekend. Eliza, our baby sitter for two summers, one of our family heroes, was getting married. And it developed that Patrick, the man she was marrying, had once briefly been a boyfriend of Heather, our oldest daughter.

The wedding was in Washington, where I had worked for four confusing years early in my career. Eliza's wedding was at St. Alban's on the grounds of the Washington Cathedral, next to the diocesan offices where I had first turned for help when I recognized I was in over my head in this work and in most of my life. Jim Anderson was the first person to whom I ever mentioned my fears about my father. That he was too powerful for me to compete with, and I was afraid I'd gone to seminary to escape the rough and tumble world of business. Jim listened, then delivered an opinion different from anything I'd ever thought. It would change the entire direction of my life.

"Your father doesn't sound all that powerful to me," he said quietly, matter-of-factly. "In fact from what I know of you and what you tell me of him, I'd say you're a braver more powerful man than he is."

The light was on in Jim's old office as we walked from the church to the reception across the cathedral close. The conversation of 30 years ago reverberated in my head.

Frank Wade, Rector of St. Albans and officiant at the wedding, had already weakened my defenses preaching a homily that was true and lean. Or rather he acted out a brief drama with the couple about this being as good as it's likely to get. He resurrected sensations from my first, failed marriage that I thought were beyond recall. I've known Frank a few years and hadn't bargained on his getting to me. Receiving communion from him unleashed a little electric current that surprised me.

Clark Grew was there, my old tennis buddy and sidekick from my days as Rector of St, Paul's, Dedham. He used to call me when he was the new green Rector of Westwood and I was a seasoned veteran, nearly nine years ordained.

"Hey coach," the voice on the other end would say, "I've got this couple who are coming to me to talk about their marriage and I'm not sure how I should be responding."

I never was either, but after a couple of sets of tennis or a cheeseburger at Charlie's, we'd flap about it until we could at least laugh at this weird business we'd gotten ourselves into.

Now I'd quit and Clark was Bishop of Ohio. We hadn't exchanged much and I wondered if we could connect the way we once did.

"How do you do retired?" Clark asked me. "How come you don't just lie around in bed all day? I mean do you say to yourself, 'It's noon, time to go for a walk? I can't picture it."

We had one of those wonderful uncluttered conversations, letting go all efforts to impress or outweigh each other. I was astonished at how anxious I had been about whether being a writer, with no status, would mean I couldn't hang with my old buddies who were still in their ascendancy.

The previous afternoon Lacey and I had visited the Viet Nam Memorial, The Wall. I felt ambivalent about going. It was built after I moved away. I had been in a church that was in bed with the Nixon Administration, craving a place alongside the city and nation's power brokers. I felt ashamed, not only at my own excitement at looking from my desk over Lafayette Park to the White House, but at my silence about my feelings that the war was wrong, stupid, self-defeating. My boss wore his battle ribbons from WWII pinned to his preaching scarf.

I was the 30, a couple of years older than the 1st Lieutenants leading patrols into the terrifying shadows where every motion of a branch might signal their end. But because I was exempt, a holy deferment, which I thought probably a violation of the first amendment, I was spared the Viet Nam or Canada decision.

There is no preparation for approaching the Viet Nam memorial, at least not for anyone who has any emotional baggage about that war. I saw the leading edge as we crested the rise walking from the car across the Mall. I wasn't sure what I was seeing until we started down the other side and the long glistening stone wall, with the 58,000 names of young Americans engraved on its face, emerged from beneath ground and climbed until it was ten feet high.

As it came into full view, my breath unexpectedly caught in my throat and I sobbed. That sob expelled stale breath that had been trapped in me for thirty years. The confusion, the ambivalence, the dread that had caused me to cleave to that breath all those years, was too weighty to unpack now. Maya Lin, the architect of the wall, although a generation younger than those of us who lived through it, found the trigger is in us that released the sphincter we had clamped shut all those years ago.

"No," the Jamaican/American taxi driver said, this time softly, almost as if to himself, "I like being an American but that don't mean I got to become a trained killer."

SUMMER OUTING

July 13, 2000

Yesterday Lacey and I went to Brattleboro to run some errands, have supper and see a movie. Driving the dirt road through the dense woods this time of year the afternoon sun makes weird patterns and shapes on the uneven road as it pours through the heavily leafed trees blowing in the always-steady breeze.

We took dry cleaning, the dry cleaner had taken the week off, struck out there, on to the framers to get framed a beguiling oil our Zimbabwean friend Mo Davy did of Alyssum, our aging terrier, take a pair of sneakers back to Sam's Department Store because Lacey didn't like them after all, then the Latchis Grill for Scrod and a salad and on to the movie, "Shaft". Why Shaft? Probably because it was playing when we finished dinner and was around the corner from the restaurant, a black exploitation film, pretty engaging, especially of my digestive system each time someone else got blown away by Shaft's piece. I managed to pick up bits and pieces of the dialogue.

Forty minutes into the movie I began thinking about the keys to the truck. I hate squandering energy dreaming up things to worry about. I was enjoying sitting there mindlessly in the dark shoveling pecan M&Ms into my mouth. I told myself to ignore myself. But it didn't work. I hoovered the remaining M&Ms and began feeling around in my pockets for the keys. My hand met some metal in my pocket. I berated myself for being

neurotic, grasped the metal and came out with my money clip, a
Filipino silver peso my father used to carry. I'd only recently
begun using it after finding it while cleaning out an old box. I
love having it, but I was looking for the key to the truck and I
wasn't glad to find the money clip now. Not in the other pocket
either. I looked behind me to make sure I wasn't sitting in front
of someone (we were in the little room at the Latchis and it was
only partially full . . . a sign of Vermont moviegoers' discerning
taste in movies). I stood up so I could reach really deep into my
pockets and search seriously. No key in either pocket. I got
down on my knees and felt all around under the seat. No key. I
counseled myself not to panic.

I walked out of the theater, trying unsuccessfully to catch the
eye of the ticket-taking lady who was eating a pizza , I wondered
if I had my stub to get back in but was too frazzled and in a
hurry now to rummage again through my pockets or to try to
explain.

I retraced our steps. The framing place was closed. I couldn't
think why I would have taken the keys from my pocket there,
hoped I hadn't. The waiter at the Latchis grill was
understanding, got down on his hands and knees with me under
our table. People at the surrounding tables looked at us as if we
were voyeurs. No keys. Sam's department store has three floors
and I'd stopped at each of them though I bought nothing; I'd
wanted to avoid being there when Lacey talked the sales person
into giving her money back for shoes she'd worn. Now I had to
see him once more when I asked if he'd found a key to a Ford
truck. He hadn't and was decent enough to act as if he didn't
remember that I'd been there with the woman who wanted her
money back for the sneakers.

I left Sam's trying not to draw attention to myself, a 60 year old
man running up the street, burping scrod and M&Ms. I turned

the corner and could see the red truck where we'd parked it. I came alongside and considered the truck, both doors locked, before cupping my face in my hands and peering inside half hoping, half hoping not to see the keys dangling in the ignition. They weren't. Nor were they on the seat. I tried not to look furtive, sure someone would think I was stealing the truck. I wondered whether to call our friends Louis and Wendy and ask them to drive a half hour to get us and drive us more than a half hour home before returning to their house by which time it would be way past all our bedtimes.

"The key's in the truck." I hadn't seen the young man walking by on the street. I actually heard what he said but it didn't make sense, I thought I'd misunderstood. How would he know the key was in the truck unless he had also cupped his face and peered inside? And why would he have done that except for some sinister reason? And if he was up to no good, why would he announce to me that he'd seen the keys in the truck?

"What?" I asked, as if I hadn't heard; he was already several steps beyond.

He stopped and turned back toward me. "Is that your truck?" I figured he'd been watching me and thought I was trying to steal it, but by now I was desperate and out of options and beyond my usual preoccupation with what someone is going to think of me. (I'm the guy who would leave the table in a restaurant and choke to death in the men's room rather than make those grotesque gestures and have someone do the Heimlich on me right there in front of everyone, maybe exploding the offending object across the room, or worse, vomiting the way George Bush did at the state dinner in Tokyo as he slid beneath the table. I mean, holy shit, who wouldn't rather die than do that?)

"Yes," I answered, "it's my truck."

"Key's in the door," he said and kept walking. I turned back to the truck and sure enough the key with the black plastic top was in the door lock and the highly visible white tag with the blue lettering from Rountree Motors was dangling from the chain. I was so happy and relieved that I let go for a moment of my embarrassment and chagrin that I could have had such an unguarded, unconscious moment, and of my wonder at how many other such moments I may have had that same day and never knew it.

And of what danger I may be putting myself and others in by being only semi-aware of my surroundings, and is this progressive, will I tomorrow or next month forget, not just the keys but the way home?

My mother admitted to me once that she was afraid driving to the grocery store, two blocks from her condo, not only because she had to make a left turn across traffic, but because she got scared every time she went that this would be the time she would get back into her car in the parking lot and have no idea how to get home.

Once several years ago I was driving the back way to the San Diego airport and came to an intersection and drew a blank. My heart raced, a drop of sweat rolled down my side and I suddenly developed a splitting headache. Lacey was in the car and, as I sat at the wheel, immobilized, she asked me what I was doing.

"I have no fucking idea!" I screamed at her. And I didn't. It was as if there was an air bubble in the line that goes to the part of the brain that has the direction sense. It's not the only time it's ever happened, but it is the only time I've suffered the embarrassment of having someone else witness it.

But this time, when I saw the truck key in the door, I was so happy I grabbed it, stuffed it into my pocket, looked up at the guy now nearly a block away and managed to choke out, "Thank you." I doubt he heard me.

The walk back to the theater was downhill all the way. The remainder of the movie was far less upsetting than the first 40 minutes had been even though several good looking people betrayed each other and some of them died gruesome deaths.

When we walked out of the theater it was 9pm and still light enough so I didn't turn on the truck's headlights until we got on the dirt road under the heavy tree canopy. I never get used to it, how late it stays light this time of year and the array of different greens in the woods as the light fades. I wish summer would last forever.

III

Poetry

EX NIHILO

An ode to the Moore Free Library

On its Centennial

In September of 1998 I sent this poem in response to an ad
that appeared on the bulletin board of our general store in
Vermont, inviting poems to mark the centennial of the
Moore Free Library in Townsend, Vermont. It won the grand
prize.

He borrowed his words with care
Hungry to create
not merely emulate
while
Standing onshore
breathing unfiltered
air.

Six times before, he'd ventured here
partnering with God
the works of creation
while Noah's passengers looked on
bemused.

Now he's certain he's gained his legs
and
can stomp the slithering serpent
into
submission.

"Let us make one like us,"
the lesser gods slyly
tempted
God
Who thought it great sport to fashion a
speaking , reading, writing
beast
who, despite these impressive tricks was
nonetheless
beast.

Now your library
among the artifacts of the period
called
Homo Erectus
(sapiens no longer)
stands
Witness to the brief geologic moment
in which
the weights and measures of physics
the forces of gravity and brevity
were thought to have been
repealed.

Creation Crowns
itself each aeon
with some One who fancies herself
central
irreplaceable
immortal
Divine.

This time the
Word made flesh
was It.

Your multi volume temple
protruding proudly
through
spider webbed
roach infested
worm aerated
forest,
speaks silently of
what
Was in the beginning
is now And will be
Forever.

A HAWK CRASHES

We built a new barn in Vermont in 1999, and to my horror,
discovered it is in the flight path of all sorts of birds. Even
now, four years later, birds still crash into it on their way to
feed on countless creatures that live in the pond beyond.

I

A smashing, crushing
explosion
against the highest window in the new
barn.

The red tailed
hawk
had been
eating organs
obeying instinct
feeding on the field
mouse
when I came through the cellar
door
and startled it.

Like a frightened
sparrow
my heart fluttered in
surprise as the noble hunter
bird

wildly thrashed its serrated
wings
to rise above danger
me.

My eyes couldn't
focus fast
enough to see what raised the
pressure in this micro weather
system
low altitude turbulence turning
its meal and my
measured moment into desperate doomsday
flight.

II

Its path passed between the sun and
me
instant eclipse and
crashed crushed
without braking, into the highest pane.

Rushing toward the
sound still not knowing
I found a chaos of fluttering
feather
and talon.

Frightened, I fled and
watched horrified
the hawk wildly flapped feathers furiously, furtively
flying but the
hawk's head twisted at a horrific
angle
made clear he'd never fly again.

I scanned the garage for some
weapon to
finish the wounded warrior, and
he struggled one last mighty
spasm, shuddered
then gave up the
ghost.

In awe I
approached the great still
beast afraid equally that he might still be
alive
and that he could not
be.

QUARTER HOUR

Thanksgiving 2000

Last night's
dream
probed an old awe.

I'd been sentenced to
death
for what I don't know
(but you who know me will understand when I say it was no
injustice)

I was being led to the execution chamber by a dispassionate
guard
Lacey walked alongside
her affect resolute
I would have thought I'd want her to be more
distressed
but I felt instead oddly comforted by her
intrepid
restrained compassion

We three walked the hall in silence until I asked,
When we reach the chamber, can you say how long it will be
until
(I recall a big pause here)
the lethal injection?

15 minutes, he said clearly with no
hesitation
I wished I hadn't asked or he hadn't answered so
certainly
Now I knew without
doubt
in 1/4 hour I'd be
dead.

My heart pounded, I felt the
blood
rush to my face
Would my knees buckle?
Lacey let me spend the moment
then took my hand but the familiar feel of her
flesh
was eclipsed by an old affair, whether it's OK to
die
when it's time
Whether what sprung from
seeming stillness
a scant six decades
ago
can be counted on to conduct
a quickened quark
to its succeeding
station

Has this dream sprung from my fecund
prayers for
Love
money

kids
time
health
leaving me at last with
me?

Wherever you go, promised the Zen master,
there you
are.

Dreams dreamed and, miraculously,
savored,
turn over
ground
left untilled until
the garden's guardian, sword aflame
unearths the answer as if you actually meant to ask
the question

15 minutes.

ADMIT IT

2001

Admit it
demands the double page glossy New Yorker ad
You're rich
defying the dusty taboo
a day late and a dollar short.
Unsightly embarrassment the stuffy
New York Trust
gray beards
craving to boogie with the
Boomers.

Yesterday another boy
fired on friends in one of our schools
while for that day we averted rolling
blackouts
and the white-knuckle holdout Dow clawed clear, barely, of
Bear terr
       I
          tory.

Admit it? OK, admits the
boy
who fired.
OK, the analyst accused of knowing
nothing about what

makes a market
rise or fall
admits, I don't know what makes a
market
or a boy
fire.

Rich? OK, I admit it, I
suppose
for the fleeting flattering fantasy
New York Trusting moment
I admit to believing being rich would
guard me sleeping and watch me waking
so the boy could never ever harm nor be
my child.

THREE SCORE
AND THEN SOME

May 2000

Sometime
a decade or so ago I
noticed I wasn't so strong or
supple
as I once was. I have no
idea
whether there was something special that woke my
awareness
or was it gentle, gradual and one day I saw it?

I once believed I'd be smarter when my body
began
to check out
you know, compensation, but I don't think
so.
Wiser? Maybe, if you believe there is
such a thing, and it's
not just another of our brainchildren to soften the
blow
when we're sliding
losing our grip on the
Darwinian edge
we once thought we'd firmly grasped for
good.

I reckoned how old I was when my
Dad
was my age.
33 and thought I'd slipped over the edge by
then. I was straddling more than one chasm,
hating the Vietnam
war
and I was pastor in a parish filled with super
patriots who hated my long curly
hair and bell bottoms as much as my politics.
At least that's the excuse I used for why they froze
me out.

Walter Reed was on my beat
for a while
I got to know one guy, about my
age
who'd taken a 30 caliber round in the
forehead
and lived
sort of, they'd screw another metal plate to his
skull
until the bone frizzled and they'd do it again but
they were running out of skull, getting close to his
brain.
He'd sit on the big Walter Reed lawn and talk of an afternoon
with the guy
who had no
arms or
legs
They kept telling him how lucky he was to have been in Nam
where the choppers got
you out in minutes.

My office looked over
Lafayette Park across the street from the
White House.
I could see into the park from my
second story perch over the fence that
President Nixon
had built to curb protest, the fence covered with anti-war
graffiti.
At a demonstration one morning a lovely long-haired
lady said to me, "If Nixon had to come out in the
morning and sit astride a bucket in Lafayette Park and do his
business
the war would be over that day." The guy with no arms
or legs
was the waste product The President managed to eliminate
in private.

I'm well past
mid life now
grousing
with old friends
about how they changed all the
rules
while we were in mid
stream until
our revolution swallowed its tail and vomited out
us.

The 60s, they now say, was about
sex
about whether the Victorian rules had finally lost their
grip
on us. But I'd say it was about what every age is about
desperation
the awful discovery that no one is in

charge
and no one knows how things will come
out
and perhaps Freud, discredited as he is, was right about
God
and how we invent God and project onto
(H)im
what we wish but can't win for ourselves.

We did
therapy
and then
divorced
and had our adolescent thrills in our 30s. We thought it right
that
our kids would be more like the rest of the
world
what with double-digit inflation and flat
wages and Arab oil
would live less like royalty than we
had.
We didn't yet know about
Ronald Reagan and
Hollywood neo-conservatism, the religious
Right nor
Gorbachev and the
evil empire gone belly
up leaving the stars and
stripes the only game in town, free to plunder the
world
and in the holy name of free
enterprise fashion our kids into zillion
aires.

Sometime a decade or less ago
I
discovered that whether Ron or George or his son W. or even our
sexy 60s
soul mate
Bill
holds the frenzied focus things unfold and cells keep
aging
their borders blurring, their nucleus softening
beguiling boundaries believed
to mark us off not only from the lesser
hemisphere but from
simpler soulless species
who walk this Way
with our forbearance.

Perhaps it's so the
Center
cannot hold
or perhaps its that the
Center
shifts as cells mutate and once neglected
ganglia gain new purpose as our sweet sister
Death
rolls her tongue around our inner
ear, coos her
siren song enticing us to
turn
into her embrace
finishing soul's longing,
waiving willful work in favor of effortless
ecstasy.

LENT 2K

Ash Wednesday

I

I saw my first ashes
Robert's "cremains"
in November 1964, a year or so
before boxes started arriving
wholesale from balmy
tropical south
east Asia.

I'd known the
guy a
little. Startled me. Thought
I saw a knuckle or
maybe
the round piece that hinges the elbow. I
broke that one playing
football
when I was 9.

"They're like the
ashes
you spread on roses," the undertaker said.
Not these. They're bones
parts of
Robert I can make
out.

II

Then there was
Ossie's
ashes.

Last time I saw Ossie
intact he
was in intensive
care. "Unresponsive," so
they said.
I whispered into his ear,
"Ossie, it's me,
Blayney."

His brow
furrowed, head shifted left
eye opened a narrow
slit
pupil fixed, staring straight
ahead.

"You need to take down those
goddam
trees beside your house,"
Ossie said, clear as
that, "they've grown too tall."

Last words. A week
later
on a tug off Martha's
Vineyard with Ossie's widow and four
big sons, all in oilskin
souwesters, driving, slanting, stinging rain,

blowing like
stink
we tossed Ossie's ashes overboard
just
as the wind shifted and inhaled
Ossie.

III

Remember O
wo/man
dust thou
art.

Fat Tuesday night we sang
"Carne vale." The
flesh
fled our bones,
our bones
burned to
ash
mingled
with the dirt and
disappeared to
dust.

Good News.
In the past 35
years
they've radically upgraded our
cremains
crushing them to fine
powder. No more
knuckles and no less
dead.

CANADA GEESE

June 2000

Canada
Geese mate for
life unlike many of
us
who part
painfully still in the
quick.
But when the geese
grease
golf greens our family
values
can be moderated to
include
a little
culling.

Perhaps that's what separates us from
geese
this ability we have to
rearrange
the decisions we make about what we
prize
so the inconveniences can be
annulled.

Last fall we gave
permission
for some young hunters to shoot
the geese on our
pond.
I'd forgotten the
conversation until I
woke
one morning to the sound of gun
fire and rushed to the porch in time
to see
the bird
struggling, flapping its
wings wildly in water until the dreadful
denouement.

Later
that same
day
I watched a goose circle the pond in a sad
salute
and remembered why
we leave ourselves an open
exit.

CHIPMUNK

June 2000

the chipmunk that
moments before fussed our
sentry terrier
into ratter frenzy by
shinnying up the bird
feeder pole,
now on
the road
smushed in shocking
splay of slippery sanguine, her
perfectly packed
organs dis
organized by the bite of the speeding
ambulance.

DEAD SERIOUS

December 2001

He'd had, he said, a rollicking affair with
death
playing
dead
he'd stretch out solemn
still
soft focusing his eyes so they stared without
seeing
He'd want you to think he found it
funny
teasing death
but like some other slices
of his life he wished us to
suppose
he could be cavalier about, about dying he was surprisingly
serious
dead serious.

DISSING BILL

January 2000

I

It's happening.

Principle

trumping expediency.

Papa used to call this
Spitting in the eyes of the

gods.

I never
Imagined it would look like
This.

George Wallace, sloe-eyed cynic in the
Schoolhouse door
Made me march.

When LBJ pretended Viet Nam was
A noble cause,
It brought me out

again.

Yes, I was young and
                                Righteous.
But in truth it was good
Fun
Then.

Taunting Nixon was a game.

Now the righteous seem
Grim and
                                Mean.

Were we?
No doubt.

II

Henry Hyde Hates Hilary
And Bill.

                                Why?

Did I hate Lyndon, George, Robert
McNamara? Tricky
                                Dick?

I fear I
Did.

I named them
Hypocrite, cynical opportunist
                                Unprincipled.
I hardly blushed
Then.

III

I like Bill. I wonder

                    Why?

He softens my
Shame and regret
That I'm not so tough and

                    Aloof

As we guys are meant
To be.

He's a
Poor pretender
Willfully wooing women like the longing lost half of his own
                              Soul.

Bill's principles perish before his hungry hunt for
                              soul.

Won't he ever learn?

I pray not.

God love his lonely lovely lost
                    Soul.

ELECTION YEAR EGO

August 2000

Last night
while Dick Cheney
was explaining to me the
moral difference
between W and Bill
(I can't seem to work up any affection for W)
I switched to "Being John Malkovich" and
got it
that the only sure way to
engage
anything or anyone
is from the safety of someone else's
body.

When it's just
me
in there
ego flapping in the breeze all naked and
exposed
it's John Philip Sousa 4th of July noisy fire colors popping
exciting distracting heart thumping then
eerie awkward after-the-storm
calm. And before you
know it
I'm on the prowl again for
entertainment.

This morning
while inhabiting the NPR body
I heard the
PT Cruiser
this year's sub for a sexy candidate
described as
Bonnie & Clyde machine gun gangster tough on the
outside
and pussy soft sweet plush pleasure on the
inside
A frame fit for
us to inhabit
this asset fat issue lean nervous making election
year.

W
must have thought we'd feel
more snug in Cheney's
stolid aging Gulf warred daddy's defense chief suited
body
But did he wonder why we wouldn't
junk
Bill's cruiser cush tush thirsty round
heeled body
and will Al
Gore bore
us with another somber suit to
stare from, an Alan
Greenspan
to warn the party's nearly over?

What we'll consider these next few months
from inside Pat
Buchanan's bruising
assault
on all that is not true
blue, red & white, Ralph
Nader's apocalyptic apoplexy, Al
Gore's grisly tedium, and W's
reborn Ranger suit
is in whose
skin
we'll watch the world to try to
quell our naked knowledge that they
nor us
have clue
one
and even being John Malkovich doesn't make me
God.

EVOLUTIONARY ENIGMA

April 2001

If you're under 50, you may wish to watch this
over my shoulder,   as
it's about the experiment   beyond
genetic striving,
a recent evolutionary enigma.

This morning I woke in a pool of
euphoria
and spent the day parsing its pieces
Crouching Tiger,   Hidden Dragon,
Mary Oliver's poetry
Marty Levin's long life
Sylvia's shoulds   and
classmates minor memories   morphed
into unexpected ecstasy.

Crouching Tiger tendered freedom from gravity's
weight   for   enchanting
people   bounding   over   roof
                              tops
            skipping cross water like a dragonfly
         never breaking surface tension, rising, soaring
         like Mary Oliver's verse, risking routes too

remote

to chart,   like
cells that outlive DNA's demands.

My friend Marty the raucous Rabbi, steadfast through thick
and thin
especially thin when lymphoma
stalked him like the luminary he
is.   And these years
later, his cancer quiet, life lately sweet
Marty gulps each instant whole, famished for what he always
craved   and still can't quite
taste. I'm leaving the pulpit, he told me, his eyes bright as
stars, and I want to talk to you about how you choose when
each morning you wake is
yours. Marty and I were ravishing Crown Books'
going-out-of-business Sale
His market basket bore books, 45 lbs. I'm dying, he said, of
curiosity since
cancer couldn't kill me. I'm ready to be reborn, and

solo

he uttered irrationally   exuberant.

My sister Sylvia says since 60 she hasn't any longer
time
for obligation's oughts because her
heart's desires deserve her
prize energy. And she gives it to them.

Classmates from
forty
years before in late life e-conversation confess clandestine in-

discretions
that could have done them
in, and now are more memorably etched than
prizes or honors. What we feared if found would
ruin us
has become best, bridging
distance
enticing us into intimacy we never knew we lacked or
wanted.

Lest this 60s sentiment seduce
you,
we who unwittingly encounter these
odd events form an
evolutionary enigma,   anomalies
graybeards beyond the bounds of
genetic gain.
And because biological experiments almost always
abort, why not
defy   gravity
flip off the free market
test Grace?

We're warned we'll break the social security/medicare
bank. Perhaps
but more likely,
our scattered cells will watch the way
we exploded orthodoxy
precariously perched on the precipice of
existence
when we passed from purpose into
fancy.

What, after all, have we to lose? After a long
life a little last
gasp
we never
bargained for
bursting with God-only-knows
what
pregnant possibility.

We can't go wrong, not now. We've
burst the boundaries
we once assumed defined the canopy.
We rode the tiger striped with fears and
phobia
that turned, if not tame, at least to terror
we learned to live and
die with.

WHO'S AFRAID OF
THE BIG BAD. . . ?

September 28, 2001

Two weeks after the terrorist attacks

Fear can cause a curious
commotion.
Though it provokes certain symptoms
nausea
headache, sweaty palms and arm
pits,
it doesn't have its own well-defined, clearly recognized
character.
Not like pain from a wound or accident, or
weariness
after hard work or exercise,
depression
driven by loss or sickness or the unkind
edge
of reality wedge
ing aside illusion.

More like an inner
ear
infection disturbing balance, blurred or tunnel
vision
suggesting the need for new
eye
glasses.

Fear that clings, that doesn't
dissipate
with the
danger,
the near collision, the stock
market's dizzying descent,
doctor's lingering look at that
mole,
her furrowed brow as she returns the stethoscope to the same
spot for a
third time;
Long breath, now let it out slowly . . .
When the fear lingers, begins to
gnaw
then rouse
anger
the body signals its
desire
to . . . to what? Sleep, flee, defecate, die, lash out, placate, hide,
confront,
go to the movies?
Whatever will shift the mix, for the moment,
geld the
beast.

Chronic fear, is, I think,
peculiar
to our kind. Our evolutionary kin can call up
adrenaline
in the instant, and if he doesn't die,
release it.
Do Impala suffer
headache, nervous nausea, heart
burn?
Does chronic fatigue make a monkey
impotent?

Perhaps there is some as yet
undiscovered
gain for us in this relentless
anguish.
But I suspect Gautama got it right that this
suffering
is meant to be our hedge against
abyss,
refusing reassurance
that reality is ample,
ego's pointless pursuit of personal
perfection,
forever
fueling fear.

FEELINGS

October 12, 2001

A month after the terrorist attacks

I spent thousands of hours and thousands of dollars
learning to identify and respect my
feelings.
I am male, tutored to ignore or override
feelings
so I hired a feeling professional
to help me retool
and I got the hang of it.
Now that I'm a facile
feeler
the next useful skill would be handling that dazzling array of
feelings
like a set of wood worker's tools
handy to be familiar with and to know
when to use which.

A bright young woman described her
feelings
in the month since America's gyroscope turned topsy.
I know myself, I can sustain fear only so long. Then,
if the issue remains unresolved, I gradually drift into
depression.
I told her I thought she summed up the national mood.

The President says go see a movie, have
fun.
The top cop says stay alert,
death
is a mere breath away
as it was in the beginning, is now and ever shall be.

Unfocused feelings infect us, mold us into
victims.
12 steps, our national pastime, makes hay with my
lust
for anything that will turn my
fear, rage, hurt, anxiety, helplessness, despair
into
hope, excitement, optimism, passion, purpose.

What's real here is both the
feelings
and the craving to shape them, inhibit the Seratonin uptake
so my cerebellum swims
serenely
in sweet sauces.
In this engagement with
terror
we will first face our fondness for
feelings
that assuage and our intolerance for
feelings
that tighten in us.
The only advantage of terrorism is our unwillingness to sit with
feelings
that trouble us.
Once we face again what we have always secretly known, that
those
feelings

are precise predictors of what will one day befall us,
just as the
feelings
we prize predict possibilities in the meantime, we come
alive
no longer insatiably hunting happiness but savoring seratonin
when we taste it
and marveling that for this one day more, for better and for
worse, we do have
feelings.

HEINZ PAGELS' SONG

November 1999

The late physicist, Heinz Pagels, believed that quantum physics is a kind of code that interconnects everything in the universe including the physical basis of life itself. In his book The Cosmic Code, Pagels, an ardent mountain climber, wrote, "I often dream about falling. Such dreams are commonplace to the ambitions of those who climb mountains. Lately I dreamed I was clutching the face of a rock but it would not hold. Gravel gave way. I grasped for a shrub but it pulled loose. And in cold terror I fell into the abyss. Suddenly I realized that my fall is relative; that there is no bottom and no end. A feeling of pleasure overcame me. I realized that what I embodied, the principle of life, cannot be destroyed. It is written into the cosmic code, in the order of the universe. As I continued to fall in the dark void embraced by the vault of the heavens I sang to the beauty of the stars and made my peace with the darkness."

Heinz Pagels was killed in a climbing accident in 1988.

I

F
  a
   ll
    ing. Into
N O T H I N G
        Heinz'
        heart went cold with fear,
his brittle being, hurtling headlong
into the
           abyss.

He tenses for hitting   bottom,
his soft cells smushing
into oblivion

        s p
       ou

II

Until he sees
the descent describes not
dissolution but
ecstasy. A taste of the topless
bottomless surprise that
quickened atoms discern and doubt
don't   trust.
A weightless timeless turn through
space   inscribing
         indelible
code in every cell.

Heinz starts to sing with

abandon.

III

Heinz' song's
heard cross the Millennial
marker.

Siren, mating, marking, mocking
song.
Daring, inviting, urging, demanding
predicting we, too will wed
    the
       p
       l
        u
         n
          g
          e
into   ecstacy.

HOLY NIGHT

December 2000

Compassion
is hard to learn
dangerous
comfort

That guy
I see every morning his
torn tennis shoes taped to his oozing
feet
picking garbage
he's watching me
pondering
as I bend low to tend my terrier's
turd
how it is we're both bound to
George W and Al, The Chief Justice and this Gross
Domestic Product

Where did you sleep last
night Mr
Garbage Picker, Al, George W, Mr. Justice Rehnquist, Blayney,
my sweet
children
and which unpolished piece of our welded together

lives
disturbed your dreams demanding we
waive
yet one more parochial border we'd counted on to
shelter
us?

IF YOU WANT MORE

If you want
more
you better
die
because this is all there is

here.

LABORING FOR THE CLICK

by Blayney Colmore

I

Work
God's curse. Why didn't we
linger
in the amiable innocent
forgiving forest
instead of lusting after the
beguiling click in
the head?

Flogging Fuller
Brushes in Brookline 40 years ago
("not another goy with a free gift,"
the lady teased when I rang her bell).
Saying Mass, preaching
presiding over mating and mortality, my work
for a trial 2/3rds of my
life, chasing the click.

II

I quit. Retired. Wooed the click without
work.

I carried this
picture
in my head of
how it
Was in the beginning, is now and will be forever
but never seems
quite.
Green garden without snake or Eve
offering me the
skinny on
life.

Click. Uncommonly the
click.
Deep drag of dope
lost in prayer
swimming into the zone
sitting Zen meditation.
Dreaming. Coming. The click. Damned, longed-for
click.

III

Click. A gate
opening? Molten metal
cooling quickly? Angel snuffing out his flaming
sword to welcome me west of
Eden
again for
the first time?

Mocking Yankee hard
head work ethic I wooed
The click in
nothingness, in silent

sitting. Nothing came and
dismal depression garbled every
sense
except a still small sometime seemingly random
click.

Who dares stand
idle on the harvest plain
while all around them waves the golden
grain? If you hope to have the
click.

I dared,
terrorizing
myself, praying the click would work,
release
me. Usher me into
Eden.

IV

It will. Soon I'll refund God's gift
greedily suck it in, then give it up
quit this work, too
exhale with no thought of another
inhale
release the final breath.

Perhaps you'll hear the rattle
click, click
        click
            click

Perhaps not.

MARTIN LUTHER KING, JR.
2002

Free at last, free at last, thank God Almighty, I am
free at last.
And he really seemed to be.
Mine eyes have seen the glory. And you believed he had.
I may not get to the Promised Land with you. You wonder if he
knew
that night. It wasn't the first time he had faced
death.
A garbage strike. Imagine risking your
life for
garbage collectors? In Memphis?

You know where Jesus was
assassinated? On a
garbage dump. Gehenna. Where they chucked what was
no longer needed or too
putrid
to let rot inside the city walls.

When I lived in the Philippines I saw people's homes on the
garbage dump.
Even though I had grown up in the American south, with grimy
colored sections
that embarrassed me to think
Gertrude lived there,
I had never seen anything like those
naked children
picking at garbage.

Until today I hadn't considered a connection between
garbage
and freedom.
Seems like freedom would be leaving
garbage
behind. Leaving it for others to deal with.

The only time I ever saw
Dr. King
I was surprised at how short
he was
ordinary seeming, wearing a hat like my father wore to work.
His suit was rumpled and he never so much as cracked a
smile.
A woman standing in the crowd, next to me,
while Dr. King spoke, startled me
spat suddenly
on the ground and muttered
"garbage".

Garbage
is what I heard someone call our new enemies
now the word reverberated, ricocheted inside me
like a forgotten trauma triggered under
anaesthesia.

One man's trash, garbage, they say, is another man's
treasure.

Freedom, the treasure for which we say are struggling against the
forces of darkness
I learned from
Martin Luther King, Jr.
requires our engaging
garbage
we thought we'd never again need to consider.

So this becomes a time to go on high
alert,
not just for those who wish us ill,
but for many we mistakenly mark as
garbage
and in whom Martin, American
martyr
insisted, God sows the surprising, unsuspected seeds of
our
freedom.

MASS

I

Atoms
impulses, ions
charged particles steaming
incandescent like dry
ice
lighting an odd
design across the CT
scan while I felt no
thing except a formal
fear.

Purple dye
probing imposter
pulsating pretending to
be my
blood, searching arterial paths that
feed the greedy untrained offending
organ.

A mass they
said.
Hell, I'd said Mass
hoping
to feed the gods so
they
would never feed on
me.

Yet now they've come for
me.
Visiting these seasoned
cells with unaccustomed
vigor
issuing invitation to brand
new
organs to dine
before this
compost spends its final
feast.

II

"We could excise
it," they pledged
"though that may excite the anger of the
blood
and cause a
flood
of cells to storm your walls."

Or radiate or
poison
you
with peculiar chemicals designed to
execute the new
organ shortly
before it corrupts
you.

How about planting radium
seeds
perennials that grow a
plant more lethal to the
young guest than to the
ripening host?

Or wait

and see
what might   h
            app
                 en
then.

III

Perhaps we need to check
again
to see
if what we
found is what we
thought.

The vandal at the
gate come to cheat
the chosen
of his
promised prize?

Or

post
modern form
less
new life
the mass we dread
knowing it comes to make
good
on the promised new
life for which we pray and long
but cannot
bear?

ME & MY SHADOW

A glimpse
     of dark
               ness
darting
          under and
around   illuminating
        my worst
primeval
                         Fear.

I thought I'd out
                    smarted the
smarmy   shadow.   And there it
was.

You know what's
               smarter
       than   my
            sneaky
            shadow?
Nothing.   Absolutely
          fucking
          Nothing!

MICE IN THE HOUSE

October 2001

Rodents reinvaded the house
one wet night a
few weeks ago.
I heard them
running, nesting in the walls.
The hair stood up on the back of
my neck. Then
Indian summer intervened and the rodents must have been
content
to forage in the fields for another fortnight, so I
forgot
my phobia for foreigners, feeling
comfortable, unconcerned
at home.

Last night the temperature plummeted
and the little
devils
again breached my walls,
made their way back into their lair,
industrious claws within walls
kitchen closet on one side, keeping-room on the
other.

"Holy Jesus!" I shouted
stirring at last the aging deaf Terrier,
"listen to that racket." She couldn't and
the cat,
lacking some genetic part,
regards rodents as sometime
sport,
yawned and stretched.

My Vermont neighbors remind me every year this is
customary.
When the flurries fly, we fly, too, to California, and the rodents
run for cover.
My neighbors are too mannerly to say what I
suspect, secretly they think
the rodents' routine
revolves
around some ancient awareness
ingenious evolutionary
inclination that serves them at least as well as my
migration
serves me.

Each fall in the weeks before we leave I
litter the attic and basement with traps, even
de-con
carrying corpses to the compost
feeding my
fantasy
of fastening my house.

What upsets me so about some
mice
making my home theirs
I cannot say exactly.
In proper perspective I suppose you'd have to call it the other
way; we made their home ours. For a while.
When we
with geese and finches
migrate back to Vermont, the ice is off the pond, the
beaver busy
jonquils
are already mostly mulch, lilacs likely
blooming
cows turned out to dance in spring sun
and the rodents
gone from our walls to the fields
to take their
chances
with the golden eagle.

ON THE EDGE

An Ode to the Museum of

Contemporary Art San Diego

I

Balanced on the Pacific rim
solid rock or shifting sand?
Forever or a spell?
We won't know in our brief
span.

II

Gotham graffiti on the foyer wall greets
skeptical fourth graders.
"That's not art," I heard a fleshy bespectacled boy
protest. "I could do
that."

High tides spray through
Irwin's breathtaking air
holes.

Plastic, punch out
ready to assemble
crucifix,

Jesus' parts (yes, all his parts)
the spikes and crown of
thorns
waiting to be broken
free and
assembled into the west's millennial
sign
of grace and gruesome
violence.

Zuang Huan
robed in rib-
cage of pork and
calligraphy
making sport of our narrow picture of
Communist China's creative courage.

5x5 squares of human hues
25 museum trustees'
pigments
so similar and so subtly
not the same at
all.

Spray gun mounted on the wall above the
surf,
mingling afta shave with
ocean aroma.

Kenyan's light
hearted picture of American
gravitas
Bill & Monica
cavorting before the whole world, even
Africa.

III

And on her seaward outside
wall
the tall ship lists beneath the ambiguous
Brave Men Run In My Family.

"Not art,"
pronounced the boy, "I could do it
myself.

But will he?

1999

MY WIFE'S MOTHER
& ZIMBABWE

I

Her breath's ferried through a
tracheotomy
supper through a feeding
tube for
this proud lady who
furnished her
uterus and her life
for my wife and her sisters on their way
from dots to awesome
women.

Not that she had no
life
of her own. She did, plenty. We all thought
she'd refuse to go on
when it came to
this.
But she hasn't. She writes
notes
in strong clear legible hand. "You look

thin" she writes when my wife walks into
her room. "They haven't brought me anything to
eat," her pen
complains. "They feed you through that
tube, Mom."
Her eyebrows lift in wonder, then her face
scrunches
as if she's tasted something
bitter.

"Bring my lipstick." She writes and reaching round
the plastic tubes she scores a startling slash on lips that no
longer
eat nor speak, in
seasoned skin embracing an intact
woman who refuses to
leave.

II

They're rioting in
Africa
sang the satirical 60s song.
Now it's our friends edging into eclipse on the dark
continent
We beg them to leave
But they don't.

Same reason, I
guess
my wife's mother doesn't leave her
body
that's been home ninety years.

"We live today," our Africa friends explain, "not
knowing, clinging to God's
grace
for each breath. We're not sure that in your
comfortable country we'd remember. No offense." None
taken. Only awe.

60 seemed sufficient for learning my
limits
what works, what falls beyond
bounds.

The venerable lady's
lipstick
our bush friends' brutish brush with
grace
shreds again any sense of
certainty
that I know my end or what when it
comes
I'll choose.

May 2000

WATCHING KENNETH STARR TESTIFY

November 19, 1998

I

Armor eyes
piercing
adolescent offenses.

Catch me if you can.
He can.

Good Vs. Evil
Light & Dark
paper scissors rock.

But which,
I always wondered,
is which.
They seem intertwined
twinned.

II

For decades I suffered the angst of being found
                                        Out
the fear that I might
                Be

And one day I
        Was

A day when the dark went light and I stood
naked
        In
        The
            Blue
                Glare
of the surgeon's lamp
shadows exorcised.

III

Ken
the doll with the effaced groin, missing
Organs
No gonads

Elicits dread in
Me.

"Teaches Sunday School" the caption under his image on the
screen
warns.

"The facts suggest," he chants
And then recites the terrible secret we already

knew
And had decided,
because it seemed like handling a poisonous Viper,
to let lie
Still.

IV

Don't you wonder
Why
we
commission these Manichean Men
to patrol our shadows?

When
we know
their lonely laser will one day
curl its fibre optic
around the labile labyrinth and
finger
our feral hungering.

V

We fear our own
Primordial
Lust
more than we fear being put to
Shame.

So we send
Ken
to snare the snipe.

Hoping he'll be kept busy holding the
Bag
And he'll never notice us tip toe
Away.

We should have known that
Barbie's
flattened flank
Would one day
Enrage, frustrate and
frenzy
Ken.

And then
Ken
would come
for Us.

PEACE KEEPER

Kosovo

I heard we hit a train.
Or was it
a school?

Will we ever again, do you 'spose,
enjoy one of Stud's
Good Wars?

Remember when being
American
meant I Like
Ike?

It's a bitch being the
richest
most powerful, world's
cardinal actor.

That sailor kissing the bent-over-backward girl in
Times Square,
the noble-faced squire grieving FDR in
Warm Springs,
G.I.s handing Hershey
Bars on the
Champs Elysees,
made me like me.

Careful, my mother warned, what you
pray for.
The most powerful nation on earth, our mantra, became
our karma.

Communism collapsed and we had the most
toys. With which,
I heard we hit a train.
Or was it
a school?

1999

SDMCA: HARBORING LEVIATHANS

Yesterday, from the Museum library I looked out to
sea
and spied
a spout, a great grey going
south
to birth her baby behemoth in warmer water.
This shaky season in which our once
seemingly tranquil waters have been
so terribly troubled,
this lovely leviathan's calm confidence reassured me.

The Museum of Contemporary Art provides the perfect
point
from which to watch whales
and rightly so.

Scant seasons since the grey, near extinction, near us
stayed submerged
sensing danger, human harboring
disastrous dreams
of owning earth,
sky and
sea.

Looking back the other way, into the Museum's
gallant galleries,
harboring haunting
images challenging convention
inviting us to
wonder whether the world might work some other
way
than our callous custom calls
necessary, normal, inevitable,
orthodox,
makes me hope we, too, might one day dare to
show ourselves where
predators previously promised
peril.

SEATTLE'S 6.8

After Seattle's 6.8 earthquake in March 2001

The 6.8 sorely
shook and scarred but didn't sink
Seattle
Had it been here in southern California
our freeways would be pasta.
Seismologists say Seattle's event erupted 30 miles
down
while ours normally mash a mere 11 miles under
us.

I've been fretting over my
work,
these Notes
how deep they
reach.

Some days this
writing wreaks
a southern California quake
near the surface upsetting some seemingly
stable structures, but, really,
reducing to rubble what
we all already understood was chimera
shit
and were ready, rightly, to relinquish.

Seattle's shock provokes the grievous sort of
angst
signaling secrets embedded deep
beneath
consciousness
compromising crust
the suddenly permeable schist no longer sheltering soul's
awe.

Do I want to tear the
cover
from our conscious, exposing to the
light
what, preserved in cool, dark
hibernation,
laid bare may stink and rot and
ruin?

That's what I used to think
I wanted
to cause our chicken hearts to hearken
all the way
        down
           to
             the
                 deepest
descent
and measure
melancholy.

Seattle, not southern California shaking,
demands we play our hand.
The drawn-out deep convulsion provides unnerving duration
time enough to step deliberately down
into the dark
ness.

I haven't stomach
to promote that primal project.
When I write to you I trust you sense a southern California slip,
not Seattle
Relief, even if it is illusion
as you feel a familiar fragment of the fragile
crust
crumble to dust,
since, yes, it must
be rearranged.

But not to trouble
the
dislocation down
too
deep to depict
the shift that will not
quickly
crush us
no matter how much we wish it
would.

SEEMINGLY STURDY
SIGNS OF LIFE

Seemingly sturdy signs of life amidst frightening fugues of death
forward phony pheromones past nostrils seeking solace.
Entropy, ebbing energy courting cruel
chaos
causing chorus of
lament
for terrible knowledge of
what?

Lost love?
Broken marriage? Cruel, unjust grinding poverty?
Perhaps the glimpse of our inevitable
extinction
evoked by arrogant assholes
physicians, poseurs posturing as people perfecting
plague protection while
AIDS
has her way with
us.

Yesterday I went and watched a friend marry someone he'd
hardly
touched
nor she him
It felt like the purest moment
until I understood the purpose for their practice of such

purity
was their hope it might arouse the alchemy they wish would
transform their tinsel to treasure beyond
measure. How sad to suppose that purity provides power to
live.
The closest we come to purity is when we lie eerily still in
death. Purity is an impoverished strategy for living since living
leads to
another alchemy that
mixes mud and shit sometimes so we can never know
which when we
taste it. And we will
taste it.

The wonder is that when we do, the e-
coli comes to nothing since the purpose of pooping is to
eliminate impurity so my body can improve its chances of
perfecting my path to
perdition.

SKATE

Swimming in the
Pacific
is unlike bathing in the
Atlantic
except perhaps for the
Amniotic pleasure
vestigial memory
retro bursting bonds of being dirt
bound
slipping back to near zero
gravity
exciting synapses seemingly gone
out.
In that, being immersed in the Pacific is kin to Atlantic
bobbing
only Much More So.

For, that west Ocean's glassy surface shows me my
kin
shark, sea
lion, bottle
nosed dolphin
orange garibaldi
and the Skate that bore
the weight

of my evolved upright
Gravitas
as I was making, faking my vertebrate way
back from
2+land breather to
primitive plasma
longing to again float free
she
stung me.

TERRIER

Our tough tiny
terrier
turned twelve this
year
and hied herself a terrible
tumor
on her spleen.
She seemed not to trouble herself until
x-rays and ultrasounds, numbing sleep, surgery
sliced her
spleen disheartening for a
day
her vigil at the window waiting for some striped
rodent
to tread her turf.

Two years before she'd turned a
tumor on her teat
taking a
multiple mastectomy with the stoic
stance
her lineage required.
Turned out to
be
no tumor at all but a bot
fly burrowed in her belly nesting for
transformation.

She's 84 in dog
years
and she's got scars to show it. She still stalks
stone
walls
and hops on her hind
legs when food or friend excites some signal in her
unfiltered
by fear of being over eager or too in
love
with life.

TERRIER'S TIME

The spring sun finally burned through winter's fog, warming our
walk.
The dog seemed perkier, wanting to go
longer
than she'd been going these past few months. Her
13 years have deafened her and
slowed her step.

She spied the cookie lady
and sprinted to her eagerly accepting her morning
offering.
When we returned she
hurried
up the back stairs for her reward for coming
home.

She noisily lapped water, then turned to
scour
the floor for the tiny treats
The first one disappeared into her
mouth
and as she unreeled her tongue to take the other treat she
collapsed
onto her side
motionless,
still as, well, as
death.

Lacey dropped to the floor beside her and felt her
heart
beating
I laid my head flat next to hers and could see her eyes
moving
She twitched once, seemed to see us, tried without success to
gain her feet
heaved a heavy sigh and
rose
as if for
Easter
seeming solemn, slightly chagrined, surprised perhaps to find
herself with
us.

We've been abnormally
attentive
since, rubbing her stomach, telling her of our
unrequited
love.
So far,
though you can tell she finds it all a little much,
embarrassing
this living beyond dying, she's humored us, willing to
walk
and eat her treats as if none of us had
noticed.

WAITING AT AN INTERSECTION

After the Terrorist Attacks 2001

Waiting today at the long light, the big busy
intersection
Torrey Pines and La Jolla Shores Drive
a Mercedes silver SUV skulked into formation behind me
its hovering hood ornament an ironic reprise of a
sixties symbol for
peace. Or a middle finger to Mercedes magnates.
I Sized up its occupants in my mirror
007 like.
At the helm a swarthy broad shouldered man, maybe American,
maybe middle
eastern
could have been wearing a winter tan. He seemed somehow
sinister, fiercely focused deep
set eyes, staring straight ahead, three day stubble, dark
mustache, salt and pepper buzz
cut. I thought he caught
my eye in my mirror and I darted my eyes here and there as if I
had all along been sweeping my surroundings. I looked again
and he was speaking to his fair passenger, California blue-eyed
blond, Armani silk scarf around her neck.
His mouth barely opened as he spoke,
his chin chopping his words.

She neither looked at him nor replied
her face composed in that seemingly unconcerned,
slightly bored 1940s gun moll
manner.

Being on Ashcroft Advent alert, I wondered whether these two
were
alert, too, to me, alert to them, and whether I would be able
pick them out
of pictures provided by police. Or prophet.
Perhaps.

At the green light I drove straight, they turned left.
At the next light a long limo with one way glass pulled
alongside
and I considered in the
black glass
my reflection.

Silver swept back hair
tinted glasses
crew neck black sweater beneath Italian leather jacket
unshaven
deeply lined, weathered features, right eyelid oddly
menacingly drooped,
somewhat swarthier than Mercedes man
my mustache much
bigger, bushier
than his.

Behold, Mercedes man,
I saw you, did you see
me?

WHAT NOW, MY LOVE?

I

Ego must die for
You
to live
my Love.

So you will do the
Work, Love,
Yes?

Excuse me, were you
speaking to me?
I felt myself
stiffen and prepare to
resist,
the sure signal that I feel
under assault.

Defend, protect. But protect what?
Why, myself, my Love.
But what self am my
Protecting?
Why myself?

To live my Love I
must
surrender self and, with
                    Jesus
                            Buddha
                    Gandhi
                                King and
Bob Dole,

sweep clean
wide spaces fit for a
royal
presence.

II

So what now, my Love?

My body, and my 200K
Volvo
have mushy shocks.
They lean and groan into
turns
they only recently mastered
with elegant
ease.

The surrender tender, it seems, is being
sweetened.
Dreams of world-class achievement and
acclaim
diffused,
released to
                    Liddy
                Mary
                        Teresa and
Coretta Scott.

It's getting clearer that
no matter what
I do or
don't
The mileage will wear smooth the
tread and I will,
wearily, willingly,
with my
Volvo,
dress up a
barren bone yard, with my
skeletal sculpture of
             vaunted vintage.

III

Set me down easy,
Love.

The bees buzz about my ears.
Your invitation
echoes in my head, even while the temple's cooling,
my blood pooling in
elbows and heels.

Gehenna, eager ego's
resting place.
Scavenger dogs lick once longing
loins.
Feral cur fulfilling failed fantasy.

What now, my Love?

10,000 X 10,000
aeons of effort turned

to dust.
In the dust the storm stirs
the simple solemn secret
the muddy Mother of all
Egos.

1999

IV

Fiction/Short Story

FLASHER

I'm hung over, like I might throw up. Looking into the mirror I am startled to see myself in the round white collar, like a halo that slipped over my head. I should have been suspicious of my motives when, three years earlier, passing a common room in the hallway of my seminary dorm, I saw a guy a class above me, strutting in full vestments like a drag queen. A wave of nausea swept over me then, too.

The Dean, a hero of mine for his iconoclasm, happened by at that moment and read my response. "Makes you want to throw up, doesn't it?" he diagnosed prophetically.

Now, three years later, it's Ordination Day. June 12th, my agnostic mother's birthday. ("Charley," she said, "I think it's nice you've found something you seem to believe in.") Hot, humid, sultry Boston, no-spring, right-into-summer day. I'm trying to fasten my white linen collar for the first time. My hands shake. I finally get it buttoned and consider myself in the mirror. Oh my God, I look Bing-Crosby—perfect for the part. I feel crazy, an impostor.

At the big family party in the private dining room at Lochobers last night, with uncles, parents, sisters, a few friends, I was the awkward center. I felt like I was spiraling down an Alice-In-Wonderland tunnel. I got drunk and funny. I had a dreaming sensation, like driving slow motion into a wreck.

They fawned over me. "Can you imagine how proud Graddy would be?" How had I let myself be cast in the role of our grandfather, the dead patriarch? He died when I was 10. His portrait, in his Bishop's vestments, presided over many a family gathering. I wonder what he believed, or if he had any scarlet secrets?

I'd been ambivalent about the church and her pretensions of owning the truth from before seminary. Yet I was intoxicated by God-hunger and longing for some manageable way into the maelstrom which was burning the boundaries of every community and institution in American culture. The years were 1963 to 1966. The President was shot, Martin Luther King wrote his Letter to the offended southern pastors from the Birmingham jail, and a deputy sheriff gunned down a seminary classmate who was registering Negroes to vote in Loundes County, Alabama.

My role models were three. Our parish priest (we called them "ministers" then) from my childhood days in Charlotte, North Carolina, who punctured the piety of the people of Christ Church over and over until they drove him out.

And two young clerics, chaplains at my old boarding school. One a brilliant, erratic, to-the-manor born, hard-drinking man five years older than I, who sponsored the school's first black student and challenged the smug hierarchy of the place as only a rich, confident product of that environment could.

And his assistant, a man a couple of years older than I, gentle, brilliant, passionate, sardonic, and brave enough to ask awkward questions that could pry rich people's sons loose from their parents' smug assumptions.

I never quite slipped the sophomore questions about God and

Camus, and wondered what might become of me, the son of an IBM executive who believed Jesus and Karl Marx framed the agenda for our culture.

Two summers teaching in the summer session of that same boarding school persuaded me that I was no teacher, and provided me hours of hard drinking and rich conversation with the two chaplains. After a weekend visit with our now aging Charlotte pastor, I decided the church was the place in which intensity and necessity might work together. Perhaps as a parish priest, an identified eccentric in a sufficiently conventional setting, I might gain some integrity and also make a living, maybe even become a force for something useful.

Come June of my third year in seminary and time for ordination. I have been through Comprehensive Exams, a week of practical exams at the hands of the board of examining chaplains in my home diocese ("Mr. Danforth, would you tell us your view on angels?" "I'm so glad you asked. Don't you think it likely that, if there were another realm of being, it would be at least as complex as the realm about whose existence we have confidence?"). I have accepted a job as curate in a large church in Akron, Ohio (called "St. Harvey's In-the-Polo Field," by my classmates). And the date for my ordination has arrived.

June 12, 1966 ushers in Boston's first heat wave of the coming summer. My sweat is pouring down my face, stinging my eyes, moistening my new collar, a dark stain spreading across the belly of my black shirt. I am to ride the MTA from Harvard Square to Park Street to the Cathedral, need to leave in five minutes. I cannot bring myself to ride the subway in this Irish Catholic town, while I am displaying this starched collar. What if someone is dying and asks for a priest? Or a crazy person with that prescience they seem to have sees into my heart and knows what a fraud I am? What if someone asks me what the seven deadly sins are? Worse, what if I feel like I'm important and holy just because of this getup? Maybe I've already sold out.

Frantic, out of time and options, I rummage through my closet. My raincoat! It still has the heavy lining from the winter. I can't stop now to zip it out. It always gets stuck and I end up cursing, frustrated. I slip it on, button it all the way up, grateful the highest button covers the offending collar. I walk the four blocks to the subway, dripping wet, am nearly knocked over by the body odor as I enter the train, wonder how much of it is mine. I stand as far to one end of the car as I can, turned away from the other riders, facing into the window. I see my reflection, stiff, sweating. The car is full. Are these people really all looking at me?

"What must they think?" I wonder, as I step off at Park Street, knowing in some inchoate part of me that my life is forever altered. This self-consciousness will travel with me wherever I go. I catch one more fleeting reflection of myself in the window as the car pulls out of the station. I'd almost forgotten how absurd I look with the raincoat buttoned to my chin.

The two heavy-set, middle-aged women whose reflection I'd watched in the window, stare at me. As I run off the train towards the stairs leading up to street level and the Cathedral steps, I see them turn toward each other and begin to talk. In my head I create their conversation as the train pulls out of the station.

"Did you see that guy with his raincoat buttoned all the way up on this hot day?"

"I sure did. What do you suppose is up with him?"

"Hate to think. Seems like the world's full of creeps these days."

"So you think . . . he's a . . ."

"Of course. Why else would he button all the way up like that? Pervert! He's a flasher."

"I'm sure glad he didn't flash us!"

"Oh, I dunno, he looked kinda small and puny. We probably wouldn't even have noticed." Raucous laughter.

The conversation in my head is drowned out by the Bach fugue as I descend the stairs into the cathedral crypt to get vested for the service.

LOSING MY CHERRY . . .

One cold and rainy December night I lost my cherry, sort of, I guess, in downtown Charlotte, North Carolina, in a second floor walk-up hotel, in a ceremony ancient if not altogether honorable.

Though I'd thought endlessly about it, dreamed, lied, hoped and lost my nerve about it, I hadn't thought I might lose my virginity that Christmas vacation. I don't know when or how I thought it might happen, but certainly not like this. I'm not sure I was confident it ever would. I listened to my classmates' stories about their many sexual adventures, never considering that they might be lying, as I was when it came my time to pony up with my experiences.

I was 17, 17 and 1/2, going to turn 18 the following summer. This was my fourth year of boarding school. I had begun to feel like a freak. Especially because I'd lived in the Philippines since I was 11, where, I assured my awe struck friends, every sort of imaginable sexual pleasure was available to teen age Americans because we looked like full grown men to the diminutive hairless Filipinos.

So, terrified as I was of misreading a signal and making an unwelcome move, I hadn't yet so much as reached beneath a girl's blouse. I didn't feel a bit certain when we were locked in our drooling embrace, whether she realized what that was poking into her ("Are you falling for me, or are you carrying a knife?" didn't become a joke until much later), or whether those were her swelling breasts heaving into me, or my desperate wish. My shortness of breath was surely a dead giveaway of how out of control I was, but she seemed calm, quiet, so I worried that she wasn't as excited as I was.

Looking back, I can hardly believe I hadn't had an honest conversation about this with anyone by then, not my father, one of my sisters, my mother or a friend. But I hadn't. A woman I know once told me she asked her older sister, after coming home from a date with a boy whom she'd fended off when he reached for her breast; "Sally, is it ok to let a guy go for second base?" Her sister, may she have a star-studded throne in heaven for her kindness, replied,

"Oh hell yes, of course, it's just great. Enjoy it!"

Aside from a few furtive tongue thrusts accompanied by tentative swinging forward of my hips, my sexual experience was one-dimensional, airbrushed Playboy centerfolds with the stapled navels. My desire was clearly intact, but I could gain no picture of how to work out the fleshy particulars.

So when I boarded the train in New York for the overnight ride to Charlotte that December evening, my hopes were high as ever, but my expectation was that I would carry those hopes back for bleak, sunless and girl-less winter, still a virgin. And a disgrace.

The Winter Assemblies, dances to introduce young men and women to adult society, which to us meant drinking, smoking and sex, were held in a Junior League Hall on Morehead Street, the boundary of Charlotte's coiffed, tree-line residential streets, where the first doctors' offices and drive-in restaurants gave notice that you were about to enter the downtown. Downtown, where fathers' offices were, was shut tight after work hours, except, so I'd heard, for some sordid goings on, mostly in the colored section. This was 1957.

My grandparents were too old to cope with a libidinous 17 year old, but this was before the days of civilian jets, and a long expensive trip to the Philippines to be with my parents was out of the question, so I spent Christmas with them. Searching for some way to fill the fourteen nights of vacation, they signed me up for the Assemblies.

The afternoon of the first dance, I persuaded my older sister's boyfriend to buy me a pint of Bourbon which I transferred to a silver hip flask with a leather case. Armed with that courage and a pack of king size Pall Malls, I drove my grandparents' car to the dance. I hadn't lived in Charlotte since seventh grade, and the austerity of Yankee boarding life had done little to prepare me for the steamy throbbing crush of coed teen energy which had transformed the children with whom I'd gone to white glove dancing school in this same hall as a boy, into a stomping, shouting , libidinous mob.

"Poison ive-e-e-ey, poison ive-e-e-y, late at night while you're sleepin', poison ivey come a creepin' ..You're gonna need an ocean . . . of calamine lotion . . . Oh you can look, but you better not touch . . ." There's Leigh, the lovely little girl who dazzled me in sixth grade, head thrown back, eyes shut, hands in the air, pelvis thrust forward, shouting the song to the red-faced Morgan, already a budding version of his paunchy alcoholic father. Tommy was the first to greet me.

"Hey, Charley. Didn't know you were going to be here this Christmas!" Tommy's eyes were hooded, like he needed a good night's sleep. We were soon greeted by Courtney, then Rex as we formed a huddle in the middle of the pounding dance floor, shouting to make ourselves heard over the din.

The evening is punctuated by visits to the driveway behind the building where we guys assemble to sip from our flasks and blow smoke rings.

*   *   *

Tommy and I had drunk the pint of bourbon when we climbed into my grandmother's car to drive downtown. Tommy said that if I let him drink from my flask, he'd take me to a whorehouse. My energy was running out of control, so I had no sense of how drunk I was. I'd driven drunk before and the sensation was familiar, having to concentrate, staring at the center line, struggling to stay awake and keep some sense of how fast we were going. I thought I was doing pretty well, especially since I had to keep waking Tommy. I'd never been north of McDowell Street, and Tommy was becoming increasingly inarticulate and vague as we went along.

"Which way, Tommy?"

"Who gives a shit which way?"

"Come on, Tommy, get it together!"

Finally, after a couple of having to go back on our own tracks, Tommy yelled, "Pull over! Right here!"

"Where?"

"Here. Right here, goddamit!"

So I did, next to a ramshackle wood frame two story building. In front a nattily dressed black man, maybe 35, leaned against a light pole, watching us park.

"Wait here," Tommy commanded, as he emerged unsteadily from the car. He walked over to the man, talked a little, shook his head and came back, getting into the car.

"Let's go," he said.

"Whatdayou mean? What happened?"

"He wants $25. Way too much!"

By this time I'm frantic. "I've got $25, Tommy. Tell him 'OK'."

Tommy looks me over, his eyes now nearly invisible beneath his sinking eyelids. "You'd pay 25 bucks for a whore?"

I'm long beyond caring. "Yes."

"OK, it's your money. Give me the cash."

I do and he gets out of the car, says something to the man and motions to me to get out. The man opens the door of the building, revealing a dimly lighted stairway. Tommy and I follow him to the top where he goes through a door and gestures to a woman sitting behind a hotel lobby counter.

"Room 3," she motions me to a room down the hall. She looks bored. I feel excited, nervous, and still pretty drunk.

I walk down the hall, hesitate in front of room 3 and then knock.

"Come on in." I open the door and a white girl, no older than I am, is sitting on a chair on the far side of the little room at the foot of an iron poster bed. She's wearing a low cut dress, a flower print; the hemline reaches midway down her thigh. She's pretty, a little overweight. Her rouged cheeks make her look excited, and certainly, to me, exciting. She's barefoot. She looks me over and smiles.

I'm not sure what's supposed to happen next.

"Take off your pants," it sounds more like a suggestion than a command and I feel myself get aroused. I'm embarrassed to take off my pants and have her see I've got an erection. I must have stumbled.

"You're pretty drunk, huh? Here, let me help you." She takes my hand and leads me to the bed. I feel a rush of love for her, and of fear. I sit on the edge of the bed and she undoes my belt and unzips my fly. Am I supposed to touch her? Her perfume is strong, nice, and the heat of her cheek next to mine almost unbearably thrilling. The last person I remember undressing me was my mother when I came home from school in second grade, with a high fever.

"I'm pretty new at this . . ." I mumble, hearing my words slur. She smiles.

"Don't worry, we'll do OK."

"Relax," she coos, as my pant leg gets hooked on my heel, and I struggle awkwardly to pull it off. I nearly tip off the bed. "Lie back, I'll get your pants off."

And she does. Then she steps out of her dress. She's not wearing a bra; her nipples are the first I can ever remember seeing except in a magazine. Her bikini panties are new to me, too. My sisters' and my mother's, that I've seen come back from the laundry, are full, over-the-hips cotton, not like these sheer nylon briefs that show her dark patch of pubic hair. As she steps out of her panties and puts them on the chair, I feel light-headed, not sure I'm going to remain conscious.

"Lie back," she suggests, and I do. She seats herself astride me and I feel my erection drain of its blood and deflate.

"Oh God," I say, "I'm so sorry."

She smiles. "Don't worry," she reassures. I feel in the hands of someone older, not my age. She reaches down and takes hold of my member, the only person to touch it since I was in diapers, except for the country club manager who fingered me once when I was getting out of the shower. I must have flinched in surprise as she took hold of me.

"It's OK, I won't hurt you."

It wasn't that I was afraid she'd hurt me; I was embarrassed to have her touching me. I would have changed my will if I could have touched her in return, which I no doubt could have, certainly she expected me to, but it felt far too bold a thing and I never tried.

By now my penis was the size of a tiny never used balloon, the kind given as party favors at children's parties. I wished I could disappear.

She was matter of fact, business like and knowledgeable about male physiology, and I was obviously not the first frightened drunk virgin teenager she had encountered. She began expertly fingering me in ways that finally encouraged adequate amounts of blood into the necessary capillaries to produce at least a semblance of an erection onto which she then quickly and efficiently mounted herself and brought me to sufficient climax to earn whatever portion of my $25 was hers.

I was vaguely aware through my alcoholic haze that I was no longer a virgin, and though I suppose I was glad that I now had my own true story to tell back at school, it all seemed hardly more of an event than the endless hours of masturbation that make up a significant percentage of a boy's life in boarding school. And, at the same time, a sacred moment I would hate to cheapen in smutty dorm conversation.

"You're a sweet boy," she said after we had both put our clothes on. And before she opened the door, she kissed me, chastely, on my cheek, my right cheek. It caused a rush of blood back into my penis that I would have killed for a few moments earlier.

BISHOP LOBASKI

Mrs. Lobaski made me a priest way more than the Bishop I'd knelt before at my ordination two years earlier, though I never heard her speak a word nor did she lay hands on me.

Mrs. Lobaski suffered a cerebral "accident". Just before she and her daughter ordered their lunch, she looked up from her menu, her features tightened in pain. "Stephanie," she moaned to her daughter, "my head!" She slipped from her chair and slumped to the floor. The ambulance arrived quickly. But Mrs. Lobaski had already suffered what the neurologist called a "fatal insult" to the brain.

Her daughter watched in helpless despair as doctors and nurses assaulted her mother. One attacked an orifice; another slashed open new ones. Stephanie couldn't take it in, that this body being violated was her mother with whom she had been laughing minutes before.

By the time Stephanie's sister and brothers arrived the next morning, the doctor had told her there was no brain activity. Stephanie understood, "brain dead" The heart and lungs were strong.

"Any chance her brain might recover?" Stephanie forced herself to ask.

"There's always a chance."

"And now?"

"We wait. Do another EEG in the morning."

The neurologist accompanied by Dr. O'Brien and me, the priest, met Stephanie and her sister and brothers in the family lounge. The new EEG showed the same flat line.

"Dr. O'Brien is our hospice doctor and Father Ryan our chaplain," he explained. "I've asked them to consult on your mother's case because we're facing tough decisions." Stephanie and her sister and brothers studied each other's faces. They'd been a close-knit family, but the years had changed them and they could no longer predict each other.

"Where there's life, there's hope. God is so great!" Sam had been "born again" in a tent meeting five years before.

"Of course that's true." Dr. O'Brien saw they could use some help. "But with the new Harvard definition we're comfortable saying that, even though the machine can keep the heart beating artificially, if there is no brain activity, the person is clinically dead."

"Maybe you and Harvard are comfortable saying that, but it's my mother, and I'm very uncomfortable with you playing God with her life." I thought Sam looked at me. I looked at Stephanie.

"Dr. O'Brien," Stephanie was desperate, "how long do you think Mother's heart might be kept going?" Stephanie avoided eye contact with Sam.

"Hard to say. Days, weeks, a month, could be years."

The family lines hardened, three wanting to turn off the ventilator. Sam was resolute; no playing God. Sam agreed to bring their mother's case before the Ethics Committee, but he made no commitments about being bound by their finding. His sisters and brother were grateful for even this morsel.

The Ethics Committee had seven members, three doctors (one was Dr. O'Brien), the rest of us from the community, a lawyer, a real-estate broker, a housewife and me. In our tenure of less than a year, this was the weightiest matter we had considered. Our procedure was to debate, and if a decision was requested, to vote.

"How long will Mrs. Lobaski's insurance pay?" the lawyer wondered.

"We shouldn't consider that, the woman's life is at stake." The real estate broker bristled.

"But is her life truly at stake," I wondered, "what with the Harvard definition."

"Do you really think almighty Harvard should make this decision?" the housewife asked. "Harvard's smart, but what's the point of our having this committee if all we do is defer to Harvard?" I was silent.

The debate raged for three hours. Seeing we weren't going to agree, we suspended debate and voted, five to two to turn off the machine, let Mrs. Lobaski's heart stop (if it would). The debate was hot. Dr. O'Brien suggested we offer to stay with the family if they decided to turn off the machine. "Look at what a hard wrenching thing it's been for us. It's their mother. Let's not disappear and leave them alone now."

I was surprised how fast Sam agreed to do it. Dr. O'Brien made our offer to stay with the family while the hard thing was done. They leapt at it.

Mrs. Lobaski (Mrs. Lobaski's body?) was alone in a small room with a metal office chair and a clutter of machines, wires and tubes running in and out of her. Eleven of us crowded around her bed. Sam asked if we could pray. We joined hands; someone asked God to protect her, and us. I wondered who would decide when the machine would be switched off. My clerical collar felt like a choker. "Prayers for the dying," I thought, "that's what you're meant to do now." But none came to me. I could have read them from my Breviary, but that would have meant dropping the hands of the people next to me, breaking the circle.

"Is it time to turn off the machine?" Dr. O'Brien asked. She explained that it could take a while before the monitor went flat. Several heads turned towards Sam. Crying softly, he nodded. Dr. O'Brien reached across Mrs. Lobaski and flipped a toggle switch. I wondered if her heart might keep on, how long we'd stand there. Her chest heaved. I was sure the people holding my hands felt my sweaty palms.

It took ten minutes. Silence, the blips slowed, flattened, jumped irregularly. My heart flopped. Dead flat. Is this it? Mrs. Lobaski looked much as before, asleep. But weird, so still. Her children sobbed. I felt I had intruded on a great intimacy. Who decided she was dead? Should I pull my hand from the hand of the person on my right, so I could make the sign of a cross on Mrs. Lobaski's forehead? I was paralyzed, like a bad dream. I wanted to run. Averting the eyes of the others in our circle, I looked out the window. A teenage couple was walking down the hospital drive, holding hands, talking and laughing. They looked carefree. My mind was shrieking.

"You two! Do you know what just happened in here?"

AFTER THE FALL
A HAIR RAISING TALE

For years Allison anticipated wearing to her mother's funeral the wide-brimmed black hat she'd found in the attic. The one with the long, luxurious fall of hair attached. Her mother hid the hat in the attic after Vanity Fair ran her picture in it, the picture with her secret lover. That hat covered more than her mother's deceit. Allison thought the hat quite the right thing to wear to the funeral, to hide her own hateful hair, and to expose her mother's embarrassing secret.

"Allison," her husband scolded, "her funeral is no place for you to get even with your poor mother."

"She's been in my hair for forty years, George." She strung out his name sarcastically, stretching her fleshy lips across her protruding teeth. "This is my last chance. Don't you meddle in my affairs with my mother."

Allison regarded them as affairs. Her mother treated her as a grown woman from the time she was 14, after her mother, enraged at her father when his receding hairline set behind the crown of his head, banished him from her bed, and then from their life. For the next fifteen years the two women enmeshed in one another's vital energies like the tangled twigs of a bird's nest.

Her mother had been born a hermaphrodite, in England, where a child born with both male and female reproductive organs was legally considered male. When she was emerging from her miserable adolescence she learned of the gender clinic at Johns Hopkins in America, which provided counseling for people who felt trapped in the wrong gender. If they were adequately endowed with the apparatus of the gender they longed to be, and had sufficient emotional and physical stamina, Johns Hopkins performed the several surgeries required.

Her mother underwent that, so successfully that, against all odds, she not only enjoyed sex with the family gardener, but she conceived Allison. Allison, offspring of a miraculously made mother, and a striking Jamaican father, emerged with chic rust-colored skin, and silky black hair, more of it than the doctor had ever seen on a newborn.

And there was the dilemma, the kink in Johns Hopkins otherwise successful remodel. Allison's mother had a man's thin receding hair and no amount of hormones helped.

And as Allison grew, so did her hair. People stopped her mother in the supermarket aisles to admire her hair. When she was six her hair reached to her waist. One night as she was leaning down to kiss her goodnight, her mother ran her fingers through Allison's hair.

"Allison, wouldn't you like to have your hair cut? Not a lot. Just enough so it wouldn't get tangled."

"No, I don't really think so, Mommy. I love my hair. I don't mind when it gets tangled."

"Think about it, Allison, darling. You're starting to play sports, and pretty as it is, that long hair is going to become a nuisance. None of your friends have hair nearly that long. Just think about it."

"I really don't need to think about it, Mommy. I like my hair just the way it is."

But Allison did think about it. That night she dreamed that she was bald and though her friends laughed at her, in her dream her mother hugged her the way she always wished she might.

On her 12th birthday, Allison was nearly killed playing in the front yard with their black & tan Norfolk terrier, Alyssum. The dog chased a ball into the street as a car sped by. Allison rushed to save her. The next thing she knew she was waking, with a splitting headache, one leg suspended above her in a sling. She reached up to her face, felt heavy bandages around her skull. Her mother was sitting next to the bed.

"Allison, oh my God, Allison, you're awake. Thank God. Oh darling, we've been so worried."

"Alyssum?"

"I'm so sorry, Allison."

"Oh, no." Allison wept.

She touched her neck below the bandage. "Mommy, my hair."

"They had to shave your head, Darling, for surgery. You're a lucky little girl, you hair will grow back."

And it did, but, Allison thought, not nearly as pretty.

The following spring someone cut a page from Vanity Fair magazine and mailed it to Allison. Allison opened the envelope and stared at the picture of her tall striking mother in a leather, fur-trimmed suit, wearing a wide-brimmed black hat. Beneath her hat, hauntingly familiar long, thick hair tumbled down her bare back, silky, black, beautiful hair with tan highlights. A handsome, broad shouldered man, not Allison's father, had his arm around her. Allison stifled a sob as she tore up the picture.

Years later, when Allison found the hat with the long black fall and the tan highlights in a dark corner of the attic in her mother's old house where she now lived, she and her mother were long since estranged. But she drove to her mother's nursing home and confronted her with it. Her mother, slouched, tied into her chair by restraints, a terry-cloth turban hiding her baldness, stared at the hat with the long, beautiful hair, expressionless, mute.

Allison returned the hat to the box in the corner of the attic where it stayed for the next 2 years. The night before her mother's funeral Allison brought the hat down to her bedroom, put it on and observed herself in the dressing table mirror while she brushed the hair for fully two hours, until it shone wonderfully.

DAVID

I wonder, David thought as he felt his member begin to unfold in his lap, if this part, too, is different about me. He had stayed still as a deer, watching Ann for nearly an hour as she sat equally still in her chair across the room. The attendant had put her next to the big bay window and the morning sun caught the blond highlights in her auburn hair. Though she was slumped, kept from sliding to the floor only by her sash, a twisted bed sheet around her waist and around the back of her chair, David still saw in her bright blue eyes some excitement that roused in him feelings he seldom had. And this stirring in his pants.

David had known since he was a small boy that he was different. He couldn't figure out precisely how he was different, but he was pretty sure his parents and his doctors didn't really know either. Not that he would argue with their diagnosing him as autistic; he understood what that meant and he believed it described him well enough. But to him it was like saying you were tall or left handed; it told something about you but nothing revealing about what it felt like to be you.

Though he was nearly thirty, and this wasn't the first time looking at a girl aroused him, over the past several months watching Alice had affected him in some new way. He wondered if anyone noticed. Mostly he hoped not.

David had spoken for the last time more than twenty-five years ago. He was four. His mother had told him he simply had to try

harder at school, that he couldn't just sit in the corner of the
room and stare.

"But mother . . ." he'd begun his reply, and then it was as if,
suddenly, a n opaque screen had descended between him and his
mother. He could still see her, even hear her, but the screen was
so thick that just the thought of trying to speak through it
seemed exhausting, futile. He remembered thinking maybe he'd
gotten sick and would get better, or maybe this screen would
happen only with his mother. Or soon go away. But when his
sister came home, there it was with her and then with his father.
That night they all acted like he was in a bad mood or was
punishing them somehow. One minutes they'd be mad at him;
"Damn it, David, you've got to stop this right now." The next
they would beg; "Come on, David, it's ok, we love you. Please
speak to us."

David remembered wanting to reassure them that he was really
the same as before, just too tired to connect. The effort of even
considering how to talk to them drained his energy and caused
him to nod off the way his father did in front of TV most nights.

The orderly came to Ann's chair. "OK, Ann, it's time for
hydrotherapy." He dropped to one knee so his face was in front
of hers. Ann was expressionless. David watched, his face offering
no clue to his feelings. Though his eyes remained fixed, he took
in every motion across the room.

"Ann, he's trying to let you know he cares about you; he likes
you. So do I, you know. I wonder what it would be like to be in
hydrotherapy together. Do they take all your clothes off before
they dip you into the water? I'd love to see you naked. I feel like
I know you in some way I've never known anyone before. Maybe
I could even find some way to let you know that."

When he looked at Ann, David sometimes thought the screen let more light through, but he wasn't sure if that was just because he hoped it was true. He was certain he could see her more clearly than he could see others, because right from the start he'd noticed how beautiful she was. Others had too thick a film for him to be able to make out much more than their blurred edges. But he saw Ann sharply, her milky skin, the silky blond hairs on her arms that he could imagine stroking the way he loved to stroke Jasmine, their Siamese cat. Even though her ankles crossed under her chair, he could tell they were delicate, and her calves, that he saw only rarely from beneath the blanket, were shapely, as if they had been sculpted by a fine artist. Her face seemed to David the face of an angel, serene half smile like she was holding a wonderful secret she was saving for some lucky person. David imagined being that person. And as he watched her, which he did many days for two or three hours uninterrupted, it seemed more and more like he could be.

"I wonder if she sees me over here." The wondering possessed David, sometimes for days at a time. The screen was between him and his reflection in a mirror, too, so even the infrequent times he found himself before a mirror, he had only the vaguest notion what he looked like. He remembered what he'd looked like when he was four, before the screen, but he knew he must look much different now. He hoped that if she did see him, he looked as appealing to her as she did to him. He figured the years of being so immobile except for when they took him to therapy, had caused his body to shrink and twist in strange ways; he could tell that without seeing his own reflection. But he hoped that Ann, he learned her name from listening to the people in the day care place talk to her, could see inside him they way he could see inside her. Sometimes her parents, who came to pick her up everyday, called her Annie. He understood they did that to let her know they thought she was special, but David thought just plain Ann suited her much better. He guessed she must be around his age, though guessing ages was hard here. He knew she was a woman, not a girl. Even though he was a man, his family, too, often spoke to him like he was a child.

"They do the same thing with Jasmine, probably because she doesn't speak. I guess speaking is what they figure makes a person an equal, an adult whom you meet as another adult."

With Jasmine the screen fell almost completely away for David. And though he didn't exchange words with her exactly, he was in some way prescient with her, knowing her feelings and what she was going to do before she did it. Jasmine's greeting, rubbing against his leg while making a weird jump, came through to David clearly, telling him she was marking him as her special companion. He had no doubt she knew it was reciprocal.

When the screen first descended David felt confused, then afraid, then despair. Not so much because he was unhappy, mostly he was content, but because of his parents' and his sister's distress. He desperately wanted to let them know he was all right and loved them. But no matter how hard he tried, they didn't get it. Even now, all these years later, though they had become resigned to it, he knew they still felt rejected, or like they had done something bad to him that caused him to stop talking to them.

"I really didn't stop talking to *you*," he wanted to tell them, "I just stopped talking." David couldn't say why, except that he didn't have the energy to make words come out of his mouth. It certainly wasn't personal, and in fact, had his parents not been so upset about it, David thought maybe there was nothing terribly wrong about it.

"David," his mother asked him in her most pleading voice one afternoon when she was driving him home from daycare, "what do you do in there by yourself in your own little world all day every day?"

David heard the anger and the sarcasm in her voice, but he thought it was a reasonable question and he wished she could discern his answer because he thought it might make her feel better.

"I'm *being* in here, Mom, pretty much like you're *being* in your world, only without the words. And even without the words, my world feels vast, rich, not little at all." He knew she couldn't sense what he had answered, and he wasn't sure she could imagine how peaceful it was being where he was. What he remembered of the wordy world he'd spent his first four years in was the din, the chaos. "I don't miss it, Mom, and I think you'd like my world better than you imagine."

As the orderly wheeled Ann from the day room, her head flopped onto her right shoulder revealing the graceful curve of her neck, the tiny, fine down David sometimes imagined licking, stirring with his breath, like sea grass in a gentle breeze.

"Good bye, Ann, and thank you for filling my morning with such pleasure."

Had it not been for his Aunt Harriet, his father's older sister, David thought he might have felt lonely, isolated. From his earliest memory David sensed her empathy.

"Your sister Harriet is a spook," David heard his mother say one night to his father, "She inhabits some other planet."

"But she's harmless," his father protested, "and she has a kind heart."

"Right," his mother agreed, "like Jasmine."

David remembered how his heart leaped when she said that. "Mom understands about Jasmine!"

"That's a little unkind, don't you think?" The way his father defended Aunt Harriet took away David's excitement. That was meanness, sarcasm, not understanding. He sensed she was about to respond to his father and swallowed whatever it was before it could tumble from her mouth. David saw that his father realized that, too.

"You have a cruel streak, Monica."

"I'm sorry, Mac, I think I'm just tired. It's been a long week."

After that David decided it was for the best that his mother couldn't understand Jasmine. Or him. Her world didn't seem to have room for the things that made David happy and that made him feel connected to Jasmine.

But Aunt Harriet's world did. Right from the start, when Aunt Harriet came to visit, David felt safe and included. She never said much, but she touched him, rubbed his head and folded over his ear lobe with her fingers, a tender gesture that made him feel close to her, special.

Once when Aunt Harriet was visiting, his parents got into an argument about him.

"Sometimes he just seems like a God damn bump on a log," his father complained. Though David still felt the sting of his father's disappointment, he no longer suffered the agony he had when he was younger. He knew his father just didn't get what it was like for him.

"Mac, David may not speak, but he hears and I'm pretty sure he's very smart," Aunt Harriet said.

"Smart? What makes you think so? How much do you think he even understands?" his father asked, his voice filled with exasperation.

"Everything and lots more than everything," Aunt Harriet answered in her soft, matter-of-fact, non-emotional tone. The way she said it made David excited, feel more important than he ever did around his parents. "And since he's sitting in the next room, I'd suggest we be aware of what we say about him."

"More than everything?" his father bit off his words. "What's that supposed to mean?"

"Mac, I don't say this to be cruel, but I'm not sure I can explain except to say that out loud words are only one and probably not either the largest or most profound level of reality or communication. I have no idea why David stopped using words, but you can bet he's still in there, still communicating, plenty."

"Are you suggesting that I may not be smart enough to communicate with my mute son?"

"I'm suggesting nothing except my conviction that David is bright and fully present in there. Though I can understand and even sometimes share your frustration over his silence, somehow I don't think it's the tragedy for him that it often feels like to us."

"You always were a dreamer," was how his father stopped the conversation. It confirmed David's sense that his Aunt Harriet did know something of what went on in him. And his mother's silence felt to David like hope, like she wanted to believe Harriet.

Six months ago, an afternoon the van delivered David home from day care, his parents were in the front hall, visibly upset. It was unusual for David's father to be home at 3:30 in the afternoon when David got home. He was on the phone.

"How long ago was she admitted?" David sensed that 'she' was Aunt Harriet. In fact that morning he had *heard* from her in a new way that startled him.

"Hey, David, it's Aunt Harriet." He was in the day room, basking in a morning of looking at Ann. The words came to him in a way that, though he had never received them like that before, he never doubted and understood immediately.

"Where are you, Aunt Harriet?"

"I'm not exactly sure, but I think maybe the hospital and I think I just came into your world in some new way."

"You must have because I don't think we could be communicating like this if you hadn't." David, though uneasy about having his peace disturbed, trusted Aunt Harriet not to abuse this channel.

They had put David on the couch in the living room that afternoon while his father talked on the phone, and he overheard what his father said.

"What's a cerebral accident? Is she likely to regain consciousness? Can she have visitors? What are the chances of her surviving this? If there's no hope of her ever regaining consciousness, what are our options? Yes, I have power of attorney. Yes, she does have a living will."

From that day until yesterday had been some of the best time David had known since he was four. They never took him to the hospital to visit Aunt Harriet, which was fine with David because he felt close to her without being there.

"I don't feel like I'm barely in this body anymore," she said to him a few days after they took her to the hospital. "Is that what you've felt like in your body all these years?"

"Something like that," David responded. "Or maybe like it's a set of borrowed clothes, not exactly mine."

"Yes, that's it exactly."

After a week of communicating like that, David decided to ask Harriet for her help with something he had been thinking about.

"Aunt Harriet, do you know who Ann is?"

"You mean that lovely young woman, with autism, whom I've often seen in the day room at your day care center?" David wasn't sure anyone else noticed her. It thrilled him to have Aunt Harriet describe her as lovely. "The one you love so?" This gave David a moment's pause. He was surprised, even felt a little caution that she knew. But the caution quickly yielded to giddiness.

"Yes, yes! That's the one. So you know. Aunt Harriet, do you suppose you could communicate with her the way you do with me?"

"Yes, I think I might."

And she had. Though neither David's parents nor any of the people who worked at the day care center detected it, Aunt Harriet opened a channel of communication that sparked what could only be called a romance between Ann and David.

"David, Ann has been watching you across the room all these years and she has fallen in love with you. She thinks you are handsome and she understands that you are a wonderful compassionate person. She says she's flattered and so happy that you have noticed her."

"Noticed her?! Tell her I adore her!"

And she had. Over the course of the next couple of months the exchange grew richer and more complex. Through Aunt Harriet they discussed their childhood and their families, even what it was like for them to have stopped speaking. Their hopes for their futures.

"You mean you and your cat know each other, too, the way Jasmine and I do?" The communication had become so total by then that, even though Aunt Harriet was the go-between, and they were unable to communicate directly, sequence of time didn't matter. Though it was still Harriet's voice, not Ann's, David was content.

"Yes, Alistair, he's Siamese, seal point, a little different from your blue point, is my best friend at home." It thrilled David that she knew Jasmine was a blue point even though he'd never revealed that to her. They both seemed to know just about everything about each other, but that in no way lessened their pleasure in this exchange Aunt Harriet was making possible.

"Aunt Harriet," David alerted her one morning, "I've been thinking about asking you to tell Ann something important that I'm not too sure about."

"I suppose you mean your sexual feelings, right David?"

Though this was new ground, David felt confiden about it, thanks to Aunt Harriet who was her usual compassionate, matter-of-fact self."

After a couple of uneasy false starts: "Tell her I think she has a beautiful figure, and she could be a model;" Aunt Harriet nudged David toward new ground.

"David, your admiration of Ann's beauty pleases her; she's glad you think she's attractive. I sense there's something more, different you want to say. Perhaps something about what sort of sensation you feel in your body when you look at her."

Aunt Harriet's prompting collapsed a dam in David that had been holding back a flood of energy, energy of which he was aware, but nonetheless astonished him with its intensity.

"When I see your breasts pressing against your blouse, my heart races and I feel faint. Imagining the nurses removing your clothes for hydrotherapy, picturing your perfect naked body makes blood rush into my penis so that it throbs and feels wonderful."

"Ann responds to watching your body just the way you said you do to hers. No one has ever aroused such thrilling feelings in her. When she learned your feelings about her breasts her nipples became hard and felt delicious rubbing against her bra. Now, when they remove her clothes for hydrotherapy, she imagines it is you undressing her, and she feels the blood rush into her vagina just like you describe happening to your penis."

It was almost as if David forgot that Aunt Harriet was in between, as if he was communicating directly with Ann. One day he was sure he detected a hint of a smile, a Mona Lisa look, come across her impassive features as they were positioned on opposite sides of the room. He hoped she saw something of the same in his face.

David had never dreamed of being so happy. He wondered if people in the jostling, noisy speaking world could ever imagine the joy he felt. And it wasn't all or only about Ann. His life at home, with his parents, and especially with Jasmine, now had added dimensions. He found he wanted to stay with them in the living room at night after dinner rather than go straight to his room and bed. And his parents seemed to understand and be happy about this new interest David took in all of them. They even thought sometimes he seemed to be following the TV program.

Occasionally his parents spoke of Aunt Harriet, usually at dinner on Thursday night. His mother went to visit her in the rehab hospital Thursday afternoons. His father almost never went.

"I talked with the charge nurse on Harriet's floor today, Mac. She says we're coming up on a decision that will have to be made in the next short period of time."

"What sort of decision?"

"Well, she was reluctant to speak for the doctor, but it seems Harriet's kidneys are showing signs of giving out. I think they suspect she'll go into kidney failure before too long."

"So what sort of decision does that mean for us?" His father sounded irritated. David felt suddenly on alert.

"Dialysis," his mother answered. "They'll have to decide whether to do dialysis, and since she's unable to make the decision, it'll be up to you. Power of attorney."

"Jesus, Monica! Dialysis, on a woman who's comatose, hasn't responded to anything for over five months, who'd starve if they didn't shove that mush down that feeding tube every day. Are they nuts?"

"Well, that's the question, Mac, whether to do it or not, because there are different views on this sort of thing, and I guess she'll die of kidney failure if they don't do it."

"And what'll she die of if they do? That's absurd; I'll never agree to do dialysis on that poor old lady. Let her go, for God's sake."

David felt his world begin to narrow, his focus tighten, like he might pass out. Strange shapes flew across his consciousness, colors, odd noises, buzzing, annoying, distracting.

"David?" His mother's voice sounded like it was coming from another room, but he could make her out leaning over him where he was curled up on the couch. "David, are you all right? Mac, I think there's something wrong with David. His face is all blotchy and he's breathing funny. David!"

That time he heard his name clearly and managed to lift his head, letting her know he heard. All the clutter began to recede, but David still felt the panic as much as before.

"Come on, David, I think it's time for bed. You look exhausted."

He was exhausted and, despite his terror at the conversation he had overheard, he was relieved to be going to bed. These past few months, since Aunt Harriet went into her coma, the time in bed before he fell asleep had become when he could communicate best with her. When he heard new dimensions from Ann and sent her news of his growing adoration. He waited impatiently for his mother to complete her nightly ritual with him. At never varied.

"You know, David, how precious you are to your father and me, how much we love you. Of course we miss hearing your voice, but even if you never speak again, you are perfect to us just the way you are. And now may God watch between us for this night. Good night, my love." She leaned down to kiss him, Jasmine's signal to jump onto the bed. Jasmine spent every night sleeping against his legs. David loved feeling her warmth against him, and the contact made their communicating easier. His mother walked from his room into the hall, leaving the door open a crack so a sliver of light fell onto the rug and the foot of the bed, coming to rest on the photograph on the wall, of David on his father's shoulders in the ocean when he was three. He knew his parents loved the picture It seemed to David like a picture of his father with someone else, not him.

"Jasmine, they're going to let Aunt Harriet die. They can't." He could feel Jasmine's concern through the skin on the back of his legs. He always wondered how she knew that was the best place for him to pick up her communicating. "I don't know how to bring this up with Aunt Harriet. How can I tell her?" Through the calf of his left leg he picked up Jasmine's reassurance that Aunt Harriet knew; he needn't fret that he was going to be the bearer of bad news."

"You know, Aunt Harriet? You know they're talking about letting you die?"

"Yes, David. In fact I put the idea in their heads. I decided to start failing my kidneys because it looked like they would leave that feeding tube in me forever."

"You mean you want to die?"

"David, I'm not sure I'd say that I want to die, but that it's time for me to die and I'm ready. Right now we're trying to make a silk purse from a sow's ear." David loved that expression, but not now.

"But Aunt Harriet, what about. . . ?"

"I know, David, that's what's been keeping me from doing this sooner. David, not only do I need to die, but you need for me to die. Unless I die, you're not going to get on with what you're ready to do. It's the right thing for both of us."

"But Aunt Harriet, Ann, what about Ann? How am I supposed to communicate with Ann?"

"Darling David, I've already let this go on too long. You and Ann no longer need me. It's time for you to communicate with each other with no one between you."

"But Aunt Harriet, Ann and I are both autistic, don't speak. We don't know how to make contact."

"And I am comatose, David, almost dead. Do you think it is easier for me to pass these communications between you and Ann than it would be for you two to do it yourselves? You two beautiful, smart young people? You think autism separates people more than unconsciousness does? Since I've become unconscious I've sometimes thought that out loud talking gets in the way of communication."

"But Aunt Harriet, you have been my lifeline for years, even before Ann."

"David, all I have done is let you know my love and respect for you. The rest you have done. The communication with Ann, that has been yours, not mine. You've been afraid, nervous about communicating directly with her, so I've been here to boost your confidence. Ann is eager to hear from you directly."

"Aunt Harriet." David felt his grip on her loosening, his body succumbing to exhaustion, as if he was trying to save her from drowning and no longer had the strength to keep her afloat. "Do you think you and I will be able to communicate like this after. . . ?"

"After I'm dead, David? Well, I've never been dead so I don't really know. I'm not sure whether being dead means going somewhere new, or having your life energy scattered into other forms and maybe other newborn people. So it may be, David, that you will find me, but I don't think you should expect me to feel familiar for a while, if ever. What I'm pretty sure is that the intensity of my love for you, which I've always felt was way more than I could muster on my own, is indestructible. So when you run into that love again, and you will, I'd say it's a good bet that's me."

"Oh Aunt Harriet, I'm going to miss being with you like this. I can't imagine not being here like this with you before I go to sleep every night."

"Well, David, we always want to bottle love when we find it, don't we? And no wonder; it's precious. But it just won't stay in the bottle. So you and Ann will carry on for a season, and a lovely season it is sure to be. This special time each evening, it belongs to you and Ann now."

"Aunt Harriet, could I ask you to do just one more thing for me? Could you go between Ann and me one more time, tell her how much I love her and that I'm going to try to communicate with her without you in between?"

"David, I decided this afternoon to spare your father the agony of making the decision about dialysis. Right now I'm using my last earthly energy to be here a moment longer, with you. It's as if my batteries have run out and my light is dim, about to go out. So you're going to have to tell Ann yourself and I know you will. I love you very much, David, and so does Ann. Good bye, David."

"Aunt Harriet." She was gone.

David didn't sleep that night; he rode the storm through his mind and heart, a fierce unrelenting gale blowing him across dark, frightening, unfamiliar seas, until dawn. His mother came into his room a half hour earlier than usual.

"David, I'm afraid I've got some bad news." Of course he knew. "I know it's going to be hard for you, I know how much you loved your Aunt Harriet. Hard as it may be, your father and I think it would be best for you to go to day care today, keep the schedule as much as normal as possible. But don't for a moment think we don't understand what a big loss this is for you, as it is for us."

There was a new orderly that morning who wheeled David into the day room. He put him in front of the TV instead of his usual spot. There was a game show on. David's heart sank; from where they had put him, he couldn't see the other side of the room.

"Alex," a familiar voice called to the man who had wheeled him into the room, "David's not a TV fan; he likes to sit over there where the sun comes in."

"Oh, OK," Alex answered, and took David to the sunny spot. As he positioned him with his back to the wall, David felt the sun's warmth on his neck. He saw Ann on the other side of the room.

"Good morning, Ann, my beloved."

GONER

"Guess I'm a goner," he'd said. I could tell by the faint echo, like a voice in a dream, it was a call from the east coast. His voice broke, only for a second; if you didn't know him you might have missed it. The only other time I'd heard him do that was when he told me his father had died; then he wept. It unnerved me, I was a little boy then. Now I felt a slow motion, underwater sense, accentuated by the metallic echo that increased as the conversation went on. I remember when I had my hernia repaired, the anesthesiologist's voice sounding like that as he explained he was starting the sodium pentathol. I wondered then if that's what it would sound like when you're going out, dying. They say hearing is the last sense to go. How do they know?

There was no mistaking the raw fear in his voice and I felt a powerful obligation to feel it, too. But I didn't. I began piling up my excuses, he'd always kept himself emotionally distant, hiding his feelings if he even had any, so why would he think I could come up with strong clear feelings for him now? I had a million excuses, crafted in years of therapy. They never helped, only made me feel worse, the Adolph Eichmann defense.

A goner? For Chrissakes, I haven't seen that word since I stopped reading comics. I don't think I've ever actually heard someone say it, at least not seriously, not about their own dying.

Therapy, I thought, you've done too much therapy. You can't even hear your own father tell you he's dying (maybe he's being dramatic, he's probably going to outlive you), without dissecting your response, as if you were reviewing a French movie.

"A goner, Dad? But why? I mean what . . ."

"The tumor's back in both lungs now, Son. It's metastasized to the liver."

"How long do they. . . ?"

I couldn't believe I'd let that question slip out. How many of my patients had asked me that, and I struggled not to seem impatient with their wanting me to outguess God, or Thor, or whoever the hell determines when that breath is the last one. I couldn't believe I'd let it slip out.

"The doctor said he couldn't say. Not long, I don't think. Weeks, months."

"Shit, Dad, that's awful."

That felt pretty real. Hope he heard it. Now what? Am I s'posed to offer some kind of miracle? I'd made it a practice to sit down when I tell my patients the news, look them in the eye, stay with them, let them do the talking, let them decide when they've talked enough. It can back up a waiting room full of people, but all the studies show it cuts way back on malpractice suits. Not that that's the measure of anything, just that people feel heard, cared for. That counts for more than medical skill, at least when things get hairy.

"So, Dad," (I was filling the void, something I'd learned not to do with patients), "would you like me to come?"

I realized I was holding my breath; what if he says yes? Or no?

"I know how busy you are."

Man, if you knew. The clinic's fiscal year closes in two weeks and I still haven't worked out my billable hours. The merger between the two hospitals is coming to a head. A couple of the younger doctors have challenged my decision to go forward. They've even questioned whether it's time for me to step down as Chief of Surgery. Alice has her opening at King Gallery next week, could be her breakthrough show. Busy? I'm drowning!

"Hell, man, are you kidding? Busy? Bullshit. The day I'm too busy to spend some time with my old man is the day I'm hanging up my spikes."

"Well of course I'd love to see you. It's been a while and . . . But you know I'll understand if you can't. "His voice got weak, I thought we might be losing the transcontinental signal, then his voice cracked again; now two of the three times I'd heard him do that had been in just the past few minutes.

"I'm exhausted, Son, I'm going to hang up and get some sleep."

"Hey, Dad, of course you're exhausted. I'll talk with Alice tonight and call you in the morning. I'm just so sorry to hear your news. You may think of yourself as a Goner, (I had a little trouble choking out the word), but to me you're my wonderful Dad, and I love you. "

I think I'd started to make a joke about Goner, but the joke went astray in mid-sentence, for which I was grateful. He and I had just begun in the past couple of years saying we loved each other. We still had to wrap it into some larger narrative.

"Of course you have to go," Alice said, that night as we were finishing our first bottle of California Merlot, almost succeeding in hiding her disappointment about her opening that weekend. "But God, Henry, what about the merger? I mean what's the Board going to say about you're taking time off right at this crucial moment?"

"Well, fuck you, Alice, I have no fucking idea what they're going to say. Maybe they'll say, Hey, everybody's got to go sometime; let your old man die on his own time. How do I know what they're going to say. I don't think you give a rat's ass about the merger or my Dad; you're only thinking about your opening."

You can't have done as much therapy as I've done and not know when you're projecting, making someone else wear your own terror. That nasty stuff I put in the Board's mouth; I knew it was mine. Same for Alice, though I could have killed her for provoking my venom.

Alice finally broke the silence during which we'd both stared down at our arugula pesto as if, like tea leaves, it could reveal our fortunes. Her voice was lower than normal, calmer.

"Henry, how long do they think he'll live?"

"Who the fuck knows?" I screamed, feeling scary out of control, my face red, hot, as I remembered asking Dad the same stupid question.

"So what do you propose?" she asked, thin-lipped. I'd provoked her and now I was going to reap what I'd sowed. "To fly six hours across the country and sit there with him until he croaks?" Her eyebrows arched as if she'd heard someone else use that word. "What if it takes two weeks, or six months?

I think Alice asked me that, but now as I think back on it I can't be sure those awful questions didn't bubble up inside me like noxious gasses, and I put them in Alice's mouth. I'm really not sure.

That night, after I'd hung my suit in the closet and brushed my wing tips and put them in shoe trees, on my way to the bathroom to put on my pajamas, I stopped in front of the full length mirror. It must have been years since I'd stopped and looked at myself like that, naked, my whole body, full on. What made me stop was that, in my peripheral vision I had seen, not myself, but my father. Unmistakably. The receding white hair, the out-of-fashion large mustache, the pockets of fatty deposit on my hips, giving my otherwise trim athletic body a slight feminine cast. The wrinkled organ, dangling comically in front of a sagging pair of balls. I must have stood staring for several minutes, finally daring to step closer and check out my face in Alice's magnifying make-up mirror suctioned onto the larger one. When did those wrinkles in my forehead etch so deeply, like furrows in a plowed field? Were the little broken capillaries in my nose from alcohol? Used to be that my beard showed heavy shadow by bedtime; now dotted white stubs scattered randomly, like grains of salt across my cheeks.

The next afternoon, sitting in an old Hitchcock ladder-back chair I remembered from my room growing up, by the hospital bed that hospice had delivered that morning and set up in Dad's living room, giving the house the feel of a death house, I held his hand as I recounted to him the story of staring at myself in my mirror last night and seeing him more than me.

His head, seemingly shrunken, was sunk deep into the down pillow, so it fluffed up around his face, hiding his ears. It muffled his voice and I had to lean forward to hear him. His breath was stale, his lips cracked, dried out from the morphine. He smiled weakly.

"I remember when the same thing happened to me about my father," he said.

Printed in the United States
5115

9 781401 048648